THE JOHNS HOPKINS UNIVERSITY STUDIES IN HISTORICAL AND POLITICAL SCIENCE

Under the Direction of the Department of History, Political Economy, and Political Science.

SERIES LXXXIII
(1965)

NUMBER 1

THE RIGHT TO VOTE:

Politics and the Passage of the Fifteenth Amendment

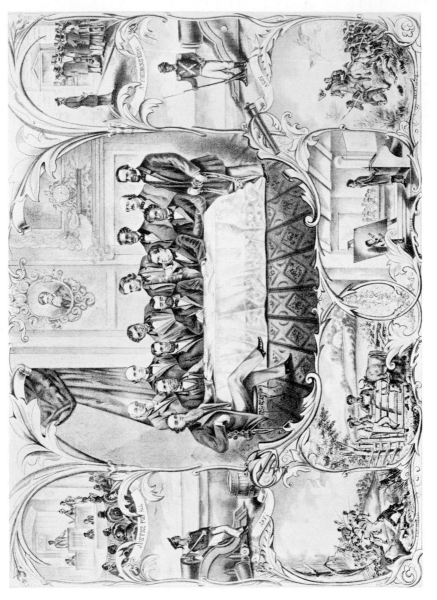

One of a number of lithographs printed to commemorate the passage of the Fifteenth Amendment and reprinted here by courtesy of the Library of Congress. The original carries the notice: "published by C. Rogan, Savannah, Georgia." The men in the central panel are (seated, left to right) E. Stanton, S. Colfax, A. Lincoln, U. S. Grant, W. H. Seward, F. Douglass, (standing) H. Greeley, S. Chase, R. Small, C. Sumner, H. Revels, B. F. Butler, W. T. Sherman.

THE RIGHT TO VOTE:
POLITICS AND THE PASSAGE OF THE FIFTEENTH AMENDMENT

By
WILLIAM GILLETTE

BALTIMORE
THE JOHNS HOPKINS PRESS
1965

The book has been brought to publication with the
assistance of a grant from the Ford Foundation.

FOR DAVID DONALD

PREFACE

That the politics of the Fifteenth Amendment might comprise a suitable topic for research was first suggested to me by Professor David Donald, then Harmsworth Professor at Oxford. Professor Donald's proposal merited consideration for several reasons. In the first place, the study of John Mabry Mathews, published in 1909, needs to be supplemented and qualified in the light of recent scholarly investigations. Then, there is the growing importance of the political power of Negro Americans in both the North and the South in this middle of the twentieth century, so similar in some respects to the role of the Negro voter in the postwar years of the nineteenth century. Moreover, as the one-hundredth anniversary of the ratification of the Fifteenth Amendment approaches, it is particularly appropriate to rediscover a crucial phase of national Reconstruction.

Today our country is attempting to match the promise of the first Reconstruction by the final achievement of its original purpose. The abolition of caste, and commitment to equality, in the Thirteenth and Fourteenth amendments and in the Civil Rights acts of 1866 and 1875 are now beginning to be enforced by executive order and federal intervention, historic decisions of the Supreme Court since 1938, and the passage and acceptance of the monumental Civil Rights Act of 1964. Slowly but surely, the Reconstruction principle of equal treatment and simple justice is now being achieved in the integration of the armed services, schools and housing, employment and welfare services, public accommodations, and transportation. Participating in this massive war on racial discrimination are the civil rights organizations which had their earlier abolitionist counterparts. Similarly, the Fifteenth Amendment and its enforcement acts of 1870 and 1871 are now being effected by the passage of the Hatch Act of 1939 and the Civil Rights acts of 1957, 1960, and 1964, with vigorous federal enforcement as well as ratification of the Twenty-fourth Amendment, which eliminated the poll tax in federal elections.

9

Federal attempts during the presidency of Ulysses S. Grant to stop political intimidation and prevent mob violence have been and are now being accelerated during the trail-blazing administrations of John F. Kennedy and Lyndon B. Johnson. The voter registration drives now being conducted in states like Mississippi and Alabama parallel the work that was done during Reconstruction by the Union Leagues in the South and Equal Rights leagues in the North. American reality in the present generation, as the late President John Kennedy put it, is beginning to match our rhetoric.

Reconstruction is repeating itself at the polls as well, for the power of the Negro voter is surely now as great as it was a century ago. From 1867 until 1892, southern and northern Negroes provided the margin of victory for Republican candidates in incredibly close elections in critical states. With the advent of the liberal New Deal coalition under Franklin D. Roosevelt, Democrats now retain key southern, border, and northern states because of Negro support in close elections. In 1948, for example, President Harry Truman would not have been elected without the electoral votes of California, Illinois, and Ohio, and his narrow margins in these states were achieved by indispensable Negro voters. Similarly, in 1960 Senator John Kennedy would have lost the election if he had not won Illinois and Michigan. He won in Illinois by only 9,000 votes, while roughly 250,000 Negroes voted. Michigan was carried by 67,000 votes, with 250,000 Negroes voting Democratic. South Carolina also was won in the same manner. Even while President Lyndon Johnson was ahead by a landslide in 1964, he carried most of the South because of the Negro vote. Almost solidly Democratic, it exceeded the Johnson plurality in four of the six southern states (Arkansas, Tennessee, Virginia, Florida), and North Carolina would probably have been lost but for those same voters. Such estimates emphasize the supreme importance of the Negro electorate in close elections, decisively counting in large states like New York, California, Illinois, Pennsylvania, Ohio, Michigan, New Jersey, Indiana, and Missouri.

Negro voting power affects congressional and state races as well. In 1956 the size of the Negro vote was greater than the plurality won by the incumbent congressman in sixty-one congressional districts in the North. Now, with a majority of Negroes living outside the South, the Negro voter in strategic northern and western big cities has eclipsed the importance of the rural southern

Negro voter during the first Reconstruction. As power increases so political prestige mounts as Negroes achieve greater political recognition. That fact is clear whether the politician be the Negro chieftain of Tammany Hall or one of the ninety Negro state legislators—including, for the first time since Reconstruction, 2 Negro state senators in Georgia and 1 in Tennessee—whether it be the present 6 congressmen or the 184 elected Negro officers in 33 of the 50 states. It is only a matter of time before Negroes will sit at the cabinet table, on the Supreme Court bench, or behind a Senate desk, or represent a Congressional district south of the Mason-Dixon line. On the other hand, the negative pattern repeats itself as well in white fears, active opposition to Negro advances, and ugly violence. Such so-called white backlash was considered strong enough by the Barry Goldwater campaign managers in 1964 to adopt the southern strategy of " refined racism," as Reverend Martin Luther King terms it. Republicans temporarily deserted Lincoln as once Democrats spurned Jefferson, yet the relative failure of nineteenth-century backlash in the twentieth century is an encouraging sign of its moral and political bankruptcy. The continuities in Reconstruction then are striking, but the major changes give ground for greater hope for Negro Americans and for the quality of American life in the future.

The emergence of the modern Negro voter has national implications. It is becoming increasingly evident that the deep South is moving toward modern border state politics, thus discarding racist for interest politics, while the border states are becoming increasingly northern in their orientation. Georgia, for example, is moving closer to a Texan political pattern, while Texas seems in many respects to act more like Missouri, and Missouri in turn, along with Delaware, is starting to approximate the style of Illinois or New Jersey. This changing political pattern, by breaking new ground for genuine two-party politics, not only helps Republican candidates in the South and border states, but strengthens the national Democratic party by ending the domination of southern politics by race. Southern Negro voting is transforming southern politics, because southern politicians love to hold office more than they dislike, or appear to dislike, Negroes. The demise of Jim-Crow politics and the further decline of the solid South presents the opportunity to use the party caucus in Congress, thus unifying, disciplining, and enabling liberal congressional Demo-

crats to govern, and even wresting control of congressional committees and leadership away from senior conservative southern
Democrats. The increased importance of interest politics in the
South, combined not only with the greater need of Negro voters
by midwestern Republicans but with reapportionment, marks the
disintegration of the conservative coalition in Congress, with its
rural midwestern Republicans and rural southern Democrats. In
other words, the consequence of the power of the Negro voter
is tremendous.

Substantial progress has been made, for example, in the broader
interpretation of voting rights by the courts, congressional approval of the Civil Rights acts of 1957, 1960, and 1964, and the
vigorous and expanding activities of the Civil Rights division
of the Justice Department. Forthcoming recommendations of
President Lyndon B. Johnson, along with future adoption of
temporary federal voting registrars in the one hundred counties
of lowest Negro registration, future decisions of the courts against
the ability to understand tests, and future registration activities of
various civil rights organizations, will help, but still more is
required. The fact remains that it is extremely difficult to prose-
cute state and local officials who administer state suffrage regulations in a discriminatory manner. Their obstruction and the lack
of agreement about the scope of federal powers over suffrage
make the need for fundamental reform imperative. The right to
vote must be made secure against any racial discrimination or
obstruction; otherwise the very integrity of the democratic process
and national authority are in jeopardy. Almost one hundred years
ago the Fifteenth Amendment was drafted as a step in that direction, but it necessarily lacked power and scope. Today the mandate
of equal opportunity in registering and voting should be completed
for the anniversary of the Fifteenth Amendment by passage and
ratification of a new constitutional amendment extending the right
to vote in all elections to all American citizens over twenty-one
years of age who have been residents of their voting districts for
at least one month, both conditions to be validated by forms
available at post offices. The time has come for federal qualifications only; the nation is ready for universal suffrage.

However, it has been argued by some that our political society
would be a better and stronger one if we kept literacy tests and
prevented illiterates, white or otherwise, from voting. Such a view

is open to argument, for the administration of such tests in the past did create a double standard by which illiterate and uneducated whites who were frontiersmen or immigrants were given the franchise under a lenient administration by eager politicians who needed their votes, while illiterate and uneducated Negroes in the South were gradually eliminated from the polls by those who profited by their exclusion. Because such tests in the South today remain open to flagrant abuse by the nature of individual administration, the level of intellectual difficulty, or the lack of equal educational opportunity, it is necessary in the middle of the twentieth century to eliminate the test itself. But even if a nondiscriminatory administration of a literacy test were possible, would such a test be desirable today? It is an academic question, for the number of illiterates is relatively small and politically apathetic, but it is hardly certain that the nonparticipation of illiterates, however inconsequential, would enhance the quality of political decision or improve significantly the democratic process in a pluralistic and changing American society. Underlying the qualitative emphasis remains the unanswered question of the standard and measure of value, such as a concept grounded on individual, group, or national interest. If interest politics rather than national interest is assumed to be the criterion, then the question must be answered as to whether a voter can be shrewd enough to know and vote in his own interest if he does not read. Many in answering would perhaps place an inflated value on education by identifying political intelligence with formal education or literacy, and exaggerate the role of rationality in the process by which voters make political decisions. Though now increasingly difficult in an urban and impersonal setting, a shrewd voter can only with difficulty still calculate his interest without recourse to newspaper or book, by watching, listening, and talking with his fellow citizens and by having a seasoned knowledge of human nature, as well as a first-hand acquaintance with men in public life. The American colonial, and early national, experience with greater illiteracy, as well as many public servants' lack of formal training, is not dissimilar to the experience of underdeveloped countries today. A further broadening of the suffrage by abolition of the literacy test would act out the irreversible logic of democratic politics in widening the suffrage in order to broaden the party base to secure victory. In addition to the practical application, there is the ultimate consideration of the philosophic demands of democratic theory. In the conflict between the imperatives of equality and the desire for quality, Jefferson placed no qualifications as to intelligence or wealth when he wrote in the Declaration of Independence that " Governments are instituted among Men, deriving their just powers from the consent of the governed." Universal suffrage is the best answer for a democratic society. However, formal suffrage qualifications are no substitute for the sound political judgment of citizens who soberly appreciate both the uses and abuses of power in governing a democratic society.

The roots of the Negro suffrage problem run deep, for the power of the Negro voter is still at stake, while the status of the Negro American remains a vital element in our constitutional politics. In fact, the problem still touches the sensitive nerve of politicians. Richard E. Neustadt writes in *Presidential Power* that the " means can matter quite as much as ends; they often matter more. And there are differences of interest in the means." Forging the means and fashioning the ends, politicians make possible what they consider necessary, but the legislative process and its product bear the seal of their time and place. The story of the Fifteenth Amendment is no exception: the details mattered, and not only because there were differences of interest in the means, but because the differences of interest marked the boundaries of their time and place, not ours. The effort of these politicians to frame and ratify an amendment revealed the tensions of their era in attempting in some measure to accommodate the high aspirations of equality with the harsh limitations of reality. In assessing their concrete problems of possible choice, it is useful to recall Oliver Wendell Holmes's remark: " It is one thing to utter a happy phrase from a protected cloister; another to think under fire—to think for action upon which great interests depend." The politicians of 1869 operated in the world of shadows and sunlight, wrestling with both principle and prejudice, and acting under both the pressure of events and the compulsion of interests.

Specifically, the purpose of this study is to tell the story of how and why the Fifteenth Amendment came to be. It is not a history of Negro voting in the 1860's and 1870's; it is not an account of the Republican party on federal and state levels during Reconstruction; it is not a study of former abolitionists in the same period;

it is not primarily a history of public opinion about the Negro as a voter; nor is it a study of the enforcement or judicial interpretation of the Fifteenth Amendment. Rather, it is restricted to an account of the immediate background, passage, and ratification of the Fifteenth Amendment, a study of one phase of the political and constitutional history of the first Reconstruction.

The many debts for help I have received from historians, political scientists, attorneys, politicians, archivists, and librarians are impossible to acknowledge here. I am grateful for permission from W. R. Brock, author of *An American Crisis: Congress and Reconstruction, 1865–1867* (Macmillan and Co., Ltd., and St. Martin's Press, Inc.), to reprint a passage, as well as permission from librarians and scholars to quote letters cited and to use unpublished dissertations. But certain persons deserve special mention.

It was my singular good fortune to have the assistance of Professor David Donald, now with the History Department at The Johns Hopkins University. Professor Donald read early drafts, weighed every word, and practically tested every piece of evidence. I should, therefore, like to thank him for his resourceful guidance and steadfast support—all of which can only be termed an example of the disciplined imagination of a great mentor.

I also thank Alexander Bickel of the Yale Law School, and Everette Swinney, for their searching observations on the second chapter, and I appreciate the help I have received from William Van Alstyne of Duke Law School. It is with pleasure that I acknowledge the interest and generous use of facilities afforded by The Honorable Peter Frelinghuysen, Jr., member of Congress from the Fifth Congressional District of New Jersey, who continues the fine tradition that his great-grandfather began by vigorously supporting the Fifteenth Amendment in Congress. I owe a further debt, for their help in various ways in the beginning of my research, to C. Vann Woodward, Yale University; The Honorable Spottswood Robinson, District Judge, United States District Court for the District of Columbia; Rayford Logan, Howard University; Robert Lively, Alpheus T. Mason, James McPherson, Princeton University; William Ward, Amherst College; Carroll Quigley, Georgetown University; Marko Zlatich, The World Bank; and Frank Lennon, Cos Cob, Connecticut.

I am grateful as well to the History Department at Princeton for the C. J. Dunlop Fellowship, enabling me to undertake research at the Library of Congress for one calendar year, to June Guicharnaud, who helped copy edit the book for publication, and to Robert Hall, who helped copy edit my Princeton dissertation, which was an early draft. Finally, I want to thank my family for their support: Samuel, Lillian, Robert, and Marsha Gillette. This book is my responsibility, of course, but the many others who have encouraged the enterprise and contributed to its development leave me with a sense of deep appreciation which I cannot adequately express.

WILLIAM GILLETTE

Fairfield, Connecticut
March 3, 1965

CONTENTS

THE RIGHT TO VOTE:

Politics and the Passage of the Fifteenth Amendment

CHAPTER I

THE KNOT OF RECONSTRUCTION

In 1864 when the days of both slavery and the Confederacy appeared numbered, northern statesmen began to consider the postwar settlement. Determining what policy should be applied to the white southerners, and whether Congress or the President should apply that policy were in themselves hard enough questions. But a more formidable problem was presented by the Negro, whose role in society would have to be redefined in the face of southern opposition, northern prejudice, and abolitionist idealism. Especially perplexing was the problem of political rights. Could and should Negroes vote? The provision of a political identity for four million slaves was a complex and controversial task, and the same problem faced northern states, for only New Englanders, except in Connecticut, allowed Negroes to vote without special discrimination.

Debate on the most important issue, Negro suffrage, began in earnest in 1864 and continued until 1870. Though emphasis shifted at times in the course of the debate, whether and how best to secure this suffrage remained the central concern throughout. Many opposed Negro suffrage in any form; others favored it. Some supporters argued that suffrage was a natural right, while others contended that it was only a political privilege. Some advocates maintained that suffrage should be impartial and qualified; others felt that universal and unrestricted suffrage was the solution.[1] Some reformers emphasized Negro suffrage; others

[1] See the fine study of abolitionist advocacy of Negro suffrage in James M. McPherson, *The Struggle for Equality: Abolitionists and the Negro in the Civil War and Reconstruction* (Princeton, N. J.: Princeton University Press, 1964), p. 327. Reconstruction terms characterizing the sort of suffrage desired were used loosely, but "equal" or "impartial" suffrage usually could mean either unrestricted or qualified suffrage. Both terms, however, meant suffrage open equally to both races. "Universal" suffrage meant unrestricted manhood suffrage except

21

insisted that women's suffrage must come either first or simultaneously. Some favored federal control of suffrage, while others wanted to keep state regulation. Many reformers wanted a congressional act; others preferred a federal constitutional amendment. The conflict between doctrinaire principle and political expediency ran deep and did much to divide Republicans throughout the country and in Congress.

During the end of 1865 and through the following year controversy centered on Negro suffrage as a vital element in a Reconstruction settlement with the South. The breach between the White House and Capitol Hill was widening enough to develop into open conflict, as President Andrew Johnson ineptly prepared to declare war on an infuriated Congress over the control and terms of the peace treaty ending the Civil War. Fear spread among Republicans that if a coalition ever formed and succeeded between Johnson administration conservatives, northern Democrats, and unrepentant southerners, the very war aims would be jeopardized. Thus preservation of the Union under such a subversive coalition would be in question if rebels ever returned to power in Washington, assumed the rebel debt, and mouthed doctrines of state rights. Similarly, abolition of slavery and caste would be undermined if southerners refused to grant their former slaves political and civil rights, and reduced them to peonage under the Black Codes. Thus, in a peace settlement, Negro suffrage was central to Northern war aims, for Republican control of Congress might be imperiled if the southern states were readmitted without being required to enfranchise Negroes; especially since by counting all former Negro slaves for apportionment roughly fifteen southern seats had been added to the House of Representatives. Freedom for the freedman, moreover, was meaningless unless he had the ballot to protect himself. Republicans felt that security for both the Negro and the Republican party must be achieved at a time when they identified Republican victory with the national interest. Under such pressing conditions in a deepening national crisis, the Republican Congress, through the Joint Committee on Reconstruction, attempted to fashion a fourteenth amendment as their peace treaty, dictating congressional terms of readmission of the southern states to the Union.

---

for age and residence requirements. The term " Negro " suffrage could mean either universal or impartial suffrage.

After much discussion and dissension in a meeting on January 20, 1866, the Joint Committee on Reconstruction recommended a moderate proposal concerning Negro suffrage, drafted by Representative James G. Blaine of Maine. Instead of prohibiting racial discrimination, it provided for reducing the congressional delegation of any state that disfranchised any portion of its Negro population by subtracting the entire Negro population from the basis for representation. In short, the resolution looked forward to future, not present, Negro suffrage. The resolution, slightly modified, then passed the House of Representatives on January 31 as follows:

Representatives shall be apportioned among the several States which may be included within this Union according to their respective number of persons in each State, excluding Indians not taxed: *Provided*, that whenever the elective franchise shall be denied or abridged in any State on account of race or color shall be excluded from the basis of representation [sic].[2]

The Senate gave the House resolution a frigid reception. Veteran antislavery men denounced it as a halfway measure because it failed explicitly to enfranchise the Negro and allowed exclusion of the Negroes at the polls to continue, under a possible penalty. Senator John B. Henderson of Missouri introduced a much stronger, more explicit amendment that " no State, in prescribing the qualifications requisite for electors therein, shall discriminate against any person on account of color or race." [3] Henderson's version, which did in fact prohibit racial discrimination, was somewhat similar to the final form of the Fifteenth Amendment, but it was significantly voted down by a decisive margin. Also defeated decisively was the proposal of Massachusetts' Senator Charles Sumner, which had an even broader scope in banishing racial caste by " no denial of rights, civil or political, on account of color or race." [4] It was clear by these defeats that a majority of Senate Republicans were not yet ready for national enfranchisement of Negroes, who, although championed by a Republican minority, were unable to muster a two-thirds majority to accept proportional reduction of representation with explicit

---

[2] U. S., *Congressional Globe*, 39th Cong., 1st Sess. (1866), pp. 535, 538.
[3] *Ibid.*, pp. 362, 702.
[4] *Ibid.*, p. 1287.

mention of race or color. The House resolution (Blaine proposal) was thus rejected as well, on March 9.[5]

The congressional stalemate was broken when Representative Thaddeus Stevens of Pennsylvania moved, in the critical meeting of the Joint Committee on April 28, to strike out reformer Robert Dale Owen's proposal, which provided for Negro suffrage after 1876 but allowed suffrage discrimination to continue until then under penalty, and instead helped to insert a new provision that simply excluded from the basis of representation eligible male citizens to whom the vote was denied. In short, both immediate and prospective Negro suffrage would be scrapped. Stevens, under mounting pressure from the New York, Illinois, and Indiana congressional delegations, had gone along to kill Negro enfranchisement.[6] The adopted plan of proportional reduction in representation, because of racial prejudice, significantly, deleted " race or color " which had been included in the original House resolution. Indirection thus weakened the second section of the Fourteenth Amendment:

Representatives shall be apportioned among the several States according to their respective numbers, counting the whole number of persons in each State, excluding Indians not taxed. But when the right to vote at any election for the choice of electors for President and Vice-President of the United States, Representatives in Congress, the Executive and Judicial officers of a State, or the members of the Legislature thereof, is denied to any of the male inhabitants of such State, being twenty-one years of age, and citizens of the United States, or in any way abridged except for participation in rebellion, or other crime, the basis of representation therein shall be reduced in the proportion which the number of such male citizens shall bear to the whole number of male citizens twenty-one years of age in such State.[7]

Accepted along strict party lines in both chambers on June 13, 1866, it was sent to the states for ratification, which was secured on July 28, 1868.

This compromise, the best amendment that congressmen could devise and still get an amendment passed and ratified, was a

---

[5] *Ibid.*, p. 1289.

[6] Joseph B. James, *The Framing of the Fourteenth Amendment* (" Illinois Studies in the Social Sciences," Vol. XXXVII, No. 37 [Urbana, Ill.: The University of Illinois Press, 1956]), pp. 109–13; Eric L. McKitrick, *Andrew Johnson and Reconstruction* (Chicago, Ill.: The University of Chicago Press, 1960), pp. 347–48.

[7] U. S., *Constitution*, Amdt. 14, Sec. 2.

modest but incomplete step toward Negro suffrage, in allowing southerners to continue excluding Negroes from voting at the possible risk of taking the unpleasant penalty of roughly fifteen less seats in the House of Representatives and thus the equivalent votes in the electoral college. Most congressmen apparently did not intend to risk drowning by swimming against the treacherous current of racial prejudice and opposition to Negro suffrage. They therefore designed a measure that would avoid the Negro issue in the North, yet exert indirect pressure on the South to accept Negro suffrage. The proportional reduction of the representation feature "was intended to reduce southern representation until the Negro would be in a position to divide, if not dominate, the political power of the South." [8] The practical need of the southern Negro vote, then, was recognized, but so too was the unpopularity of Negro suffrage everywhere. Such compromising sentiments were voiced by radical Republican Senator Jacob Howard of Michigan in presenting the report of the Joint Committee to the Senate on May 23, 1866:

The committee were of [the] opinion that the states are not yet prepared to sanction so fundamental a change as would be the concession of the right to suffrage to the colored race. We may as well state it plainly and fairly, so that there shall be no misunderstanding on the subject. It was our opinion that three-fourths of the states of this Union could not be induced to vote to grant the right of suffrage, even in any degree or under any restriction, to the colored race.[9]

So a way was found in the second section indirectly to help Negroes in the South without antagonizing whites in the North.

Voters in the North, in referendum after referendum, rejected Negro suffrage by a generally substantial vote. Such unmistakable opposition, nearly always in the majority, understandably intimidated Republican politicians, for in state after state the verdict was the same. During 1865 five jurisdictions voted down Negro suffrage in popular referendums. Then, in September, it was defeated in the conservative Republican Territory of Colorado by a vote of 4,192 to 476, or a majority of 3,716. In October, a very conservative Connecticut cast 33,489 votes (57.17 per cent) against Negro suffrage to 27,217 (44.83 per cent) for, which was a negative majority of 6,272, with the forces opposed to suffrage

---

[8] James, *Framing*, p. 180.
[9] *Globe*, 39th Cong., 1st Sess., p. 2766.

carrying every county but the abolitionist stronghold of Windham. During November two northern states with firm Republican loyalties produced the same result. Wisconsin opponents in thirty-four counties cast 55,454 ballots (53.28 per cent) against 46,629 (46.72 per cent) in twenty-three counties in favor—a negative majority of 8,825, while the state Republican ticket ran nearly 12,000 ahead to win the governorship with 54.67 per cent of the vote; and in Minnesota 54.88 per cent of the vote was opposed. Finally, in December, 1865, voters in the southern-oriented District of Columbia rejected Negro suffrage by 6,521 to 35 in Washington city and 812 to 1 in Georgetown. In June, 1866, settlers in the northern-oriented Nebraska Territory defeated Negro suffrage in a close vote, for the majority against the discriminatory state constitution in question was only 100 (3,938 to 3,838). During 1867 the elections were more significant, but the result was the same in Kansas, where the majority against was 9,071 or 55.05 per cent while again the vote was closer in Minnesota, where the majority against was only 1,298. But in the most important referendum in Ohio in the same year, voters decisively rejected Negro suffrage in a vote actually cast by a majority of 38,353, while twelve counties voted Republican for governor but opposed Negro suffrage. Ohio was the acid test and the answer was negative. Michigan in April, 1868, rejected the proposed state constitution, which provided for Negro suffrage—although the issue was not a separate question in the referendum—by a vote of 71,733 to 110,582, or a negative majority of 38,849. Missouri also in 1868 struck down Negro suffrage by a majority of 18,817 or 57.27 per cent. New Yorkers followed the national trend by rejecting the issue in 1869 by a majority of 32,601.

In Iowa and Minnesota only, voters accepted Negro suffrage on November 3, 1868, with Minnesotans favoring it by 56.80 per cent, Iowans by 56.50 per cent—a majority of 24,265. Significantly, victory came on a presidential election day in but two solidly Republican states, and with the use of sharp tactics in Minnesota: placing the suffrage question on the presidential ballot to discourage ticket splitting, and concealing the issue by labeling the question not " Negro suffrage " but rather " revision of section 1, article 7." Minnesota Democrats termed the referendum a swindle. In contrast, the Iowa referendum was fully described to the voters, who could agree or disagree to strike the word

" white " from five provisions of the state constitution. However, Negroes were still forbidden in Iowa to run as candidates for the legislature. In Wisconsin the state supreme court ordered Negro suffrage in a decision handed down in 1866 and based on a successful referendum in 1849. By the end of 1868, then, no northern state with a relatively large Negro population had voluntarily accepted full Negro suffrage. Although there was substantial support for it in a few marginal elections, and notable success in two states, the pattern of defeat was most conspicuous, and even the victories in Minnesota and Iowa were not of earth-shaking proportions because of their timing or tactics in monolithically Republican states with few potential Negro voters and with an infinitesimal percentage of Negro inhabitants. Unfortunately there was no ground swell of popular support or any great decisive change in public opinion between 1865 and 1868 as registered in referendums on Negro suffrage. Instead, white Americans resented and resisted it. After agonizingly grappling with the problem, politicians soon recognized that only federal action could circumvent state inaction. But such a course was hazardous and might have to be postponed until the right occasion.[10]

[10] A comparison between the Iowa and Minnesota votes reveals no great electoral differences, despite the fact that the Iowa vote is a fairer reflection of voter choices. In fact, more was at stake in Iowa, for the Negro population was both absolutely and proportionately higher, numbering 5,762 by 1870 in a state where anti-Negro sentiment was strong enough to divide Iowa Republicans on the issue in 1865. By contrast, Minnesota Negroes numbered only 759 by 1870 in a state more New England in its orientation. Quite understandably, then, the suffrage question ran well behind the vote for Republican Presidential candidate Ulysses S. Grant by 5.42 per cent in Iowa, while only trailing the Grant vote by 2 per cent less in the obscured referendum in Minnesota.

Minnesota was the only state in the Union to vote several times on the Negro suffrage issue between 1865 and 1868. Support did increase in 1867 over the 1865 vote, and then again in 1868, but Minnesota was a strongly Republican one-party state, never electing a Democratic governor between 1860 and 1899. The hard core opposition to Negro suffrage came from ten counties along or near the Mississippi River. All these counties were strongly Democratic and voted against Negro suffrage in all three referendums. These counties were clustered in two groups: one in south central Minnesota, consisting of Ramsey, Carver, Dakota, Scott, Le Sueur, and Sibley counties; the other in the center of the state, in Morrison, Benton, and Stearns counties. Perhaps these counties were settled by Southerners or their descendants, but at any rate there is complete correlation between Democratic loyalty and anti-Negro intensity. On the other hand, there is only some evidence of a relationship between Negro settlement and anti-Negro feeling. Negroes were concentrated in usually urban areas in four counties in 1870. Two of these—Ramsey (St. Paul) and Dakota—were consistently opposed

At this juncture open war, long brewing between the executive and legislative branches in Washington, blazed forth. All attention and energy were focused on the congressional election campaign of 1866. President Johnson, opposing the Fourteenth Amendment and insisting on his policy alone, made his celebrated " swing around the circle " by train from Washington to St. Louis. Speaking extemporaneously as well as intemperately, the President was egged on by hecklers to lose his temper, and repetitions of this caused Johnson to become his own worst enemy. As a result the congressional election returns proved a disaster for Johnsonian conservatives and marked a complete repudiation of presidential Reconstruction. *The Nation* declared that the " conductor of the train has found out that the train has run over him, instead of

to Negro suffrage in all three elections. Winona county similarly opposed Negro suffrage in 1865 and 1867, but favored it in a close vote in 1868. Yet Hennepin county (Minneapolis), with a large proportion of the state's Negro population, was consistently progressive, favoring Negro suffrage in all three elections, though by a close margin in 1865.

It would thus appear that at least in Minnesota people opposed Negro suffrage more out of Democratic sympathy than out of fear of Negro presence. The Minnesota election returns on Negro suffrage are given below, but there is a slight discrepancy between these figures taken from *Tribune Almanac* and the official returns, which indicate that the 1867 majority was slightly larger and the 1865 majority slightly smaller. The unofficial returns, nevertheless, are used, because a county breakdown was unavailable in the official returns examined:

MINNESOTA ELECTION RETURNS ON NEGRO SUFFRAGE AMENDMENT

		1865		1867		1868
Against equal suffrage		14,838		28,759		29,906
For equal suffrage		12,170		27,461		39,322
Whole vote		27,010		56,220		69,228
Majority	against	2,670	against	1,298	for	9,416
% against		54.88%				43.20%
% for		45.12%				56.80%
Counties against		24		18		10
Counties for		21		30		40

See the New York *Times*, April 7, 1868; *Tribune Almanac for 1866*, pp. 46, 53, 55, 57, 69; *Tribune Almanac for 1867*, p. 70; *Tribune Almanac for 1868*, pp. 45–46, 56–57, 62; *Tribune Almanac for 1869*, pp. 74–75, 85; *Tribune Almanac for 1870*, p. 53. See but compare Leslie H. Fishel, Jr., " Northern Prejudice and Negro Suffrage, 1865–1870," *The Journal of Negro History*, XXXIX (January, 1954), 8–26; and Fishel, " The North and the Negro, 1865–1900: A Study in Race Discrimination " (Ph. D. dissertation, 2 vols., Dept. of History, Harvard University, 1953), I, 70–119. See also on the Iowa election, James Harlan to William E. Chandler, July 28, 1868, Chandler MSS, Library of Congress; John S. Runnells to Chandler, September 14, 1868, *ibid.*

his having run away with it." [11] As a whole, the elections were a vote of confidence in congressional Reconstruction and marked, in effect, approval of the Fourteenth Amendment. The anti-Johnsonian Republican coalition that controlled Congress was reinforced and reinvigorated. Congressional Republicans of bolder stripe preferred to interpret the election results as solid support for Negro suffrage everywhere, rather than just opposition to Johnsonian policy or personality alone.

If supporters of Negro suffrage still felt they lacked enough votes in Congress to confer it directly and nationally by a constitutional amendment, they continued to press for it wherever it was clearly within congressional power, as in the District of Columbia. Just as antislavery leaders before the war had attracted support for their cause by urging emancipation in the federal capital, so advocates of universal suffrage hoped that enfranchising Negroes in the District would serve as a pattern for the whole nation. As early as December, 1865, such bills were introduced, and the bill of Representative William D. Kelley of Pennsylvania was finally passed on January 18, 1866, 166 " yes " to 54 " no." Although House Republicans earlier, in a caucus, had rejected universal Negro suffrage and instead supported a qualified form of it, on the floor Democrats using obstructionist tactics succeeded, with more radical Republicans, in passing the measure. Opposing on the final vote were only fifteen Republicans, most of whom represented the border states, some the old Middle West, and a few the Far West, but none from the East. The more conservative Senate never voted on the Kelley bill because Republicans wanted to avoid the controversial Negro suffrage issue, and there was fear that even if the bill passed the Senate it could not override a presidential veto there. Parliamentary squabbling and the excessive heat of that June of 1866 also contributed to inaction.

Significantly it was only after the decisive election returns were counted that the Senate was encouraged to approve Negro suffrage in the District, with only two Republicans disapproving, on December 13, 1866. The next day the House approved the measure, this time with only nine Republicans voting in the opposition, mainly from the border states. Observing acidly that those congressmen who supported Negro suffrage for the District of Columbia were

[11] *The Nation*, November 15, 1866.

from states which prohibited it, President Andrew Johnson vetoed the bill on January 7, 1867. Concluding that neither the Negro nor Washingtonians were ready to accept Negro suffrage, Johnson felt the bill was the wrong thing by the wrong method at the wrong time. Republican congressmen retaliated by overriding the presidential veto on January 8, 1867. The Negro could now vote in the nation's capital.[12]

Congress was not to be trifled with during that January, 1867. Its mood reflected the victories of the 1866 fall elections, and this development occurred before the new Congress convened. Another bill, in effect enfranchising Negroes in federal territories, had passed the House before the congressional elections on May 15, 1866 (with eight Republicans opposed—seven less than the District vote four months before), but, like the District bill, was not passed by the more conservative Senate. However, after the elections, on January 10, 1867, the Senate passed a similar measure, with only one Republican, Peter G. Van Winkle of West Virginia, in opposition. On the same day it was supported by the House. President Johnson, apparently in a state of resignation after the District of Columbia defeat, acquiesced, and Negroes after January 31, 1867, had the formal right to vote in federal territories.[13]

---

[12] Edward McPherson, *The Political History of the United States of America during the Period of Reconstruction* (2nd ed.; Washington, D. C.: Solomons & Chapman, 1875), pp. 115, 160 (all subsequent citations will be cited as "E. McPherson" referring to this work alone); the New York *Times*, October 16, 1867; William Lloyd Garrison to George W. Julian, February 11, 1866, George W. Julian MSS, Library of Congress; *Globe*, 39th Cong., 2nd Sess., pp. 109, 138, 303–6, 313, 344.

[13] *Globe*, 39th Cong., 2nd Sess., pp. 382, 399, 994–95; E. McPherson, pp. 116–17. Negroes were voting in April in Republican controlled Colorado Territory. Presumably it was Democrats in the Dakota territorial legislature who agreed to Negro suffrage in December, 1867. Although racial discrimination in voting was now voided by congressional action, apparently Washington Territory Democrats and Republicans as well postponed action to strike the word "white" out of their laws by failing to take such action during January, 1868. Democrats were in strong control of the territorial legislatures in Idaho and Montana, and appear to have not stricken "white" from their election laws in the latter state. A federal law, creating the Territory of Wyoming on July 25, 1868, prohibited racial discrimination in voting and holding office. The legislative assembly complied and went a step further by establishing women suffrage as well on December 10, 1869. However, the legislature outlawed miscegenation. Party lines seem unclear in Arizona, New Mexico, and Utah, but information is difficult to obtain concerning these states and Idaho. In general, however, Southern mores appear strong in both parties throughout the western territories, for latent racial prejudice and overt discrimination were not uncommon, especially with many southerners migrating to ranch and mine.

Still another part of the nation was accorded Negro suffrage in January, 1867, by congressional insistence. Congress laid down as a condition of statehood that the Nebraska Territory must enfranchise the Negro. On January 30, 1867, President Johnson vetoed the measure, but Congress again ignored presidential opposition and overrode the veto on February 9. Strongly Republican, the Nebraska legislature accepted Negro suffrage and Nebraska was admitted into the Union as the thirty-seventh state. Thus in one month all the territorial subdivisions under the direct control of Congress had received Negro suffrage.[14]

The climax of the suffrage drama in the Thirty-ninth Congress was the decision to adopt the fifth section of the First Reconstruction Act of March 2, 1867. Congress now required Negro suffrage as a condition for readmitting the former Confederate states to the Union and seating their representatives in Congress. Thaddeus Stevens had justified universal Negro suffrage in the South by concluding that " if it be just, it should not be denied; if it be necessary, it should be adopted; if it be a punishment to traitors, they deserve it." [15] One Floridian felt that exclusion of whites and inclusion of Negroes in voting was desirable, because the guilty would be disfranchised and the deserving enfranchised.[16] But other southerners bitterly complained of the double standard of their being forced to endure Negro suffrage with all its revolutionary consequences, while northerners refused to allow it in their part of the country, where there were not enough Negroes to cause any problem.[17]

This brief review of the congressional record on Negro suffrage between 1865 and 1868 indicates that a very substantial Republican majority, except for those northeastern and middle western advocates of universal Negro suffrage, was completely opposed to Negro voting immediately after the war. During 1866, however, this position cracked in the House of Representatives, though border state and some older middle west Republicans remained actively hostile. By February, 1867, congressional Republicans had enfranchised the Negro in the District of Columbia, federal terri-

[14] *Globe*, 39th Cong., 2nd Sess., pp. 481–82, 485, 487, 851–52, 1096, 1121.
[15] *Ibid.*, p. 252.
[16] O. B. Hart and C. L. Robinson to D. Richards, January 8, 1867, William P. Fessenden MSS, Library of Congress.
[17] McKitrick, *Andrew Johnson*, pp. 473–85; L. E. Jones to John Sherman, March 6, 1867, John Sherman MSS, Library of Congress.

tories, and Nebraska, by very substantial majorities, and the following month they demanded enfranchisement of the southern Negro. But since it was the same Thirty-ninth Congress that had first failed to act and then did act affirmatively and hurriedly after the elections, it is an open question whether the shift of congressional support came about because sincere supporters of Negro suffrage were too timid during 1866 or because pragmatic politicians, following the latest fashion and most recent election returns, wanted a radical reputation in a hurry in 1867. In any case, these politicians, whether stirred by idealistic impulse or moved by political expediency, appeared—because of the timing—to be acting under the pressure of events and the compulsions of interest.

While congressmen could easily legislate for the District or Nebraska, and with more effort for the South, national enfranchisement of the Negro—which meant Negro voting in the North—was out of the question. The decisive disapproval of Henderson's amendment in the voting on the Fourteenth Amendment, and the equally decisive approval of Negro suffrage in the District of Columbia, would lead one to the conclusion that there was a substantial consensus among Republicans in Congress to enfranchise the Negro everywhere except back home in the North. Enfranchising the northern Negro was another matter, and there were serious differences among Republicans over how to handle the question. In fact, state opposition to Negro suffrage remained strong enough to intimidate congressmen.

Probably the single most important influence to slow the pace of the movement to enfranchise the Negro was the 1867 elections, which stressed the issue of Negro suffrage in the North. Capturing the heat of the Ohio campaign, Burke Hinsdale wrote that " both sides are making their strongest appeal to prejudice—the one [Democrats] harping on the ' nigger ' and the other [Republicans] harping on the ' copper-head.' " [18] When the returns were counted the dimension of the devastating defeat took shape. Republicans first received setbacks in the spring in Connecticut by losing the governorship and almost losing the legislature. Then, during

[18] Burke A. Hinsdale to James A. Garfield, August 19, 1867, in Mary L. Hinsdale (ed.), *Garfield-Hinsdale Letters, Correspondence between James Abram Garfield and Burke Aaron Hinsdale* (Ann Arbor, Mich.: University of Michigan, 1949), p. 96.

September, Maine Republicans ran poorly and a Democratic governor replaced a Republican in California. In October and November state elections Democrats made spectacular gains by capturing both houses of formerly Republican legislatures in Ohio and New Jersey, the House of Representatives in Albany, as well as all state offices in contest and a chief-justiceship in Pennsylvania. The Democracy became further intrenched in the border states, while running surprisingly strong in the Middle West. As Democrats picked up seats in Congress by special elections, they simply reversed Republican electoral majorities of 1866 with the same voter turnout. In Ohio, for example, Republicans won ten out of nineteen Congressional districts in 1866, but the Republican state ticket in 1867 carried three districts. Because of the size of the turnout in Ohio and because referendums on Negro suffrage went down in decisive defeat in Ohio, Kansas, and Minnesota, not to mention the discussion of it elsewhere, Republican losses were widely interpreted as repudiating extension of Negro suffrage in the North.[19]

Politicians and editors responded quite predictably to the Republican fiasco. Democrats and conservative Johnson administration men celebrated and paraded. President Johnson saluted Ohio and regarded the elections as an endorsement of his policy. New York City Democrats fired cannon, set off bonfires and fireworks, and listened to bands and speeches. Democratic Mayor John T. Hoffman told Democrats at a rally that "Radical fanaticism"[20] was repudiated and no longer would radical firebrands try to elevate Negroes by stepping on poor whites who were also trying to get ahead. Mayor Hoffman's remark brought the wildest applause of the evening. In short, Democracy was delighted, and now had great expectations.[21]

[19] *The Nation*, November 21, 1867; the New York *Times*, October 16, and November 10, 1867; the Cincinnati *Commercial*, October 29, 1867; Jesod R. Grant to Richard A. Wheeler, December 27, 1867, Jesod R. Grant MSS, New York Historical Society; Selden Henry, "Radical Republican Policy Toward the Negro During Reconstruction (1862–1872)" (Ph. D. dissertation, Dept. of History, Yale University, 1963), p. 379. Henry estimates that in 19 northern and border states the Republican loss between 1866 and 1867 was 164,125 votes, or slightly less than the total Democratic gain, in 1867 over 1866, of 164,427. The total turnout was remarkably constant—3,190,537 in 1866 and slightly higher by 302 in 1867's total turnout of 3,190,839.

[20] The New York *Times*, October 10, 1867.

[21] See editorials of Democratic New York *World* quoted in [New York] *National Anti-Slavery Standard*, November 16, 23, 1867.

Recrimination characterized much of radical Republican reaction to the elections of 1867. The ardent abolitionist Wendell Phillips, among others, denounced what he felt was the cowardly stand of Republican politicians in the recent campaign for Negro suffrage and felt that it could have been achieved nationally when the time had been ripe in 1865 or 1866. His remedy for the fiasco was a larger dose of radicalism, by impeaching President Johnson and firing his supporters, thus distracting the people so that Congress would pass a simple law enfranchising Negroes throughout the country.[22] The *Independent* mixed wishful thinking with realistic prediction by first reassuring its readers that since the " Party of Justice having God on its side is sure of the final victory," [23] Republicans cannot abandon the principle of Negro suffrage in the North; yet it also acknowledged that national equal suffrage might be delayed until after the presidential campaign in 1868. For its part, the *National Anti-Slavery Standard* turned its guns on those who were flirting with the movement to nominate the so-called political sphinx, General Ulysses Grant, as the Republican presidential candidate. One correspondent declared that expediency should not rule the hour because that meant sacrificing principle; instead, unswerving loyalty to principle was the only answer, for otherwise the " half-closed eye of expediency is more easily satisfied than the broad vision of principle." [24] Beneath such ostentatious confidence or righteous recrimination there appeared widespread panic in the radical ranks.

Symptomatic of the crisis and soberly anticipating it, Thaddeus Stevens started to draft a new constitutional amendment to enfranchise the Negro before the Fourteenth Amendment was even ratified. It was not the first time that Stevens shifted on the issue, for like many Republicans he was markedly cool toward the subject in 1865, appeared not its most vigorous proponent in the Joint Committee while drafting the Fourteenth Amendment, but vigorously endorsed Negro suffrage for the South in 1867, and now during the summer and fall started drafting a version of a proposed fifteenth amendment that would give Negroes the vote everywhere. Hoping to save the Republican party from defeat by granting universal Negro suffrage by an amendment, Stevens

[22] The New York *Times*, November 2, 1867.
[23] The *Independent*, November 14, 1867.
[24] [New York] *National Anti-Slavery Standard*, November 9, 1867.

wrote: "We must establish the doctrine of National jurisdiction over all the States in State matters of the Franchise, or we shall finally be ruined—We must thus bridle Penna. Ohio Ind. et cetera, or the South, *being in*, we shall drift into democracy." [25] By implication, other radical plans, such as Charles Sumner's proposal to merely pass a law, now appeared visionary—such was the traumatic force of the 1867 election reverses upon radical opinion.

Neither Democratic exultation nor radical desperation characterized moderate response to the elections. Without accepting the Democratic interpretation that the elections marked repudiation and the possible ending of congressional Reconstruction in the South, moderate Republicans still did agree with their Democratic opponents that the meaning of the elections was an overwhelming repudiation of extremism. Extremism had succeeded before, because Democrats were no serious competitors to Republican supremacy, and thus Republican politicians "grew too strong to be wise," [26] losing prudence and restraint after the successful 1866 elections. When radicals started ignoring arrogantly and arbitrarily the great vital center of moderate opinion; when they were manning the 1867 campaigns with exclusively radical supporters; when they were forcing the issue of Negro suffrage in the North, recklessly and relentlessly, as a party principle; when they were talking of "rights of suffrage" and "logical sequences" to people who cared nothing about rights and who didn't know what a logical sequence was; then they were earning defeat by alienating many moderate Republicans in the recent campaign. The New York *Times*, in an editorial, posed squarely the question of the future usefulness of the Negro suffrage issue, thus answering radical demands:

It is all very well to say that the Republican party cannot abandon it [universal Negro suffrage]—that they must "fight on," and "rally afresh to the combat," and "keep the banner of eternal justice very high," and all that sort of thing. So it may, and so it should; but it does not intend to be beaten in the next election. The party does not see very well how the cause of justice and the rights of the negro, are to be aided by the election of a Copperhead President; and it does not intend to permit any

---

[25] Thaddeus Stevens to Edward McPherson, August 16, 1867, quoted in Richard N. Current, *Old Thad Stevens: A Story of Ambition* (Madison, Wis.: The University of Wisconsin Press, 1942), p. 288.

[26] The New York *Times*, October 10, 1867.

such result. It will go in *to win*, and it will nominate as its candidate the man who is most sure to be elected.[27]

Moderates recognized, then, that for the future advantage of the party the unpopular Negro suffrage issue had been temporarily eclipsed, for " the negro has been covered up and laid away under Democratic majorities." [28] Burke Hinsdale observed that " politics have taken on a conservative complexion—Republican politics I mean. The negro will be less prominent for some time to come." [29]

The corollaries of the election reverses seemed equally clear to Republican moderates. First, Republican congressmen would be put on their best, not their radical, behavior. Moderates were premature in view of subsequent impeachment proceedings, but clearly, such radical proposals as southern land confiscation were dead. The defeats in 1867 also provided moderates with a convenient excuse to rally their forces and use the election fiasco as an excellent weapon to stampede the nomination of Grant as a sure winner in preference to the questionable candidacy of the champion of Negro suffrage, Chief Justice Salmon P. Chase. Moderates advertised that under Grant's leadership the Republican party would be united by a popular war hero running on a sound and statesmanlike—i. e., moderate—platform. All in all, moderate Republicans had little to complain about the defeats of 1867, for their power was thereby strengthened in 1868.

Generally, Republican politicians were either scared or shrewd enough to trim their sails and set course according to the prevailing winds, which had shifted abruptly during the fall of 1867. One Republican, writing to Senator William P. Fessenden of Maine, expressed the new consensus that prejudice against the Negro was too strong to tolerate schemes to enfranchise him in the North. Congress should march forward under the brave banner

[27] *Ibid.*, October 17, 1867.

[28] *Ibid.*, November 10, 1867. See also *ibid.*, October 10, 11, 14, 15, November 7, 8, 10, 11, 1867. The Ohio correspondent minced no words about radical reaction to the Ohio campaign: " I see that some of the New-York newspapers are inclined to find many wonderful things at the bottom, which the people of Ohio do not see. The New-York *Tribune* gives the Republicans credit for a marvelous amount of moral courage, in leading an advance for impartial suffrage . . . but it will be some time before the Republicans make another ' advance' in the line of impartial suffrage." *Ibid.*, October 21, 1867.

[29] Hinsdale to Garfield, October 22, 1867, Hinsdale (ed.), *Garfield-Hinsdale Letters*, p. 112.

of equal suffrage for the South, " but the Northern states may not yet be ripe and you may have to allow them to educate for some time longer." [30] Just as the farmer at harvest may not be able to reap his grain all at once but must wait longer for some of it to ripen, John Binney concluded it was prudent to win with General Grant in the presidential election of 1868, and then " this measure of universal negro suffrage will be carried possibily soon after the Presidential election—but must not be done till then." [31]

Consequently, managers at the Republican national convention, held in Chicago on May 20–21, 1868, hoped to keep the party's stand on Negro suffrage as bland and noncontroversial as the assured presidential nominee, Ulysses S. Grant. But controversy over a suffrage plank developed even before the convention assembled. Radical Republicans were worried that a weak suffrage plank would evade the issue in the North, abandon the Negro everywhere, and ultimately destroy the party. More moderate Republicans implored politicians to go slow on the issue or lose elections. Yet despite a vigorous struggle in the Committee on Resolutions, the moderate position won out in a close vote.[32] A double standard was rationalized: handing Negro suffrage in the North over to the northern states, the resolution also declared that the " guarantee by Congress of equal suffrage to all loyal men at the South was demanded by every consideration of public safety, of gratitude, and of justice." [33] The fight over the suffrage plank was confined to the Platform Committee and did not erupt on the floor of the convention, where on May 20 the platform was accepted.

Much reaction was favorable. Moderate and radical Republican newspapers sighed in apparent relief. The New York *Times* correspondent reported that convention delegates had praised the suffrage plank as " prudent, sagacious, and sound." And a *Times* editorial applauded the platform for rejecting the extremist posi-

[30] John Binney to Fessenden, March 19, 1868, November 2, 15, 1867, Fessenden MSS; Binney to Schuyler Colfax, November 2, 1867, *ibid.*

[31] *Ibid.*

[32] [New York] *The World*, May 21, 1868; J. C. Lee to James A. Garfield, January 25, 1869, James A. Garfield MSS, Library of Congress; *Globe*, 40th Cong., 3rd Sess. (1869), Appendix, p. 154. Carl Schurz apparently wrote the platform. See the New York *Times*, December 12, 1868.

[33] *Proceedings of the National Union Republican Convention* (Chicago, Ill.: Evening Journal Print, 1868), p. 84.

tion of Thaddeus Stevens and Charles Sumner and for assuming that normally each state should determine suffrage regulation. Because the Negro was free and secure in the North, argued a writer in the *North American Review*, he had no right to complain of disfranchisement, but because the opposite was true in the South he needed the ballot to protect himself.[34] The logic was flimsy, but the desire to avoid the Negro issue was strong.

Criticism of the plank ranged from mild disagreement to violent denunciation. The New York *Post* suggested that northern Negro suffrage should perhaps have been included. The Democratic *World* dismissed the plank as pure politics because it provided one law for the northern white, who could deny even qualified suffrage to the Negro, and another for the southern white, who could submit only to universal Negro suffrage. The *World* charged that the Republicans feared northern voters who opposed Negro suffrage. The New York *Herald* concurred, cynically observing that the plank was as elastic as Indian rubber.[35]

Veteran abolitionists were furious. Thaddeus Stevens thundered that the Chicago platform and the suffrage plank were " tame and cowardly." [36] The *Anti-Slavery Standard* termed the plank a " palpable lie " and advocated an amendment to the federal constitution guaranteeing universal suffrage.[37]

Republican victory was soon assured by the Democrats. Rejecting Salmon P. Chase and his idea of universal suffrage and amnesty, they nominated Horatio Seymour and Frank Blair, the latter a violently outspoken critic of Negro suffrage. The Democratic platform denounced the Reconstruction acts and warned that " any attempt by Congress, on any pretext whatever, to deprive any State of this right [the regulation of suffrage by the states], or interfere with its exercise, is a flagrant usurpation of power. . . ." [38] This platform did not, however, mention Negro

---

[34] Boston *Morning Journal*, May 22, 1868; the Chicago *Republican*, May 21, 22, 1868; New York *Tribune*, May 23, 1868; the Cincinnati *Commercial*, May 22, 1868; the New York *Times*, May 22, 29, 1868; Adams S. Hill, " The Chicago Convention," *North American Review*, CCXX (July, 1868), 175–76.

[35] [New York] *The Evening Post*, May 25, 1868; [New York] *The World*, May 21, 28, 1868; compare [Washington, D. C.] *Daily National Intelligencer*, May 25, 1868; the New York *Herald*, May 22, July 9, 1868.

[36] Thaddeus Stevens to Charles L. Spene, June 24, 1868, Draft, Thaddeus Stevens MSS, Library of Congress.

[37] [New York] *National Anti-Slavery Standard*, May 30, June 13, 1868.

[38] *Official Proceedings of the National Democratic Convention, Held at New York, July 4–9, 1868* (Boston, Mass.: Rockwell and Rollins, 1868), pp. 58–60.

suffrage. It did not endorse southern Negro voting as the South
Carolina Democrats wanted, nor did it denounce Negro suffrage in
both the North and the South, as eleven state conventions—
notably those of Delaware and the midwestern states—had asked.
Instead, it declared that Negro suffrage should be left to the
states, a position that had been expressly or tacitly approved by
ten state Democratic conventions. The platform was thus a compromise, similar in motive if not in position to that of the Republicans. The party gave up its clear chance to attack inconsistencies
in the Republican suffrage plank to enable southern Conservatives
to woo the Negro voters.[39]

Democratic newspapers were more partisan in praise of their
party's platform than Republican journals had been. The Washington *National Intelligencer* called the platform "unambigu-
ous,"[40] while the New York *World* more moderately supported
state regulation, concluding that Negro suffrage would remain
and that it was futile to fight it.[41] The Philadelphia *Age*, however,
was unhappy with the plank because it "was covered with the
thin veil of expediency."[42]

Republican papers either ignored the Democratic suffrage plank
or criticized it. The *Anti-Slavery Standard* assailed the entire
Democratic platform because, though it ostensibly left the question of Negro suffrage to the states, all knew that Democrats
would drive the Negro from each poll in every state. The Democratic platform, argued the New York *Times*, complained of
Negro supremacy but said nothing about white man's government;
it called for immediate restoration of all states and their rights,
but did not specify whether with or without Negro suffrage,
concluding that such a plank provided the occasion when "trickery
comes into full play."[43]

Despite the fact that both party platforms dodged Negro

[39] Charles H. Coleman, *The Election of 1868: The Democratic Effort to Regain
Control* (New York: Columbia University Press, 1933), pp. 24, 61, 200, 203,
286. Apparently U. S. Senator James A. Bayard of Delaware wrote the suffrage
plank.
[40] [Washington, D. C.] *Daily National Intelligencer*, July 9, 1868.
[41] [New York] *The World*, June 19, July 8, 1868.
[42] [Philadelphia] *The Age*, May 23, 1868.
[43] Coleman, p. 205; [New York] *National Anti-Slavery Standard*, July 11, 1868;
the New York *Times*, July 8, 1868. Compare [Philadelphia] *The Press*, July 8,
1868.

suffrage, politicians in the campaign used the issue to attack their
opposition. In New Jersey, Democrat Samuel J. Bayard protested
the Republican scheme for "exclusive white sovereignty at the
North and actual Negro supremacy at the South." ". . . Notwith-
standing the Chicago platform," he continued, "there can be no
doubt that if the people continue to place their confidence in the
Radicalized Republican party negro suffrage will be forced on the
Middle and Western States, with or without their consent." [44]
Republican Robert G. Ingersoll in a campaign speech in Maine
accepted the Democratic charge that Republicans favored Negro
suffrage:

> But say these Democrats, you have allowed the Negroes to vote. Yes,
> we have. In days of Washington, negroes voted, and the question now
> is, if that were so are modern Democrats fit to vote with negroes now?
> Is not a negro who is an honor to the black race, better than a white man
> who is a disgrace to the white race? . . . it was our duty to see that no
> man who had fought for the flag should be under the feet of him who
> had insulted it.[45]

For the benefit of Negroes and radicals some Republican newspapers argued that Democratic victory would mean an end to
Negro suffrage in the South. But in general candid Republican
counter-offensives, like Ingersoll's, were conspicuously played down
in the more moderate newspapers. Still the issue would not fade
away.[46]

In the November elections Grant won with a plurality of only
300,000. The southern Negro vote, exceeding 450,000, was indispensable to a Republican popular, but not electoral, majority.
Three southern states did not participate in the election and six
others voted under so-called carpetbag régimes, which prevented
many whites from voting. Republican majorities were uncom-
fortable in Indiana, New Hampshire, North Carolina, and Pennsylvania. In Alabama, Arkansas, and Connecticut the majorities
were slight, whereas in the western states of Nevada and Cali-
foria, Grant's majority was infinitesimal. Had the Democrats
nominated a stronger candidate, they might have won, since a
small shift in the popular vote of a few key states would have

[44] Broadside, 1868, Samuel J. Bayard MSS, Princeton University Library.
[45] Broadside, September 7, 1868, Robert G. Ingersoll MSS, Library of Congress.
[46] Coleman, pp. 287, 369–70.

changed the outcome. In any event, Democrats made gains in the new House of Representatives.[47]

The election spelled trouble for Republicans, who worried that the southern Negro might jump their camp. Southern Democrats and conservatives were able to recruit roughly 50,000 Negro voters in the South.[48] Foster Blodgett, a Georgia politician, observed in a letter to William Clafflin, chairman of the Republican National Committee, that Democrats tried to woo the Negro voter in Georgia with barbecues, uniforms, and badges. Actually, the Democrats were successful in the second Congressional district, which " has a large majority of colored voters, [but] went against us in the last election. This has opened our eyes to the fact that Democrats can influence in various ways, many blacks to go with them." [49] Republican Congressman W. Jasper Blackburn of Louisiana told his colleagues that he knew that southern Democrats, though " they have howled and are still howling against negro suffrage, stole it and appropriated it in the last election [1868] in my State [Louisiana]; and I think I know that the northern Democracy both expected and greatly desired this."[50] The Washington *National Republican* and other newspapers also observed a tendency in many southern Democrats to woo Negro voters. Although the total number of southern Negro voters recruited to the Democrats was relatively small, the disproportionate reaction may have revealed the deep anxiety of Republican politicians.[51]

Republicans were even more worried about southern Negroes who might desert the polls rather than mutiny by supporting Democrats. They were told that Negroes had been coerced to stay away from the polls by bribery, threats, superstition, and

[47] Grant, with 52.7 per cent of the vote, had a popular majority of only 309,000 out of 5,716,000 votes cast. *Ibid.*, pp. 372–78, 384, 362–64; [New York] the *Independent*, November 12, 1868; W. Dean Burnham, *Presidential Ballots, 1836–1892* (Baltimore, Md.: The Johns Hopkins Press, 1955), p. 101.

[48] Coleman, pp. 369–70.

[49] Foster Blodgett and John Caldwell to William Claflin [Chairman, Republican National Committee], July 4, 1868, Chandler MSS.

[50] *Globe*, 40th Cong., 3rd Sess., Appendix, p. 242.

[51] [Washington, D. C.] *The National Republican*, December 12, 1868; the New York *Herald*, November 12, 1868; the New York *Times*, January 4, 1869. Prominent Democrats supported this development. R. Abbey to Samuel J. Tilden, July 3, 1868, Samuel J. Tilden MSS, New York Public Library; [Washington, D. C.] *Daily National Intelligencer*, December 29, 1868.

violence, particularly in New Orleans, Louisiana, and north Georgia, which voted Democratic, but also in South Carolina, Mississippi, Tennessee, and Florida.[52]

Many correspondents of the secretary of the Republican National Committee, William E. Chandler, expressed doubts about the reliability of southern Negro voting. One Tennessee Republican felt that the " future of the Republican party in the South is by no means secure. Sometimes I feel discouraged when I realize fully the disloyalty, the obstinacy and the blind folly of the Southern whites; the ignorance, inexperience and the changeableness of the negroes. This element cannot be relied upon, and is going to give us trouble." [53] Another Republican from Atlanta wrote Chandler that the

Negroes are too dependent upon their employers to be counted upon with certainty—They are without property, and cannot sustain themselves but a few days at most, without being fed by their Masters; they are without education or sufficient intelligence to appreciate the power the *Ballot* gives them, add to which a system of intimidation persistently practiced by the Rebels, appealing to their fears through their superstition, and you have a mass of poverty, ignorance, stupidity, and superstition under the influence of fears both real and imaginary, to organise and control, upon whom but little reliance can be placed.[54]

Even while some Republicans came to realize that it would take further guarantees to ensure the Negro vote in the South, other leaders of the party were anxiously canvassing the returns from the northern states. Despite elaborate attempts at evasion, the Negro suffrage issue hurt border, Pacific coast, and northern Republicans. A referendum on Negro suffrage was defeated in Missouri and had not helped Republicans there either. In Ohio, Congressman James M. Ashley attributed his defeat to the Negro suffrage issue,[55] and though Iowa and Minnesota had voted to enfranchise Negroes, the struggle had not been easy. In short,

[52] The New York *Times*, December 2, 3, 8, 16, 1868.

[53] J. M. Forney to William E. Chandler, December 27, 1868, Chandler MSS.

[54] Volney Spalding to Chandler, September 1, 1868, *ibid*. In a reference to the Negro vote in the South, the chairman of the Republican National Committee perhaps indicated his lack of confidence. See Claflin to Chandler, October 23, 1868, *ibid*.

[55] Coleman, *Election of 1868*, pp. 362–65; Joseph J. C. Clarke to Chandler, October 22, 1868, James M. Ashley to Chandler, October 15, 1868, Chandler MSS; the New York *Herald*, November 17, 1868; [Washington, D. C.] *The National Republican*, November 14, 28, 1868.

prospects for both northern and southern Republicans were not bright.

Republicans had to do something. The Philadelphia *Press* inaugurated the new campaign three days after the election, advising the Republicans editorially that " victory is nothing unless you secure its fruits," [56] one of which was the enfranchisement of the northern Negro. The *Press* went on to sound the first explicit call for the Fifteenth Amendment after the elections: " Let the Fortieth Congress . . . propose an amendment to the Constitution conferring the power to vote for national purposes and officers on colored men, under equal conditions with white men. . . . [Thus] where the colored men vote, there the cause of Republicanism is entirely safe, and will be." [57] In full agreement William D. Kelley, stanch advocate of Negro suffrage, wrote that " Party expediency and exact justice coincide for once. . . ." [58]

Moderate and radical Republicans were quick to endorse the *Press* proposal. The veteran *National Anti-Slavery Standard* championed a constitutional amendment on the ground of justice as well as expediency, contending that the Negro vote in the North, especially in the border and middle Atlantic states and in Connecticut and Ohio, would make these states safely Republican. The *Independent* endorsed Negro suffrage everywhere by the method of such an amendment. Moderate journals supported an amendment because it lent strength to the moderate claim that Congress did not have the power to pass a bill enfranchising Negroes in the North. It was even reported that President-elect Grant favored it. By the middle of November it was clear that probably Republicans would pass some sort of constitutional amendment, and congressmen voiced this intention in early December.[59]

Though the need for an amendment was widely recognized in Republican circles, the form and scope were matters of disagree-

---

[56] [Philadelphia] *The Press*, November 6, 1868.

[57] *Ibid.*

[58] [Philadelphia] *The Press*, November 6, 1868; William D. Kelley to R. Lyle White, October 27, 1868, quoted in *National Anti-Slavery Standard*, November 14, 1868.

[59] [New York] *National Anti-Slavery Standard*, November 14, December 12, 1868; [New York] the *Independent*, November 12, 19, 26, 1868; the New York *Times*, November 6, 7, 8, 16, 1868; [Washington, D. C.] *The National Republican*, November 14, 17, 1868; the New York *Herald*, November 17, December 1, 9, 1868.

ment. The entire debate on Negro suffrage, which had raged within and without the Republican party from 1864 to 1868, was telescoped into editorials during December, 1868, and January and February, 1869. The old and academic question of whether suffrage was a natural right or a political privilege was raised anew. A New York *Times* correspondent asked whether Negroes, women, former rebels, Chinamen, and Mormons should vote and, if so, at what age. The journalist concluded that suffrage was purely an arbitrary rule, not an inherent right, and that the point at issue was expediency, the practical benefits accruing to any change in suffrage regulations.[60]

Other issues were raised. Whether male suffrage should be universal or qualified was discussed. The New York *Tribune*, for example, wanted all eligible males to vote, regardless of color or Civil War record. The *Anti-Slavery Standard* went further, advocating universal male suffrage. Journals examined the question of how suffrage might best be secured, by congressional act or by constitutional amendment. The *Tribune* attacked Senator Charles Sumner for arguing that a simple law could impose Negro suffrage, pointing out that what a Republican Congress could extend, a future Democratic Congress could withdraw.[61]

Another critical postelection debate centered on whether suffrage was a state or federal matter. The *Tribune* felt that consistency demanded uniform suffrage regulations. The *Daily Morning Chronicle* of Washington agreed that state suffrage regulations ought to be federally controlled since United States senators were elected by state legislatures. The New York *Times*, on the other hand, favored federal control of federal elections but not of state elections, arguing that state elections should be independent of federal regulation and free from the risk that a change in the political control of Congress would make the subject a political football. Other Republicans argued about whether an amendment should be directed chiefly toward abuses in the South or toward those in the North.[62] The knot of Negro suffrage was hard to untie.

[60] The New York *Times*, December 22, 1868.
[61] New York *Tribune*, November 13, 1868; [New York] *National Anti-Slavery Standard*, December 12, 1868; New York *Tribune*, December 16, 1868.
[62] New York *Tribune*, December 1, 1868; [Washington, D. C.] *Daily Morning Chronicle*, November 16, 24, 1868; the New York *Times*, November 19, December 12, 1868.

In retrospect, the postwar movement to enfranchise the Negro was neither steady nor progressive nor inevitable. From the Appomattox of the Confederates to the Appomattox of the Johnsonians, Republican politicians acted scared. During 1865 and through 1866 there was sustained opposition to Negro suffrage, or its federal imposition, clearly in evidence in the Fourteenth Amendment votes in Congress. But the landslide Republican victories of 1866 advanced Negro suffrage in places where victory was assured and retaliation fairly remote, such as Washington, federal territories, and the more daring experiment in the South, where southern white intransigency had forced Congress' hand. Yet advance was abruptly halted by routs of Republican tickets and suffrage amendments in 1867. Withdrawal took shape in calculated evasion in the platform plank and Grant's candidacy in 1868.

Defeat in postwar state referendums, disaster in 1867 state elections, and danger signals in the federal elections of 1868 taught Republicans that something must be done, but they were not agreed on what it should be—only that it must be done by this final session of the Fortieth Congress, before the Democrats arrived in force.

CHAPTER II

PARALYSIS AND PASSAGE

The congressional debates on the Fifteenth Amendment were long and complex during January and February, 1869. Since Congress was to decide not only who should vote but whether state or nation should validate the voter, the measure was regarded as the most important business of the third (lame duck) session of the Fortieth Congress. Throughout the nation, and especially in the newspapers, the proposed suffrage amendment generated much controversy over the prospect of the Negro as a voter.

Debate on the amendment, often extending into all-night sessions, taxed the patience of congressmen, consumed three hundred pages in the *Congressional Globe*, and produced incredible parliamentary tangles. Moreover, the protracted struggle between the Senate and the House, and the shifting coalitions of obstructionists in each chamber, complicated and prolonged voting.

Yet throughout the congressional debate there was little question that the enfranchisement of the Negro was the object of a proposed constitutional amendment,[1] and it was widely recognized in Congress and throughout the country that its primary goal was the enfranchisement of Negroes outside the deep South. To be sure, it would permanently guarantee suffrage to the southern Negro by law, but, despite a certain amount of intimidation, he was already exercising the franchise, first under military reconstruction, then under the new southern state constitutions. It was, on the other hand, the unenfranchised northern Negro who would principally benefit by the proposed amendment, and presumably would thereafter loyally support his Republican friends.

[1] U. S., *Congressional Globe*, 40th Cong., 3rd Sess., pp. 558–61, 645, 721–22, 725, 1008; Appendix, pp. 92–93, 97–98, 102, 104–5, 126, 147, 199, 206, 241, 295. All subsequent references in this chapter to the *Globe* refer to the Fortieth Congress in its third session unless otherwise indicated.

This was candidly admitted by the more moderate framers and sponsors of such a measure. Republican Congressman George S. Boutwell of Massachusetts estimated that roughly 146,000 Negro citizens in the North would be enfranchised as follows: " Seventeen hundred in Connecticut, ten thousand in New York, five thousand in New Jersey, fourteen thousand in Pennsylvania, seven thousand in Ohio, twenty-four thousand in Missouri, forty-five thousand in Kentucky, four thousand in Delaware, thirty-five thousand in Maryland." [2] In addition, Boutwell stressed Negro voting in the border states of Kentucky, Maryland, and Delaware.[3] Republican Senator William M. Stewart of Nevada also emphasized the importance of the northern Negro voter, who became the " balance of power in many of the largest and most populous of the Northern States," [4] he said, when assessing the value of a suffrage amendment in retrospect.[5] During the debate Stewart accented the potential Negro vote in the border states, observing that " You give the negroes in Maryland the ballot and they will demand their other rights, as they did in Tennessee. Give it to them in Kentucky and Delaware, they will demand and obtain all their rights." [6] Stewart concluded that the power of the ballot

---

[2] *Ibid.*, p. 561. See also his reference to the northern Negro vote, *ibid.*, pp. 555, 557, 558, 560.

[3] *Ibid.*, p. 559.

[4] U. S., *Congressional Record*, 51st Cong., 2nd Sess. (1890), pp. 678, 682. See also George R. Brown (ed.), *Reminiscences of Senator William M. Stewart* (New York: Neale Publishing Co., 1908), p. 232.

[5] Brown, *Reminiscences*, p. 238.

[6] *Globe*, pp. 1299, 1629. The word "moderate" as used in this study is a description of an individual's state of mind in relation to that of others who are more "radical" on the suffrage question in general and on the framing of the Fifteenth Amendment in particular. A moderate stand, then, is somewhat less than an extreme position on any given suffrage issue. Congressional moderates wanted to keep the question of a suffrage amendment within the bounds of constitutional propriety, political expediency, restraint, and reasonableness. The moderate position was between those who wanted comprehensive suffrage reform and those who wanted no changes. The extremism of those suffragists, generally veteran antislavery men, who wanted to reform the electoral college, guarantee Negro officeholding, invalidate state suffrage qualifications in general and the literacy test and poll tax in particular, or pass a bill instead of a constitutional amendment, was ultimately rejected. Similarly, the extremism of those Democrats who opposed the need for a constitutional amendment and the desirability of Negro suffrage was also repudiated by the moderates. The moderate position was not a complete, precise, or rigid ideology; since it could not afford to sew itself up in doctrinaire positions; it was instead pragmatic, ambiguous, and flexible in general attitude. The terms and formulation of the moderate position changed as much as the congress-

has had a potent effect on the South in electing Republicans and now that power should be applied throughout the nation.

Disagreeing by varying degrees with the more modest frame constructed by the moderates, more radical Republicans nevertheless joined them in admitting that a constitutional amendment would principally enfranchise the northern Negro. The stanch advocate of Negro suffrage, Republican Senator Charles Sumner of Massachusetts, emphasized that the interests of the Republican party and those of the nation were identical and that both would be promoted by Negro suffrage in the North:

You need votes in Connecticut, do you not? There are three thousand fellow-citizens in that state ready at the call of Congress to take their place at the ballot box. You need them also in Pennsylvania, do you not? There are at least fifteen thousand in that great state waiting for your summons. Wherever you most need them, there they are; and be assured they will all vote for those who stand by them in the assertion of Equal Rights.[7]

Senator Oliver P. Morton (Republican, Indiana) declared that the " great body of the men upon whom the right of suffrage is to be conferred by this amendment are men who have long been free, who live in the northern States—not men just emerged from slavery, but a comparatively educated class living throughout the entire North." [8] Democrats, who were under no illusion

men supporting that flexible position, but the fundamentally moderate approach to frame a constitutional amendment that was neither too much nor too little remained and, in the end, triumphed. Moderates wanted only piecemeal, and not complete, suffrage reform; they wanted an amendment sufficiently balanced to appeal to both Congress and state legislatures; in short, moderates wanted a suffrage amendment limited in purpose, conservative in form, and practical in effect. The conclusion that the Fifteenth Amendment in its final form was a moderate measure parallels the findings of Joseph B. James about the Fourteenth Amendment.

[7] *Ibid.*, p. 904.

[8] *Ibid.*, p. 990. Morton added that the " argument that might be made against enfranchising men just emerging from slavery cannot be made against the colored men of Indiana, of New York, and of the entire North." Similar views of the primary objective of the Fifteenth Amendment can be found in the speeches of the following Republican senators, in the *Globe*: Orris S. Ferry (Conn.), p. 855; Frederick T. Frelinghuysen (N. J.), p. 979; Edmund G. Ross (Kan.), pp. 982–83. The same conclusion was reached by the following Republican representatives, as found in the Appendix of the *Globe*: George F. Miller (Pa.), p. 92; Charles M. Hamilton (Fla.), p. 100; William Loughridge (Iowa), pp. 199–200; and a similar expression was made in the *Globe* by John P. C. Shanks (Ind.), pp. 694–96. Southern Republicans, in their speeches in the *Globe*, appeared to consider the Amendment an extension into the North of principles already in operation in

about what a constitutional amendment was designed to achieve, fought hard against it in any form, for they knew that Republican supremacy in the North was at stake.[9]

Newspapers of both parties also recognized the main object of such an amendment. The conservative Washington *Daily National Intelligencer* felt that it meant introducing Negro suffrage into the North and riveting it to the South.[10] The outstanding Democratic paper in New York City, the *World*, observed that Congress was intent on passing the amendment in order " to reconstruct the elective franchise in the Northern States." [11] As for Republican commentators,[12] a Connecticut newspaper reported that President-elect Ulysses S. Grant favored Boutwell's amendment because the North should be like the South.[13] One Washington paper estimated that, by enfranchising Negroes in the North, a constitutional amendment would enfranchise roughly one-fifth to one-tenth the total national Negro population.[14] With characteristic understatement, the New York *Times* concluded that the " ability to justify negro enfranchisement throughout the South depends somewhat upon the readiness of the North to abate its own hostility to negro enfranchisement." [15]

This is not to deny that a secondary objective of the amendment was to protect the southern Negro against future disfranchisement, against state constitutional changes that Southern whites might attempt when they regained power. Stewart, for example, told the Senate that the right to vote for the Negro in the South was the only guarantee against oppression and the only way for a

their section, a nationalization of impartial suffrage: Representative Simeon Corley (S. C.), p. 95; Senator Charles M. Hamilton (Fla.), Appendix, p. 102; Representative John R. French (N. C.), Appendix, p. 147. Significantly, petitions to Congress in the *Globe* concerning an amendment originated in the North and concerned the northern Negro with one exception: pp. 60, 77, 120, 143, 156, 378–79.

[9] Democratic members of Congress, in their speeches in the *Globe*, questioned the propriety and popularity of Negro suffrage in the North: Senator Thomas A. Hendricks (Ind.), p. 673; Senator James Dixon (Conn.), pp. 707, 827; Representative Albert G. Burr (Ill.), p. 699; George W. Woodward (Pa.), Appendix, pp. 206–7; Senator George Vickers (Md.), p. 911.

[10] [Washington, D. C.] *Daily National Intelligencer*, February 1, 1869.

[11] [New York] *The World*, February 8, 1869.

[12] The New York *Times*, February 2, 1869; the New York *Herald*, January 18, 1869; [Washington, D. C.] *Daily Morning Chronicle*, January 21, 1869.

[13] Hartford *Daily Courant*, February 3, 1869.

[14] [Washington, D. C.] *Daily Morning Chronicle*, February 4, 1869.

[15] The New York *Times*, February 15, 1869.

man to protect himself.[16] He implied that the right of the Negro to vote was in danger in Georgia and elsewhere in the South, and had to be made secure.[17] The only solution, he felt, was to make Negro suffrage the immutable law of the land to ensure peace,[18] and that the existing southern Negro vote would enable an amendment to be ratified.[19] Republican Representative Samuel Shellabarger of Ohio stated the widespread view that loyal state governments in the South would collapse without loyal Negro voters to support such governments,[20] whereas Republican Representative W. Jasper Blackburn of Louisiana expressed the hope that southern Democrats would accept southern Negro voting once northern Negro voting was accepted.[21]

In the course of framing, various versions of a suffrage amendment were clearly directed toward protecting the southern Negro vote by outlawing literacy tests and poll taxes.[22] Also, various guarantees were framed to protect the right of Negroes to hold public office, a timely issue in the South, where Negro legislators in Georgia had recently been expelled from their seats because of their race. But when the acid test came both the bans and the guarantees were scrapped. The pattern of the framing and passage of the Fifteenth Amendment indicates that the primary objective was to make Negro voters in the North; the secondary objective, to keep Negro voters in the South. The pattern of ratification strongly supports this finding: the North mattered more than the South.

Congressmen first wrestled with the tricky question of whether Congress should enfranchise Negroes by passing an ordinary bill, by launching a constitutional amendment, or by doing both. Acting for the judiciary committee, Representative Boutwell raised the question when he introduced both a bill and a proposed constitutional amendment on January 11, 1869.[23] Lawyer, Massachusetts governor, member of the Joint Committee on Reconstruction, a manager in the presidential impeachment, and subsequently senator and Secretary of the Treasury, Boutwell was both a party regular during Reconstruction and a stanch radical who had a

---

[16] *Globe*, p. 668.
[17] *Ibid.*, p. 1629.
[18] *Ibid.*, p. 668; Brown, *Reminiscences*, p. 232.
[19] *Globe*, p. 561.

[20] *Ibid.*, Appendix, p. 97.
[21] *Ibid.*, Appendix, p. 242.
[22] *Ibid.*, Appendix, pp. 97–98.
[23] *Ibid.*, p. 286.

long record of endorsing universal Negro suffrage. Defending his double-barreled approach, Boutwell argued that his bill enfranchising northern Negroes was needed at once to secure ratification of the amendment by state legislatures in several hostile states. He supported both the constitutionality of his bill and the necessity of his constitutional amendment to guarantee permanently Negro voting in the future, regardless of which party controlled Congress.[24]

The Boutwell approach was applauded by abolitionists,[25] but was given a frigid reception by moderates. Moderate Republican editors and politicians first attacked Boutwell's plan on the grounds of constitutionality. Molding public opinion and mustering congressmen, they bombarded his arguments. Reflecting a wide consensus, they argued that Boutwell's bill ignored the clear constitutional provision and the states' practice of setting suffrage qualifications, and thus found no reason for Congress under the Boutwell bill to "play the usurper, and, under the form of law, accomplish what is at the moment constitutionally impossible."[26] James A. Garfield, writing for not only the Ohio delegation but most Republican congressmen as well, declared that his contingent would oppose Boutwell's bill, because it "presupposes the existence in the Constitution of the very powers which his proposed amendment would put into it."[27] Such a point of view was even endorsed by Democratic Senator Charles A. Eldridge of Wisconsin, who dismissed the bill with the devastating remark that if the amendment was necessary, "it must be a most pregnant admission that the bill is unconstitutional."[28]

But the Boutwell bill was also buried on grounds of strategy, both radical and moderate Republicans assisting at the funeral. If the bill succeeded but the amendment failed, it was argued, then a mere bill could repeal what the Boutwell bill extended—

---

[24] *Ibid.*, pp. 555–61, 644.

[25] [New York] *National Anti-Slavery Standard*, February 6, 1869. The extreme reformist position echoed Charles Sumner's argument that a mere congressional act could enfranchise the Negro, and thus found Boutwell's arguments irrefutable, holding that they also proved that the Constitution provided for a Negro officeholding guarantee, woman suffrage, and a broad ban on suffrage tests.

[26] The New York *Times*, January 25, 1869; see also *Globe*, p. 560.

[27] Garfield to J. L. Lee, January 27, 1869, Garfield MSS; [New York] *The Evening Post*, January 27, 1869. Ohio Republicans did not oppose Negro suffrage in principle, but wanted it in the form of a constitutional amendment.

[28] *Globe*, p. 644.

namely, Negro suffrage. Thus one newspaper advised Boutwell not to whet a knife that might some day cut his and the Negro's own throat,[29] but instead place a firm guarantee of Negro voting in the federal constitution almost out of reach of fickle public opinion and repeal.

Beneath the arguments against a bill lay the traumatic experience of disaster at the polls. The Negro suffrage issue had been badly handled for the most part by Republican politicians in 1867. Now the time had come not to repeat the costly double mistake of being too bold and yet not bold enough. Frontal assaults against " inveterate prejudices " [30] were self-defeating and had set back the cause of Negro suffrage by roughly two years. Rejecting the suicidal strategy of direct vote in each state, as difficult as it had proved unnecessary, Republicans preferred the bolder method of amending the federal Constitution as an easier and surer method than separate state referendums. Such means would encounter the least opposition and would succeed because of the indirect method of legislative action alone, thus avoiding the pitfall of a direct popular vote. Since Republican candidates were more popular than the proposition of Negro suffrage, the politicians could do the job by passing and ratifying an amendment. Republicans had traveled a hard road long enough, and therefore agreed that the longest way around was the shortest way home.

Boutwell surrendered on January 28 by shelving his bill.[31] By asking states to grant powers at the same time that he was persuading Congress to exercise them, he had rendered his position precarious from the beginning. The issue of a law or an amendment, or both, was now settled: Congress would have to frame an amendment rather than a law, because many Republicans felt that Congress lacked both the constitutional power and political desire to do otherwise. An amendment rather than a bill would recognize general state control of suffrage regulations. Since white voters in the North would not voluntarily accept, on their own initiative, Negro suffrage in state referendums, or long tolerate a congressional act enfranchising the Negro throughout the nation,

---

[29] [New York] *The Evening Post*, February 25, 27, 1869.

[30] See the suggestive editorial in *The Nation*, October 24, 1867, commenting on the election reverses of 1867, as well as the speech of Senator Henry Wilson on January 28, 1869 (*Globe*, p. 672).

[31] *Globe*, p. 686.

a constitutional amendment was required. Amending the federal Constitution was the only way both prudent and practical: the timing now seemed right and the price not too high.

The final form of Boutwell's proposed amendment stipulating that " the right of any citizen of the United States to vote shall not be denied or abridged by the United States or any State by reason of race, color, or previous condition of slavery of any citizen or class of citizens of the United States," [32] and including an enforcement section, had only two serious competitors. The first, Ohio Republican Samuel Shellabarger's amendment, was more radical. Shellabarger, who had authored the " forfeited rights " theory and designed comprehensive disfranchisement of white southerners in the congressional program of Reconstruction, was a radical and strong advocate of Negro rights. His substitute was designed to confer suffrage on all males over twenty-one years old except former rebels, and thus was intended to protect southern Negro voting.[33] Moreover, unlike Boutwell's amendment, it proposed by implication to abolish all state literacy and property tests and probably all registration requirements as well, and did not forbid forever the enfranchisement of former Confederates. On the other hand, less radical than Boutwell's measure was Ohio Republican John A. Bingham's proposal. Bingham was a constitutional and political moderate and a consistent supporter of Negro rights, having written the first section of the Fourteenth Amendment. His suggestion of setting a one-year residence requirement on males over twenty-one, and of enfranchising not only Negroes but all ex-Confederates as well, could capsize the southern Republican boat.[34] All three proposals were negative in

[32] *Ibid.*, p. 726.

[33] *Ibid.*, p. 728. The Shellabarger version read as a substitute for the first section: " No State shall make or enforce any law which shall deny or abridge to any male citizen of the United States of the age of twenty-one years or over, and who is of sound mind, an equal vote at all elections in the State in which he shall have his actual residence, such right to vote to be under such regulations as shall be prescribed by law, except to such as have engaged, or may hereafter engage, in insurrection or rebellion against the United States, and to such as shall be duly convicted of infamous crime."

[34] *Ibid.* The Bingham version read as a substitute for the first section: " No State shall make or enforce any law which shall abridge or deny to any male citizen of the United States of sound mind and twenty-one years of age or upward the equal exercise, subject to such registration laws as the State may establish, of the elective franchise at all elections in the State wherein he shall have actually resided for a period of one year next preceding such election, except such of said

that they prohibited the states from exercising specified powers.[35]

Serious voting did not get underway until January 30 and then showed that moderates were in control. The House rejected Shellabarger's radical proposal by a vote of 62 " yes " to 125 " no," 35 not voting. No Democrat voted for Shellabarger's version, because it provided permanent proscription of ex-Confederates. The House then voted down Bingham's more conservative version by a count of 24 to 160, 38 not voting. On this proposal Democrats divided: half voted in effect to grant amnesty to ex-Confederates, while the other half joined most Republicans to defeat the measure. Finally, the Boutwell amendment (House Joint Resolution 402) passed the House with the required two-thirds majority, 150 affirmatives to 42 negatives, and 31 not voting.[36] No Democrat voted for it and only four Republicans voted against it.[37]

While representatives debated the merits of Boutwell's plan, senators were considering the amendment proposed by William M. Stewart (Republican, Nevada), an energetic, shrewd, and resourceful western moderate, who had made his fortune in silver mining before turning to politics. After the war he had opposed Negro suffrage, sympathizing with the plight of southerners, to whom he was related through his wife's family. Like most Republicans, however, he became first disenchanted with white southerners, who fought postwar reforms, and then with Andrew Johnson. Gradually shifting ground, Stewart finally endorsed Negro, but not Chinese, suffrage.[38]

citizens as shall engage in rebellion or insurrection, or who may have been, or shall be, duly convicted of treason or other infamous crime."

[35] *Ibid.*, Appendix, p. 97. One of the Republican leaders in the House and a stanch radical, Benjamin F. Butler of Massachusetts, took the unusually conservative position that the literary test, which Massachusetts had, should not be abolished. Objecting to Bingham's desire that former Confederates regain the ballot, Butler instead insisted that the Negro be protected first at the polls. (*Ibid.*, p. 725.)

[36] *Ibid.*, pp. 744–45; E. McPherson, p. 400.

[37] Reportedly furious over the defeat of his pet measure, John Bingham led the lonely group of Republican opponents. He was joined by conservatives Jehu Baker (Republican, Ill.) and Isaac R. Hawkins (Republican, Tenn.), and by another Republican, Daniel Polsley from precarious West Virginia. (E. McPherson, pp. 399–400; the New York *Herald*, January 31, 1869.) Various publications commended passage by the House (Hartford *Daily Courant*, February 1, 3, 1869; [Washington, D. C.] *The National Republican*, February 3, 1869; *Harper's Weekly*, February 13, 1869).

[38] *Record*, 51st Cong., 2nd Sess., pp. 678–82.

Given the responsibility of framing a constitutional amendment for the Senate judiciary committee, on a motion by Roscoe Conkling (Republican, New York), Stewart went about his task more carefully than had Representative Boutwell. He talked to President-elect Grant, who favored an amendment, and canvassed state delegations for advice and support before fashioning his proposal.[39] Although couched in an essentially negative form, Stewart's amendment began by positing the right to vote, thus making his version slightly more affirmative than the original version offered by John B. Henderson (Republican, Missouri), if not more affirmative than Boutwell's.[40] It also, unlike Boutwell's, guaranteed the right of the Negro to hold office, apparently in an effort to elicit southern Republican support. The judiciary committee approved Stewart's proposal, which was close to the final version of the Fifteenth Amendment.[41] Introduced on the Senate floor on January 28, 1869, it stipulated that " the right of citizens of the United States to vote, and hold office shall not be denied or abridged by the United States or any State on account of race, color, or previous condition of servitude." [42]

Consideration was not immediate. Dilatory tactics consumed Senate time as business piled up, and Stewart had to fight to get his proposal discussed and voted upon.[43] Backing Stewart, Senator Morton argued that delay in passage might jeopardize ratification, since state legislatures would soon be adjourning and the longer the fight for ratification lasted the harder it would be to win, especially if it affected the 1870 and 1872 elections.[44] Yet Senate debate dragged on for three days. The House then passed the Boutwell amendment, whereupon the Senate dropped Stewart's plan to consider the Boutwell version for six additional days, until February 9.

[39] Brown, *Reminiscences*, p. 234.

[40] James G. Blaine, *Twenty Years of Congress: From Lincoln to Garfield* (2 vols.; Norwich, Conn.: Henry Bill Co., 1884–86), II, 413.

[41] The measure was not approved unanimously. Lyman Trumbull (Republican, Ill.) opposed it, while Thomas A. Hendricks (Democrat, Ind.) and Frederick T. Frelinghuysen (Republican, N. J.) were absent from the committee meeting. Stewart, Conkling, George F. Edmunds (Republican, Vt.), and Benjamin F. Rice (Republican, Ark.) joined to endorse the measure. (The New York *Herald*, January 16, 1869.)

[42] *Globe*, pp. 668, 828.

[43] *Ibid.*, pp. 541–43, 668–70, 939.

[44] *Ibid.*, p. 824.

Stewart pressed for a final vote. Debate consumed thirty-two hours in a consecutive session, through the night of February 8 and the next day, with only two short recesses. During the session twenty-four roll calls were taken, thirty propositions presented, and seventeen amendments to the pending Boutwell amendment acted upon.

The speeches and voting spelled trouble for a constitutional amendment. Senate Democrats denounced the whole enterprise because Republicans were scrapping the campaign plank of 1868 which had promised northerners that Negro suffrage would remain a local matter for each state to decide; now that the elections were over, the tricksters were planning to impose Negro suffrage on Northern states by amending the Constitution, all for the sake of getting the Negro vote in the North. If the amendment was a trick it certainly was not a treat for the Democrats, who maintained that the black race was either inferior or unable to vote intelligently. Democrats thus tried in every conceivable way to kill the Boutwell amendment, first by opposing its consideration, then by moving adjournment to obstruct its passage, and finally by supporting recommittal. Positively, Democrats tried to enfranchise ex-Confederates, restrict the scope of an amendment to federal elections, and change the method of ratification to either a popular referendum or election of delegates to a state convention.[45] Yet Democratic opposition, if annoying, was not serious, because there were only a dozen Democrats in the Senate.

Republican dissension was a graver matter, since it could paralyze action and kill passage. There were three overlapping groups that impeded Republican congressional action. Moderate Republicans, especially from the Northeast and from the West, wanted Negro voting but also wished to retain freedom of state action either in conferring suffrage and setting voting qualifications, especially the literacy test, or in restricting Irish or Chinese by the nativity test. In short, moderates were not at all agreed on the price worth paying for Negro suffrage. Radical Republicans from the North championed Negro suffrage and wanted firm guarantees that it would be permanent and effective, but they were not in agreement on the form required or on the scope of reform desired. Those from the South, with varying gradations of radi-

[45] *Ibid.*, pp. 671, 825–27, 1003, 1030, 1040–41, 1043.

calism, were primarily interested in keeping and protecting southern Negro voting, but there was less cohesion on the means to secure it, and still less on guaranteeing Negro officeholding and the means to be undertaken for its achievement. There was, in short, no unity in purpose nor resolution in method among congressional Republicans. The differences created problems.

As in the House, the intent of the amendment was clear: it was not a positive requirement of universal suffrage but a negative injunction that voters could not be disbarred by race only. Orris S. Ferry (Republican, Connecticut) remarked that, though an amendment would give half a million Negroes the vote in eighteen northern states, it would remove from the state only the power to disfranchise on grounds of race.[46] This restricted prohibition was precisely what southern Republicans and northern Radicals objected to. Since the proposed amendment failed to state exactly who should vote, Willard Warner (Republican, Alabama), along with Shellabarger in the House, concluded that " the *animus* of this amendment is a desire to protect and enfranchise the colored citizens of the country; yet, under it and without any violation of its letter or spirit, nine tenths of them might be prevented from voting and holding office by the requirement on the part of the states or of the United States of an intelligence or property qualification." [47] Desiring a suffrage that was uniform, equal, and universal, Warner suggested that federal voting qualifications and the abolition of literacy and property tests be made an explicit part of the amendment.

Senator Morton, reflecting views of many northern Republicans, agreed that the pending amendment did not go far enough. Former war governor of Indiana, a devoted Unionist, and a fiery partisan, Morton had long walked the tightrope between prejudice and principle in Indiana politics. He first opposed Negro suffrage after the war, because Negroes lacked the education and financial independence to become responsible voters, and also because it was hypocritical to force Negro suffrage on the South but not on the North. Morton then shifted ground and finally embraced Negro suffrage as a political necessity. Both the Boutwell and Stewart measures, Morton noted, allowed the states to retain control over suffrage, except for the prohibition of racial tests;

[46] *Ibid.*, pp. 855–57.   [47] *Ibid.*, p. 862.

each, therefore, tacitly conceded that states could disfranchise Negroes with literacy or property tests. Thus " all the existing irregularities and incongruities in suffrage "[48] remained. Southern states could " cut off the great majority of the colored men from voting in those states, and thus this amendment would be practically defeated in all those states where the great body of the colored people live."[49] Morton proposed as an alternative that qualifications for federal elections and elections for state legislators be made explicit, affirmative, and uniform, in order to prevent the states from evading the amendment.

The first critical test of Stewart's leadership was the vote on Michigan radical Republican Jacob Howard's explicit and sternly affirmative proposal to specify " African suffrage ":[50] " Citizens of the United States of African descent shall have the same right to vote and hold office in states and territories as other citizens electors of the most numerous branch of their respective legislatures."[51] Those senators who supported Howard's proposal did so for opposite reasons, wanting either to strengthen or weaken the amendment by explicit reference to the Negro. At their core, chiefly from New England but all from the North, were such veteran antislavery and radical Republicans as Charles Sumner of Massachusetts and Benjamin F. Wade of Ohio, who wanted to strengthen the amendment. Pacific coast men, such as Cornelius Cole and Henry W. Corbett, and one Rhode Islander, Henry B. Anthony, supported the Howard measure because they wanted to exclude from the amendment naturalized citizens of Chinese or Irish descent. However, since the antislavery and restrictionist

---

[48] *Ibid.*

[49] *Ibid.* Though Morton favored Jacob Howard's proposed amendment, which explicitly referred to " citizens of the United States of African descent," even Howard's amendment still left the states the power to impose education and property tests to disfranchise Negroes (*ibid.*, pp. 862–63). Jacob Howard insisted that the amendment should say what Congress meant—that is, that the Negro should be given the vote. He then stated: " Give us, then, the colored man, for that and that only is the object that is now before us. The sole object of this whole proceeding is to impart by a constitutional amendment to the colored man . . . the ordinary rights of citizens . . . I do not wish by any form of words to conceal the fact or to blur the fact that I am in favor of extending to this class of men the right to vote. . . ." Howard offered a proposed amendment to that effect which was explicitly direct and plain, stating that " Citizens of the United States, of African descent " should be allowed to vote. (*Ibid.*, p. 985.)

[50] *Ibid.*, p. 1012.

[51] *Ibid.*

forces could muster only sixteen recruits, the proposal was defeated on February 8 by a coalition of thirty-five Democrats and Republicans, both northern and southern, with fifteen senators not voting,[52] clearly demonstrating that the radical group could not impose its will on the Republican majority.

The crucial vote in the Senate came February 9 on Henry Wilson's plan to abolish all discrimination or qualification for either voting or holding office because of " race, color, nativity, property, education, or religious belief." [53] In effect, the question was whether an amendment should confine itself to Negro suffrage or undertake comprehensive reform of suffrage regulations, including abolition of qualifications for holding public office. If the former, then the question of education and property tests had to be decided. On the first vote, with twenty-three men ominously absent, the Senate rejected Wilson's proposal by only five votes. The defeat, a slim victory for Stewart's more moderate and limited version of the amendment, resulted from an unsteady alliance of four divergent groups against the Wilson plan: the Senate Demo-

---

[52] *Ibid.* Other Republicans who formed the antislavery bloc were Zachariah Chandler of Michigan, John M. Thayer and Thomas W. Tipton of Nebraska, Benjamin F. Wade of Ohio, and James M. Harlan of Iowa.

There is a certain historical irony in the fact that sometimes during the course of framing the best friends of the Negro seem his unwitting enemy, as in the case of the Howard proposal. Without an explicit statement of Negro or African descent, an amendment could be capable of growth, for it would gain stature, if judges had a free hand, by augmenting federal authority and expanding its powers of enforcement. Historian W. R. Brock observes that the Fifteenth Amendment " was weak from the outset because it linked suffrage with race; it was a law for negro [sic] enfranchisement and could be enforced only so long as some people had an interest in doing so. If the Fifteenth Amendment had declared in unequivocal terms that all males over the age of twenty-one who were citizens of the United States had the right to vote it might have been recognized as a cornerstone of democracy and attracted popular support [and would have been easier to enforce and more difficult to evade]. As it was the Fifteenth Amendment enacted ' impartial suffrage ' which meant that the States could impose any qualification they chose provided that it was not based on race; this meant that the white majority of the nation had no particular interest in its enforcement." W. R. Brock, *An American Crisis: Congress and Reconstruction, 1865–1867* (New York: St. Martin's Press, 1963), p. 288. It is one thesis of this study that no such amendment as Brock suggests could or, as Henry Wilson framed it, did pass Congress by the necessary two-thirds margin, or could have been ratified by the needed three-fourths of the states. In short, Brock's observation, however acute, ignores the real choices open to the framers. In defense of the radical Republicans and to their credit, they did champion universal suffrage and supported measures to enforce it. The trouble was that their timing was somewhat premature—by about a century.

[53] *Ibid.*, p. 1029.

crats; a few compromising southern Republicans; Republicans
from Rhode Island and the Pacific seaboard who worried about
the possible overthrow of state voting regulations, which they
believed to be implicit in the Wilson amendment; and a hard core
group of Republicans from the Northeast, who preferred and
consistently supported Stewart's more restricted proposal.[54]

The Republicans who were disposed to follow Stewart's leadership consisted of Stewart's colleagues on the judiciary committee—
Frederick T. Frelinghuysen of New Jersey, Roscoe Conkling of
New York, and James W. Nye of Nevada—and other moderates,
such as Charles D. Drake of Missouri, Edwin D. Morgan of New
York, and Justin S. Morrill of Vermont. This group, to which
not a single southerner or Pacific coast senator belonged, voted
without exception to reject the more extreme proposals of both
Howard and Wilson, and opposed recommittal.

Yet Stewart's victory was short-lived. Only a few hours later,
on the same day, February 9, the Senate reversed its earlier course,
voted now on a modified Wilson amendment, which guaranteed
the right to hold office but did not, as in the preceding version,
bar states from setting qualifications for holding office, and by
a majority of four votes accepted this slightly less extreme but
still comprehensive reform of suffrage regulations. What had
happened? The unsteady and divergent coalition led by Stewart
had cracked because many of the absentees had now shown up.
Apparently under potential constituent or actual congressional
pressure, and by reason of the critical change in the pending
amendment, three southern Republicans changed their minds and
three more, conveniently absent from the first vote, joined the
affirmative side. The decisive six southern recruits and the now
overwhelming support from southern Republicans (ten) indicated
that in a showdown they were not entirely free agents, yet their
lack of support on the first Wilson proposal, which attracted

[54] *Ibid.* The 23 absentees, including 6 Democrats, were Charles R. Buckalew
and Simon Cameron (Pa.), Zachariah Chandler (Mich.), Aaron H. Cragin (N. H.),
James R. Doolittle (Wis.), Charles D. Drake (Mo.), George F. Edmunds (Vt.),
Orris S. Ferry (Conn.), John B. Henderson (Mo., permanently absent), Thomas A.
Hendricks (Ind.), William P. Kellogg (La.), Thomas C. McCreery (Ky.), Lot M.
Morrill (Me.), Thomas W. Osborn (Fla.), James W. Patterson (N. H.), Samuel
C. Pomeroy (Kan.), John Pool (N. C.), Willard Saulsbury (Del.), William
Sprague (R. I.), John M. Thayer and Thomas W. Tipton (Neb.), Willard Warner
(Ala.), William P. White (Md.).

only four out of their thirteen votes, showed that they seemed
to care more about Negro voters electing whites to public office
than about Negro voters electing Negro officials. The veteran
antislavery Republicans not only stood firm but picked up several
votes from the Republican southerners and middle westerners as
well. Thomas A. Hendricks (Democrat, Indiana), a most vigorous opponent of a suffrage amendment, shrewdly backed the
Wilson amendment as a measure so extreme that it could never
be adopted. The hard core of moderate northeastern Republicans,
along with Nye—the Stewart men—stayed with Stewart on this
second, decisive vote, joined by Pacific coast Republicans and most
Democrats.

For the moment Stewart had lost control of the constitutional
amendment.[55] Exalted by their victory, the radicals, within minutes
after the vote on the Wilson amendment, also approved a proposed
sixteenth amendment—Morton's plan [56] to reform the electoral
college to ensure that the choice of the electors was the same as
that of the voters. By ignoring the limits of Republican power,
Wilson and Morton had transformed a limited amendment for
a limited purpose into utopian reform virtually unlimited in purpose and commitment. Such an effort was misguided, because
both failed to distinguish between what was desirable, what was
possible, and what was essential. With the moderate suffrage
amendment now wrecked, Stewart, his committee colleagues, and
his loyal supporters could do nothing but support, with grave
misgivings, the Wilson-Morton proposals.[57] Physical exhaustion,
acute frustration over failure to agree upon a moderate proposal,
the desire of some moderates to appear liberal to their constituents
on the issue of broader suffrage, and the Republicans' desire to
close ranks and support what was of necessity the party position,
all contributed to passage.[58]

Reaction to the Wilson-Morton plan in the moderate Republican
press was not friendly. *The Nation* condemned the proposal as
tantamount to saying that " intelligence is of no importance in
politics, and that a ' brute vote ' ought to count for as much as

[55] *Ibid.*, p. 1040. See also Henry, " Radical Republican Policy toward the Negro,"
pp. 258–59.
[56] *Ibid.*, p. 1042.
[57] *Ibid.*, pp. 1041–43, 1044.
[58] Boston *Daily Journal*, February 15, 1869.

a human one." [59] In a telling aside, the journal concluded that abolition of an education test would prove so absurd " as to give countenance to the story which is afloat, that it was inserted for the express purpose of having the amendment defeated." [60] The New York *Times* was also annoyed by the " sweeping and revolutionary " [61] scope of the Wilson version, further criticizing the officeholding guarantee because its unpopularity would arouse intense opposition in the fight for ratification. Preferring the Boutwell version, the *Times* in effect endorsed impartial suffrage rather than universal Negro suffrage.

On February 15 the House took up the Senate version of the constitutional amendment. The legislative situation was awkward for the House sponsors of a moderate measure. Boutwell, in particular, felt that his position was embarrassing: " I was counted as a radical and in favor of securing to the Negro race every right to which the white man was entitled. My opposition to the Senate amendment seemed to place me in a light inconsistent with my former professions." [62] Ignoring factional labels, Boutwell continued to work for his more moderate proposal and opposed the Wilson-Morton version, which was much more radical than his own in that it guaranteed Negro officeholding and electoral college reform, while it abolished residential, religious, property, and literacy tests. Speaking before the House in an attempt to rally more radical Republicans, he contended that the right to vote carried with it implicitly the right to hold office.[63] Also, he avoided the issue of education and property tests, understanding that rejection of the Senate proposal would also mean rejection of the ban on the literacy test and the poll tax, whose adoption many thought would unite opposition to defeat ratification in the state legislatures.[64]

Despite the efforts of Republican John A. Bingham, who approved the Wilson version perhaps in an attempt to kill the

[59] *The Nation*, February 11, 1869.

[60] *Ibid.*, February 18, 1869.

[61] The New York *Times*, February 15, 1869.

[62] George S. Boutwell, *Reminiscences of Sixty Years in Public Affairs* (2 vols.; New York: McClure, Phillips, 1902), II, 46.

[63] *Globe*, pp. 1224–26.

[64] Boston *Daily Journal*, February 15, 1869.

amendment altogether,[65] the House rejected the Senate's amendment and requested a conference committee. Oddly enough, on this vote Boutwell lost the support of fifty-four Republicans, half conservative and half moderate, who had voted with him on January 30.[66] In two weeks his position among Republicans had weakened; a sustained attack might destroy it completely.

But help from an unexpected quarter advanced Boutwell's cause. The unrepentant radical Wendell Phillips surprisingly thundered forth the common sense of moderation; he declared that Boutwell's simple, direct, and modest proposal alone had a chance of being ratified. Though personally favoring a guarantee of Negro officeholding, he felt that passage of anything stronger than Boutwell's measure would be foolish, and loudly wondered whether the Wilson proposal wasn't a trick to defeat the amendment after all. Advising prudence, Phillips concluded that " for the first time in our lives we beseech them [Congressmen, especially the more radical ones] to be a little more *politicians*—and a little less reformers. . . ." [67] Moderate publications praised Phillips' advice. *The Nation* urged Senators " to consider not Eternal

[65] *Globe*, pp. 1224–25.

[66] *Ibid.*, p. 1226. Cf. *ibid.*, p. 744; E. McPherson, pp. 399–400, 402–3. Although the Wilson version received only 37 votes, that total was an increase of 13 over the affirmative total for Bingham's amendment. There was a decline of 27 nays, 52 congressmen did not vote, and many supporters of Boutwell were Democrats. On subsequent votes on the Wilson version and the second Bingham version, 11 more radical Republican congressmen, mainly from the Middle West and Pennsylvania, who had voted for the moderate position with Boutwell on January 30 to defeat the first Bingham version (*ibid.*, p. 744) and later deserted Boutwell by not voting on the Wilson version on February 15 (*ibid.*, p. 1226), finally supported the second Bingham version on February 20 (*ibid.*, p. 1428): William B. Allison (Dubuque, Iowa), Ephaim R. Eckley (Carrollton, Ohio), Jacob H. Ela (Rochester, N. H.), James A. Garfield (Hiram, Ohio), John A. Griswold (Troy, N. Y.), Norman B. Judd (Chicago, Ill.), Ulysses Mercur (Towanda, Pa.), S. Newton Pettis (Meadville, Pa.), Robert C. Schenck (Dayton, Ohio), Caleb N. Taylor (Bristol, Pa.), and Frederick R. Woodbridge (Vergennes, Vt.). Eleven more conservative Republican congressmen, mainly from the South and the middle Atlantic states, who had voted moderate with Boutwell to defeat the first Bingham version and later deserted Boutwell by not voting on the Wilson version, finally opposed the second Bingham version: John M. Broomall (Media, Pa.), Henry L. Cake (Tamaque, Pa.), Burton C. Cook (Ottawa, Ill.), John R. French (Edenton, N. C.), James H. Goss (Union Court House, S. C.), George A. Halsey (Newark, N. J.), Samuel Hooper (Boston, Mass.), Horace Maynard (Knoxville, Tenn.), Lewis Selye (Rochester, N. Y.), J. Hale Sypher (New Orleans, La.), and Henry Van Aernam (Franklinville, N. Y.).

[67] [New York] *National Anti-Slavery Standard*, February 20, 1869; Boutwell, *Reminiscences*, II, 46–50.

Justice but the possibilities of the occasion." [68] The *Times* remarked that for once even Phillips had come into "accord with the rational, moderate Republicans. . . ." [69] But the more moderate Republican consensus in the newspapers found now no counterpart in Congress.

Differences over a suffrage amendment were intensified when on February 17 the Senate considered the original amendment by Stewart after the House had rejected the Wilson plan. In effect, the House had thrown the responsibility of defeating a constitutional amendment on the Senate. [70] Deadlock over the banking and appropriation bills, as well as the suffrage amendment, only aggravated standing differences between the two chambers, and relations between them deteriorated as senators fought against the "alleged rights" of the House, while representatives strove to check the "pretensions" of the Senate. [71] Democrat Charles R. Buckalew of Pennsylvania exploited this occasion by reminding his fellow senators that the House, under the leadership of Thaddeus Stevens (who had died in August, 1868), had had its own way for six years. Defending Senate prerogatives and maneuvering to block agreement between the chambers, Buckalew warned that unless it put a halt to House aggression, the Senate would become a House of Lords and the House a House of Commons. This struggle for institutional pride and power further complicated debate on the suffrage amendment as the Senate refused a conference with the House. [72]

Serious differences among Senate Republicans over the scope and shape of suffrage resulted only in floundering harangues. Friends of an amendment tried bravely to restore order. Now dropping his scheme to reform suffrage regulations and the electoral college, Oliver P. Morton called upon senators to stop wrangling and start acting; otherwise, he predicted, a suffrage amendment might be talked to death. He argued that every day lost meant the ratification fight would be proportionately harder, since the state legislatures would soon adjourn. The indispensable

[68] *The Nation*, February 25, 1869.
[69] The New York *Times*, February 19, 1869.
[70] The Cincinnati *Daily Gazette*, February 16, 1869.
[71] The New York *Times*, February 15, 19, 1869.
[72] *Globe*, pp. 1285–86; the New York *Times*, February 21, 1869.

object, he continued, was that "colored people shall not be debarred from the right of suffrage on account of color, race, or previous condition of slavery." [73] His words marked a break in the ranks of radical Republicans. Stewart seconded Morton and also endorsed Boutwell's proposal. [74]

However, various groups refused to budge. Democrats tried to delay consideration; Charles Sumner tried to return the entire matter to committee; [75] southern Republicans were reported on the verge of rebellion, because, while gaining no practical benefit from the Boutwell measure, they could not even secure readmission of Negroes to the Georgia legislature. [76]

Finally, on February 17, the Senate came to a vote. Morton led the less extreme of the radical Republicans into Stewart's more moderate camp to reject the more extreme and comprehensive Wilson proposal. [77] Reactionary Democrats joined with diehard radical Republicans in support of Wilson's measure, the latter voting out of conviction, the former out of expediency, in order to prolong the House-Senate deadlock for the remainder of the abbreviated session. But this unholy alliance could not secure the needed two-thirds majority. [78] Strong southern Republican opposition to a more moderate measure collapsed as these southerners split three ways. Prospects for a moderate measure looked good.

But then, reversing itself on the same day, the Senate killed the Boutwell amendment: it could not win the approval of two-thirds of the senators present. The moderate forces had suffered their worst defeat. A combination of twelve Democrats, seven radi-

[73] *Globe*, pp. 1287, 1292.

[74] *Ibid.*, p. 1292.

[75] *Ibid.*, p. 1297. Sumner believed that Congress already possessed the power to legislate on suffrage without an amendment and that any mention of race might imply that caste could be legislated. He thus feared that states might disfranchise Negroes because they were Negroes if an amendment failed to be ratified.

[76] *Ibid.*, pp. 1299, 1301; [New York] *The World*, February 18, 1869; Boston *Daily Journal*, February 20, 1869; The Louisville *Courier-Journal*, February 20, 1869.

[77] The vote was 33 "yes" to 24 "no," with 9 absences. The absence of Charles Sumner was evidence of a lack of cohesion among the diehard radicals. (*Globe*, p. 1295).

[78] Henry finds that the same combination had blocked Lincoln's program of emancipation and colonization in the early war years; had prevented recognition of the Lincoln Louisiana government in the winter of 1865; had helped to defeat the representation resolution; and had caused trouble for the Fourteenth Amendment (Henry, "Radical Republican Policy Toward the Negro," p. 263).

cal men, and eight southern Republicans defeated the measure, while eight men, by not voting, saw to it that a two-thirds majority would not be secured.[79] William P. Fessenden delivered a fitting epitaph on the Boutwell amendment when he charged that the Republican party, with more than a two-thirds majority, could not agree because it was " so cut up and divided, and there are so many opinions among the members composing it." [80] Senator James W. Nye placed the blame, with more precision, upon Sumner and Pomeroy, who had sought to gratify their own whims; upon Wilson who had obstructed passage after his own proposal was rejected; and upon southern Republicans.[81] Although moderates had gained important votes by splitting southern and northern

[79] The vote was close: 31 affirmatives to 27 negatives, with 8 absent. Democrats James A. Bayard (Del.), Charles R. Buckalew (Pa.), Garrett Davis (Ky.), James Dixon (Conn.), James R. Doolittle (Wis.), Thomas A. Hendricks (Ind.), Thomas G. McCreery (Ky.), Daniel S. Norton (Minn.), David T. Patterson (Tenn.), Willard Saulsbury (Del.), George Vickers (Md.), and William P. Whyte (Md.), joined seven Republican antislavery men: George F. Edmunds (Vt.), James W. Grimes (Iowa), Samuel G. Pomeroy (Kan.), Edmund G. Ross (Kan.), Charles Sumner (Mass.), John M. Thayer (Nebr.), and Henry Wilson (Mass.), as well as eight Southern Republicans: Joseph C. Abbott (N. C.), Joseph S. Fowler (Tenn.), Alexander McDonald (Ark.), Thomas W. Osborn (Fla.), Frederick A. Sawyer (S. C.), George E. Spencer (Ala.), Willard Warner (Ala.), and Adonijah S. Welch (Fla.), to defeat the Boutwell amendment. The 8 Republican absentees were John Conness (Cal.), Henry W. Corbett (Ore.), Timothy G. Howe (Wis.), Lot M. Morrill (Me.), William Sprague (R. I.), Thomas W. Tipton (Nebr.), Waitman T. Willey (W. Va.), and John B. Henderson (Mo.), who was absent apparently throughout the third session. (*Ibid.*, p. 1300.)

[80] *Ibid.*

[81] *Ibid.*, pp. 1300, 1306. Sumner's record reminds one of Winston Churchill's observation that " the maxim ' Nothing avails but perfection ' may be spelt paralysis." Sumner, wanting things his own way, refused to play the politician who tries to bridge the gap between fact and perfection. At the time, there was considerable criticism of Sumner and his followers for their refusal to accept the Boutwell version. The radical weekly *Independent* (February 18, 1869) criticized Sumner for being " so enamored of his bill, declaring manhood suffrage by act of Congress, that he takes no interest in the amendment." Devastating criticism was also leveled in retrospect (Boutwell, *Reminiscences*, II, 46–47; Brown, *Reminiscences*, pp. 242–45). Earlier during the battle abolitionist Wendell Phillips had written Sumner that there was no chance for Sumner's bill to pass Congress and suggested that at least the proposed constitutional amendment could pass, concluding that " I most earnestly beseech you to show yourself (which I know you are) most *thoroughly* willing and *desirous* that the Amendment should pass. Do not let any silence of your's be construed, in any quarter to mean that your Bill so exclusively absorbs your interest that you are content to let the Amendment slide and shift." (Phillips to Sumner, January 24, 1869, Sumner MSS, Houghton Library, Harvard College.) See abolitionist opinion in J. McPherson, *Struggle for Equality*, pp. 424–30.

Republicans, the Sumner-Wilson coalition could block any other proposal, even if it could not get its own way. Incapable of passing either a radical or a moderate amendment by a margin of two-thirds, the Senate would have to begin again.

Debate on Stewart's original measure, which had been temporarily side-tracked by Boutwell's amendment, now resumed. Democrats launched a violent offensive, trying to stall proceedings, but their many proposals were voted down.[82] On February 17, after a twelve-hour debate, the Senate accepted Stewart's amendment thirty-five to eleven, with twelve absentees.[83] This measure was just enough more radical than Boutwell's because of the mild officeholding provision to win twelve additional votes—seven southern, four mid-western, and one New England; thus a few more radicals were induced to absent themselves. The opposition was composed entirely of Democrats, except for one lonely conservative Republican from Tennessee. But the fight was far from over. Rumor was that some of the more radical Republicans who had voted for the Stewart amendment were sufficiently dissatisfied to advise representatives to reject it.[84]

The House took up the Stewart amendment on February 20, but prospects for adoption were not at all encouraging. For one thing, the Stewart proposal retained the officeholding guarantee, while the House version did not. Further, the Senate had refused a conference with the House.[85] Bad tempers in the Senate were producing hot tempers in the House.

In this charged atmosphere Boutwell sought to prevent agitation and even mutiny among his restless troops. He tried to confine House consideration to debate on officeholding, but more conserva-

[82] *Globe*, pp. 1309–18.
[83] *Ibid.*, p. 1318. Cf. *ibid.*, p. 1295. Six southern Republicans had refused to recede from the Wilson amendment but then approved the Stewart amendment: Joseph C. Abbott of North Carolina, Thomas W. Osborn of Florida, John Pool of North Carolina, Benjamin F. Rice of Arkansas, George E. Spencer of Alabama, and Willard Warner of Alabama. Frederick A. Sawyer of South Carolina had been absent, but supported Stewart's amendment. Three midwesterners duplicated the six southerners: James Harlan of Iowa, Edmund G. Ross of Kansas, and Benjamin F. Wade of Ohio. Alexander Ramsay of Minnesota switched from absent to affirmative. Henry Wilson of Massachusetts, who had fathered the comprehensive reform, joined the moderate forces.
[84] [New York] *The World*, February 19, 1869.
[85] The New York *Times*, February 21, 1869.

tive Republican obstructionists had other ideas.[86] Bingham suggested banning all suffrage tests, in an effort apparently to sabotage the amendment by advocating the very proposal—Wilson's —which the House and the Senate had already rejected.[87] John A. Logan, a wily Republican politician from anti-Negro southern Illinois, wanted to scrap the Negro officeholding guarantee,[88] no doubt accurately reflecting the will of his constituency, where opinion against Negro officeholding ran strong, as it did in Indiana, Ohio, West Virginia, Pennsylvania, New Jersey, and Connecticut. The practical effect of both proposed changes was to intensify existing differences between the chambers. Benjamin F. Butler, leader of the radical Republicans, repudiated these tactics and advised representatives to take what they could get and accept the more moderate Stewart amendment.[89]

But the House was in no mood to accept Butler's advice, though it did defeat Logan's proposal to strike out the officeholding provision.[90] In what James G. Blaine later termed a " capricious change of opinion," [91] the chamber adopted Bingham's ban on nativity, property, and creed (but significantly not on education) as tests of suffrage—a ban the House had, in effect, rejected previously in the Wilson proposal. The vote was close, ninety-two to seventy-one, with fifty-nine crucial absences.[92] Although the

[86] *Globe*, p. 1426.
[87] *Ibid.*, p. 1425.
[88] *Ibid.*, p. 1426.
[89] *Ibid.*
[90] Thirty-three Democrats subjoining 37 Republicans supported the measure. Interestingly enough, 16 middle Atlantic Republicans, especially from Pennsylvania and New York, joined 11 Republicans from the Middle West, along with 10 Republicans from other sections, to oppose Negro officeholding. (*Ibid.*, p. 1428; E. McPherson, pp. 405–6; the Cincinnati *Daily Gazette*, February 22, 1869.)
[91] Blaine, *Twenty Years*, II, 417.
[92] *Globe*, p. 1428; E. McPherson, p. 406. Cf. *Globe*, p. 1226. The switch in the voting in the House between the Wilson version and the second Bingham version was interesting. No Democrat changed his vote from affirmative to negative, but 19 Democrats, including the prominent Samuel J. Randall, changed from voting " no " on the Wilson version and "yes" on the Bingham version: William H. Barnum (Conn.), James B. Beck (Ky.), Benjamin M. Boyer (Pa.), Albert G. Burr (Ill.), Charles A. Eldridge (Wis.), John Fox (N. Y.), Charles Haight (N. J.), William S. Holman (Ind), James M. Humphrey (N. Y.), J. Procter Knott (Ky.), James D. McCormick (Mo.), William D. Mungen (Ohio), William E. Niblack (Ind.), John A. Nicholson (Del.), Samuel J. Randall (Pa.), William E. Robinson (N. Y.), Lewis W. Ross (Ill.), Frederick Stone (Md.), and George W. Woodward (Pa.). Even heavier was the Republican switch, consisting of 30 more radical Republicans, especially from the Middle West and Middle Atlantic

House had performed a legislative somersault, its reason was clear. The combination now endorsing the ban differed from the coalition that had previously rejected it. Earlier, a combination of Democrats and moderate Republicans had saved the moderate measure; now the Democrats—with the sweetener that education tests, which would bar southern Negroes, would not be banned—joined the radical Republicans to effect a radical result. The Democrats were taking advantage of Republican division to play radicals against moderates, confirm House-Senate differences, and freight the amendment with unpopular provisions to ensure the failure of ratification. The Bingham amendment thus sailed through the House,[93] its authors, as well as John A. Logan and the Democrats, bearing chief responsibility for its passage.[94]

Since the stalemate between the houses of Congress appeared final, newspapers revised early predictions and now viewed the amendment's chances as exceedingly slim.[95] Benjamin Perley Poore wrote that a suffrage amendment " hangs like Mahomet's coffin,

sections, who now, on February 20, voted affirmatively instead of negatively on the second Bingham version, where they had formerly opposed his first version on January 30 and the Wilson version on February 15: James M. Ashley (Toledo, Ohio), Jacob Benton (Lancaster, N. H.), James G. Blaine (Augusta, Me.), Reader W. Clarke (Batavia, Ohio), Amasa Cobb (Mineral Point, Wis.), John F. Driggs (East Saginaw, Mich.), John F. Farnsworth (St. Charles, Ill.), Thomas W. Ferry (Grand Haven, Mich.), Joseph J. Gravely (Stockton, Mo.), Charles M. Hamilton (Mariana, Fla.), Benjamin F. Hopkins (Madison, Wis.), Chester D. Hubbard (Wheeling, W. Va.), Morton C. Hunter (Bloomington, Ind.), Alxexander H. Jones (Ashville, N. C.), George W. Julian (Centreville, Ind.), William H. Koontz (Somerset, Pa.), James M. Marvin (Saratoga Springs, N. Y.), William Moore (May's Landing, N. J.), James K. Moorhead (Pittsburg, Pa.), Leonard Myers (Philadelphia, Pa.), Carman A. Newcomb (Tunnel, Mo.), Halbert E. Paine (Milwaukee, Wis.), Green B. Raum (Harrisburg, Ill.), Worthington C. Smith (St. Albans, Vt.), Henry H. Starkweather (Norwich, Conn.), Charles Upson (Coldwater, Mich.), Cadwalader C. Washburn (LaCrosse, Wis.), William B. Washburn (Greenfield, Mass.), B. F. Whittemore (Darlington, S. C.), William Williams (Warsaw, Ind.), and George W. Woodward (Wilkes-Barre, Pa). The next largest change was the significant dodge of 21 Republicans and 12 Democrats who had voted against the Wilson version but did not vote on the second Bingham version. Some of the most sincere and yet moderate members who consistently voted to limit the amendment to Negro suffrage were George S. Boutwell, Benjamin F. Butler, John C. Churchill, Thomas A. Jenckes, and William D. Kelley.

[93] *Globe*, p. 1428; E. McPherson, p. 406.

[94] New York *Tribune*, February 22, 1869; [New York] *National Anti-Slavery Standard*, February 27, 1869. The New York *Times* (February 23, 1869), was most unhappy with the new House version.

[95] The New York *Times*, February 24, 1869.

between the Senate and the House." [96] The Democratic *World* concluded that the Senate and House were at war upon technicalities,[97] but the *World* failed to see that these technicalities had practical importance for southern Republicans, tactical importance for Democratic and Republican obstructionists, and psychological importance for members of both chambers jealous of their institutional prerogatives. Important segments of the press dismissed the question of Negro officeholding as essentially irrelevant.[98]

A conference committee would have to iron out the differences between the Senate and the House. Selection of committee members, to be made by the presiding officer of each chamber, was of course critical. The House chose Bingham, Boutwell, and Logan. A moderate on a constitutional amendment, Boutwell would favor neither the officeholding guarantee nor the ban on literacy or property tests. Bingham, too, would oppose the officeholding guarantee, while Logan would eventually reject both officeholding and a broad ban on suffrage tests.[99] Radical newspapers objected to the choice of Logan and Bingham on the grounds that they would engineer the demise of the officeholding guarantee.[100] As for the Senate delegation to the conference committee—William Stewart, Roscoe Conkling, and George Edmunds—only the last could be expected to support general bans on tests for suffrage and officeholding. In other words, the committee appeared well chosen to favor a moderate measure.[101]

---

[96] Boston *Daily Journal*, February 20, 1869.

[97] [New York] *The World*, February 20, 1869.

[98] In a powerful editorial the moderate Republican organ, the New York *Times*, commented that Negro voting was most important and probably the right to be voted for was already secured by American citizenship. But that the amendment went much further for Negro officeholding was unimport, because there was no great need or demand for Negro officials. Moreover, the right of the Negro to hold office did not mean that many Negroes would be appointed or elected to office. (The New York *Times*, February 19, 1869.) A more radical journal, *Harper's Weekly*, also played down the issue. Although it endorsed Negro officeholding in the Georgia legislature, the magazine concluded that the officeholding provision should be discarded from the amendment if its inclusion meant that the amendment could not pass Congress. (*Harper's Weekly*, XIII [March 6, 1869], 146.)

[99] Boston *Daily Journal*, February 20–22, 1869; the Springfield *Daily Republican*, February 19, 22, 1869; [New York] *The World*, February 20, 1869; the *Independent*, March 4, 1869; Boutwell, *Reminiscences*, II, 46–47; the New York *Times*, February 26, 1869.

[100] [New York] *National Anti-Slavery Standard*, February 27, 1869.

[101] The New York *Times*, February 25, 1869. Southern Republican senators felt

On February 24 the conference committee met for three hours. Stewart later reported that Bingham and Logan favored the Stewart, or Senate, version without the officeholding guarantee. Stewart and Conkling agreed, because they felt the right to vote included the right to hold office. Over Edmunds' objection, and in Boutwell's absence, the committee dropped demands for officeholding and the ban on most suffrage tests, and recommended the Stewart rather than the Bingham amendment. In short, the committee had recommended an amendment closely paralleling Boutwell's but identical to Stewart's in form.[102] The proposed Fifteenth Amendment read as follows:

The right of citizens of the United States to vote shall not be denied or abridged by the United States or by any State on account of race, color, or previous condition of servitude.
The Congress shall have the power to enforce this article by appropriate legislation.[103]

The conference committee had jettisoned Negro officeholding, because it feared that the country was not yet ready for so radical a measure and that its inclusion might jeopardize ratification.[104] Northern Republicans, moreover, cared less about electing southern Negro officials than counting northern Negro votes. Because both houses had previously agreed to an officeholding guarantee, the conference report amounted to a moderate victory rather than a compromise between Republicans favoring a stronger or a weaker amendment. The provision to abolish state literacy, property, and nativity tests was also omitted, because it would also jeopardize ratification. That a refusal to ban these tests weakened the amendment was of course widely recognized in the South, but in the North it was precisely this omission which would promote ratification and rally moderates.

This amendment was also a moderate one in that its wording was negative. It did not give the federal government the right to set up suffrage requirements, but left the fundamental right with

the same way and voted against submission to a conference committee (*ibid.*, February 24, 1869).
[102] *Ibid.*, February 26, 1869.
[103] *Globe*, p. 1623.
[104] Georges Clemenceau, *American Reconstruction, 1865-1870, and the Impeachment of President Johnson*, ed. F. Baldensperger, trans. M. MacVeagh (New York: Dial Press, 1928), pp. 271-73.

the states. Framed negatively, it did not directly confer the right of suffrage on anyone, and the negative wording might obscure the major objective, which was to enfranchise the northern Negro: such a formula required no positive legislation to impart force or indicate meaning. Instead, Negro suffrage in the North would be secured by the express restraint on the states not to set racially discriminating tests for suffrage. Behind the negative constitutional form lay a positive political reality.[105]

An insistent question remains about the nature and scope of federal enforcement power under the Amendment, specifically the second or enforcement section stipulating that " Congress may pass appropriate legislation." [106] While newspaper editors argued the question of the meaning of that section, and such diverse men as Chief Justice Salmon P. Chase and Henry Adams expressed opinions,[107] most Congressional framers and supporters must have remained discreetly silent, for closely reasoned arguments were conspicuous by their absence. It would appear that radical and moderate Republicans did not care to open this Pandora's box, for fear that frank and full discussion would serve no useful purpose but would further divide Republicans and increase difficulty of passage and ratification. Debate, then, was largely avoided, and real differences over the reach of federal enforcement powers were papered over by the convenient device of an enforcement section, leaving the meaning of the word " appropriate " up to the courts for future interpretation and application, as well as up to Congress for future legislation.[108] Because of this artful dodge, the contentious constitutional issue of federal powers over voting in the states was avoided.

The combination of a negative first section and an affirmative second section was significant.[109] Before sending their vessel down the ways on its long voyage into law, the builders attempted to construct a hull seaworthy enough to withstand foul weather, and

[105] See Table 1, p. 82.

[106] U. S., *Constitution*, Amdt. 15, Sec. 2.

[107] See below, Chap. III, n. 30.

[108] By the amendments offered and rejected, it is clear that the framers did not intend to establish federal qualifications for suffrage or to abolish state literacy tests. Debate on federal powers of enforcement was evasive at best and inconclusive at least. It is thus hazardous to read either too much or too little meaning into the second section.

[109] Letter from Everette Swinney, February 1, 1965.

tried to rig a sail to take the shifting winds of the future. Thus the first section was shaped to make it impossible, if the Democrats ever returned to power in Washington, to repudiate Negro voting, North or South. It was therefore worded as a negative restriction or self-enforcing prohibition to rule out any attempt by the federal government or the states to nullify the right of Negroes to vote on the grounds of race. Here the framers said what they meant and meant what they said. Then the shipbuilders fashioned a second section worded as an affirmative grant of enforcement power. Here, providing Republicans controlled Congress and the presidency, the enforcement problem could be handled when the time was ripe and the need was clear. Presumably such enforcement power was intended primarily to accomplish the other major objective of the Amendment, to give the federal government a means to enforce Negro suffrage in the South, but also possibly provide a means to inspect election returns from Democratic strongholds in the North. In their considered omissions and cautious formulation,[110] their recognition of the needs of party and principle, their calculation of the demands of the future as well as the present, and their acknowledgment of the existence of prejudice, the framers intended to sail close-hauled.

On February 25, 1869, the committee report was submitted to the House, whose rules strictly forbade debate on the conference report. Voting along party lines almost to a man,[111] the House accepted it (S. 8).

[110] It was widely recognized at the time that the framers proposed to deal not with the whole problem but only with the worst of it. See Thomas M. Cooley (ed.), *Commentaries on the Constitution* . . . (2 vols.; Boston, Mass.: Little, Brown, 1873), II, 689. Judge Cooley, writing in 1873, recognized that Congress confined its efforts to its limited and special object: "What is particularly noticeable in the case of this article is the care with which it confines itself to the particular object in view. The pressure of a particular evil was felt; the reproach of a great wrong was acknowledged; and that evil was to be remedied, and that wrong redressed. There was no thought at this time of correcting at once and by a single act all the inequalities and all the injustice that might exist in the suffrage laws of the several States. There was no thought or purpose of regulating by amendment, or of conferring upon Congress the authority to regulate, or to prescribe qualifications for, the privilege of the ballot."

[111] Republicans voted 144 "yes" to 3 "no," while Democrats voted 41 "no" to none "yes," with 35 not voting (*Globe*, pp. 1563–64; E. McPherson, p. 399). The 3 Republicans who opposed the conference report were Isaac R. Hawkins from conservative west Tennessee, who had opposed the original Boutwell version; William Loughridge of Iowa; and Rufus Mallory from anti-Chinese Oregon. Of

Reaction to the conference report in the Senate was hostile, and, because of its permissive rules, consideration was slower. It was argued that a conference could only iron out disagreements, not nullify agreements; [112] others termed the change in the amendment's wording unparliamentary, unauthorized, and unprecedented.[113] The Senate, remarked a Democrat, was about to accept what two weeks ago it had rejected—that is, the Boutwell plan [114] —and to be sure, inconsistency characterized each phase of passage.

On behalf of the conference committee, Stewart defended the proposed Fifteenth Amendment as the only formula with a chance for ratification. He pointedly remarked that though each Senator wanted a different set of reforms, the central issue was the security and extension of Negro suffrage. Threatened in Georgia and Tennessee, Negro voters had yet to be enfranchised in Maryland, Kentucky, and Delaware. Stewart asked his associates to recognize the pivotal fact that the " ballot is the mainspring; the ballot is power; the ballot is the dispenser of office." [115]

Last ditchers, like Frederick A. Sawyer (Republican, South Carolina), representing some diehard southern Republicans, also criticized the report. He felt the deletion of the officeholding provision would hurt ratification in the South, if perhaps it helped it in the North.[116]

Other radicals reluctantly acquiesced, and the break in the radical ranks was permanent. Jacob Howard advised his antislavery colleagues to accept the conference report. Qualifying his endorse-

---

the 28 Republicans who did not vote, a majority came from the Northeast and especially from the Middle Atlantic states of Pennsylvania and New York. There was also a strong representation of Republican absentees from Ohio. Of the 3 Republicans from New York, 2 came from counties that subsequently approved of Negro suffrage, while all 3 Republican congressmen from Ohio represented counties that had previously rejected Negro suffrage. Perhaps the New York Republicans abstained because the proposed federal amendment was too weak, while the Ohio Republicans felt it was too strong. Save for 1, the 7 abstaining Democrats might have been affected by Negro voting in the North or by strong attitudes toward it. Democrats who might be concerned with Negro suffrage were George M. Adams and Lawrence S. Trimble of Kentucky, William H. Barnum from western Connecticut, John Morrissey of New York city, Charles Sitgreaves of New Jersey, and, most significantly, the influential Samuel J. Randall of Philadelphia.

[112] *Globe*, pp. 1625–26.
[113] *Ibid.*, pp. 1623–24.
[114] *Ibid.*, p. 1625.
[115] *Ibid.*, p. 1629.
[116] *Ibid.*

ment, Howard added that he entertained no illusions about the proposed Fifteenth Amendment, which outlawed racial discrimination clearly enough, but did not unequivocally confer on the Negro the right to vote; thus Negro suffrage would in no way be protected.[117] Henry Wilson also criticized the form of the amendment and regretted the committee's failure to obtain either officeholding or comprehensive suffrage reform. Despite this, Wilson admitted he would support the half-way measure rather than no measure at all.[118]

Inclined, like many advocates of an amendment, to sweeping measures, Oliver P. Morton professed great displeasure with the report. He objected sharply to the omission of officeholding and general suffrage reforms, and vowed never again to resort to a conference committee. But though his criticism constituted a personal attack on Stewart's leadership, Morton was first a realist and next a reformer. "I go upon the principle of taking half a loaf when I cannot get a whole one," [119] he stated. "But nevertheless I want to say that it is pretty hard to accept a halfloaf when a whole one or almost a whole one has been offered to us and has been rejected by the committee of conference." [120]

On February 26, at 9 P.M., the Senate grumblingly accepted the conference report (S. 8) by a partisan vote of thirty-nine " yes," thirteen " no," and fourteen absent. With the sessions of the state legislatures and the Fortieth Congress drawing to a close in four working days, there was no choice but to accept the amendment as reported out of committee or let it die. Its final supporters included important representatives of the antislavery northern and southern Republican groups.[121] Outright opposition included the Democrats, conservative Republican Joseph S. Fowler, who was politically isolated from other Tennessee Republicans, and John Pool (Republican, North Carolina), who probably felt the amendment lacked power. The bulk of the absentees consisted of the

[117] *Ibid.*, p. 1625.
[118] *Ibid.*, pp. 1626–27.
[119] *Ibid.*, pp. 1627–28.
[120] *Ibid.*
[121] *Ibid.*, pp. 1639, 1641; E. McPherson, p. 400. The more radical Howard, Wade, and Wilson joined the bandwagon, as did a majority of southern Republicans and virtually all men from the unstable group of northern Republicans, led by Morton. Sheer exhaustion may have contributed to passage. (Boston *Morning Journal*, February 27, 1869).

diehard antislavery men, Sumner, Pomeroy, Edmunds, Grimes, Ross, and Yates, along with three southern Republicans: Joseph Abbott, Frederick Sawyer, and George Spencer. According to a press reporter, Abbott, Edmunds, and Pomeroy were present but did not vote.[122] Because of sensitivity to the issue among their constituents, absentee Republicans Simon Cameron (Pennsylvania), Henry Corbett (Oregon), and William Sprague (Rhode Island) may have had sound political reasons to have dodged the vote.

In striking contrast to the grudging acceptance of the proposed Fifteenth Amendment by many congressmen was the applause that it received in the press. The more moderate Republican papers were especially delighted. A Grant organ, the Washington *National Republican*, termed the final version " sufficiently comprehensive." [123] The New York *Tribune*, fairly moderate on the suffrage question by 1869, characterized it as " wise and judicious." [124] Henry Adams, although missing the real significance of the Amendment, found little to which he could object in the " neck-tie with which it [Congress] proposes at last to adorn the statue of American Liberty. . . ." [125] Adams concluded that the " dogma that suffrage is a natural right, and not a trust, is by implication denied. The ' right ' to hold office, as well as to vote, is not asserted. Educational and even property qualifications are not excluded." [126] Even the more radical Republican press fell quickly into line by arguing that something was better than nothing. The *Independent*, which had originally supported the broader version with an officeholding guarantee and a general ban on property and educational qualifications, abruptly changed course. Announcing that the Amendment was hardly perfect and would soon need to be supplemented, the *Independent*, nevertheless, observed that it " is a flood-wave that will float the Constitution still further toward the final high-water mark of Liberty, Equality, and Fraternity." [127] It appeared, then, that a consensus existed immediately after congressional passage, as Republican

---

[122] The New York *Times*, February 27, 1869.
[123] [Washington, D. C.] *The National Republican*, February 27, 1869.
[124] New York *Tribune*, February 25, 1869.
[125] Henry B. Adams, " The Session," *North American Review*, CVIII (April, 1869), 613.
[126] *Ibid.*
[127] [New York] the *Independent*, March 4, 11, 1869. Cf. *ibid.*, February 18, 1869; April 7. 1870.

editors rallied round the proposed Fifteenth Amendment and endorsed its ratification.

The Fifteenth Amendment had a limited object—first, to enfranchise the northern Negro, and second, to protect the southern Negro against disfranchisement,[128] and it was chiefly the work of moderates in Congress. It offered too little to southern Republicans, who wanted greater protection of Negro voting and a mild guarantee of Negro officeholding; it offered even less to the many veteran antislavery northern Republicans who sought, in addition to firmer guarantees for southern Negroes, general suffrage reform and even national control of suffrage. On the other hand, for Democrats who feared the Republican Negro voter in the North and in the South and disliked any federal interference in state and local elections it proved too strong, as it did for restrictionist

[128] John M. Mathews, *Legislative and Judicial History of the Fifteenth Amendment* ("Johns Hopkins University Studies in Historical and Political Science," Ser. XXVII, Nos. 6–7; Baltimore, Md.: The Johns Hopkins Press, 1909), pp. 20–21. On the basis of their arguments in the debates over a Negro suffrage amendment, Mathews discovers four groups of congressmen: nationalists, state rightists, humanitarians, and politicians. Though one can agree with Mathews that the politicians were of critical importance in securing final passage, their stated objectives and strategies were at variance. What seemed most to matter was how a particular proposal would affect constituents in a congressman's state or district. Such considerations affected not just a few but most congressmen. Furthermore, Mathews' groupings oversimplify the complex shifts and realignments that attended each step in the passage of the Amendment. For example, Mathews takes Howard's proposal to embody the views of the "political" group, when in fact the "humanitarian" or antislavery group supported it and Stewart's moderate or "political" group opposed it. (*Ibid.*, p. 32; *Globe*, p. 1012.) Similarly, the vote on the Wilson proposal is attributed to a coalition of "politicians" and "humanitarians," yet most moderates or politicians opposed it (Mathews, p. 33; *Globe*, p. 1040). The term "humanitarian" to designate one group is itself ambiguous for some veteran advocates of Negro suffrage. William D. Kelley and George S. Boutwell worked to pass the Fifteenth Amendment, while many others opposed it altogether. In short, some "humanitarians" were practical, others impractical. If "politicians" and "humanitarians" were divided, can the fight be reduced semantically to a simple struggle between "nationalist" Republicans and "state rightist" Democrats? The answer must be no, since the sustained struggle over an amendment indicates that state rights was only one of several issues worrying congressmen. Democrats, in a decided minority, could not have prolonged the fight on the state rights issue alone, unless other issues mattered to Republicans and unless some Republicans supported the state rights cause. Splits among Republicans caused the trouble, which was not philosophical and doctrinaire but political and practical in character. Mathews' distinctions lack political meaning.

Republicans from the Pacific and Atlantic seaboards, who worried about Chinese or Irish voters.

The moderate measure that was to become the Fifteenth Amendment found itself initially blocked by those who wanted a stronger or a weaker amendment, or no amendment at all. But the effective coalition against a moderate version suffered from the instability of its component parts. Congressmen changed their minds and their camps, camps disintegrated, coalitions collapsed, and Senate and House haggled. The absence of a Republican consensus allowed obstructionists to manipulate the shifting coalitions to advantage, for factional differences were strong, party discipline was weak, and the task of rallying a two-thirds majority for passage seemed insurmountable. House Democrats were particularly adept at playing one fluctuating Republican group off against another. In the Senate the veteran antislavery group joined a number of Southern Republicans to stall legislative action.

But a realistic reaction set in before the doctrinaire extremists or stubborn provincials could either impose their own will or, what was more likely, completely frustrate that of others. End-of-session timing, the common sense of moderation, the persistent leadership of Stewart and Boutwell, and the priority of strategic necessity over both local expediency and reformist utopianism brought a majority of Republican congressmen to rise above principle to pass the Fifteenth Amendment, the Amendment that had been devised to suit moderate tastes and secure party needs. Including, as it did, just enough to accomplish its primary objective—the enfranchisement of the northern Negro—the Fifteenth Amendment contained little that would alarm its marginal supporters without whom it could not survive passage or ratification. In essence, the Amendment satisfied these requirements by establishing impartial rather than universal suffrage.

CHAPTER III

THE FIGHT FOR RATIFICATION

The chances for ratification of the Fifteenth Amendment appeared uncertain in late February and early March, 1869. Yet the Republicans who were supporters of the Amendment had four sources of satisfaction. To begin with, the Amendment was a party measure that ought to command the support of Republican politicians in the thirty-seven states, three-fourths of which had voted Republican in 1868. Secondly, congressional passage was timely, for seventeen Republican state legislatures were still in session in March, and these legislatures could act on the Amendment before elections. Also, during January and February, President-elect Ulysses S. Grant had made it clear to Senator William Stewart, Congressman Rowland E. Trowbridge, and other Republicans that his administration would work for ratification,[1] and shortly afterward at Stewart's urging, in his first inaugural address on 4 March 1869, he strongly endorsed it:

The question of suffrage is one which is likely to agitate the public so long as a portion of the citizens of the nation are excluded from its privileges in any State. It seems to me very desirable that this question should be settled now, and I entertain the hope and express the desire that it may be by the ratification of the fifteenth article of amendment to the Constitution.[2]

Finally, there was the possibility that Congress would require ratification by the southern states not yet readmitted to Congress, as in fact it did. Partisanship, timing, presidential support, and required ratification constituted telling advantages.

[1] Brown, *Reminiscences*, pp. 233, 238; Rowland E. Trowbridge to Rutherford B. Hayes, February 15, 1869, Rutherford B. Hayes MSS, Rutherford B. Hayes Library, Fremont, Ohio; Sacramento *Daily Union*, January 18, 1870.

[2] James D. Richardson (ed.), *A Compilation of the Messages and Papers of the Presidents, 1789–1897* (10 vols.; Washington, D. C.: Bureau of National Literature and Art, 1896–99), VII, 8.

But the opposing forces were also formidable. Although twenty states out of the thirty-seven allowed the Negro to vote, these were not enough to secure ratification. Moreover, that Negroes voted in these states did not in all cases indicate popular support for the Amendment, because Congress had forced Negro suffrage on eleven southern states by the Reconstruction acts and on Nebraska by the statehood act, and the state supreme court had ordered it in Wisconsin. Only five New England states, along with Iowa and Minnesota, had given the Negro the ballot voluntarily, and all of those had few Negroes among the population. Other northern states, including those with relatively large Negro populations, had rejected Negro suffrage in postwar referendums. Besides, public opinion strongly opposed Negro rights, and the state legislators who outraged this consensus would commit political suicide.

Probably the most important obstacle in the path of ratification was the anticipated political effect of the Fifteenth Amendment. In the closely divided states of the North, Democrats and Republicans alike clearly recognized the strategic importance of the northern Negro vote. The enfranchisement between 130,000 and 171,000 Negro voters in the border states, the Northeast, the Middle West, and the Far West could change the political complexion of state and national politics.[3] This Negro vote would be Republican, and it might cost the Democrats Maryland, Delaware, and New Jersey, while assuring the Republicans control of Connecticut, Indiana, Ohio, and Pennsylvania.

The Democrats needed only ten states to defeat ratification. They controlled five legislatures in session in March, 1869. Probable rejection by four additional states and one doubtful state would assure defeat.

Among Republicans, too, forces were at work to defeat ratification. The doctrine of state rights would induce some of them to join the opposition. Local pressures against Negro suffrage, as well as fear of Chinese and foreign suffrage under the Fifteenth Amendment, might force Republican legislators to sabotage ratification because the Amendment was too inclusive. There was also loud grumbling among more radical Republicans, reformers, and southern Republicans, who complained that the Amendment did

[3] See Table 1, p. 82.

not go far enough because Negroes were neither protected against literacy and property tests for suffrage, nor guaranteed the right to hold office.

In late March it seemed likely that the Amendment would be ratified.[4] But ratification bogged down during the summer and fall, and by the winter of 1869–70 the situation became very critical for those favoring it. Trouble brewed among Republicans, while Democrats tried every device to defeat ratification. However, the formidable Republican advantages overcame fierce opposition, and by the beginning of February the fight [5] was over. In March, 1870, the Fifteenth Amendment became law.

The debate on the ratification of the Fifteenth Amendment was the same in the substance of the arguments throughout the country, but what differed from section to section was the emphasis on issues, the tone and temper of the debate, and the tactics employed.

Political issues centered on the desirability of enfranchising Negroes outside the South. Veteran abolitionist and antislavery Republicans, arguing that justice demanded suffrage in the North, claimed that the Amendment would guarantee equal and impartial rights to all citizens. The underlying theme was the abolitionist doctrine of political equality and opposition to color bars or caste legislation.[6] Political equality, desirable for its own sake, would broaden the base of the electorate, so that the power of the government would be derived from the consent not of a part but of all the governed.[7] Implicit in this argument was the belief that suffrage was an inherent not a conventional right.

Many moderate Republicans accepted the abolitionist rhetoric but limited its practical application. Political equality was praised, for example, but the Chinese were excluded from its enjoyment. Moderate and conservative Republicans, who constituted a majority of the Republican state legislators, pointed out that political equality had nothing to do with social equality.[8] Unlike the doctrinaires, who received their nourishment from principle, most Republican legislators simply argued that if the Negro was good

[4] See but compare Clifford L. Lord and Elizabeth H. Lord, *Historical Atlas of the United States* (New York: H. Holt, 1944), p. 164.

[5] See Table 2, p. 84.

[6] Commonwealth of Pennsylvania, *The Legislative Record*, 93rd Sess. (1869), pp. 658–59.

[7] *Ibid.*, p. 864.

[8] *Ibid.*, pp. 512–13, 818, 911, 942.

TABLE 1: POTENTIAL NEGRO VOTE IN THE NORTHERN STATES AFFECTED BY THE FIFTEENTH AMENDMENT

Rank of State by Negro Population	State	Per Cent of Negroes in Population in 1870 a	Press Estimate of Negro Voters in 1870 b	One-fifth Estimate of Negro Voters in 1870 c	Negro Population in 1870 d	Rank by State of National Negro Population in 1870 e	Presidential Majority in 1868 f	Rank by State of Per Cent of National Party Support for Presidential Candidate in 1868 g	Majority Party for Presidential Candidate in 1868 h	Per Cent of Vote for Majority Presidential Candidate in 1868 i	Rank by State of Total Turnout of Voters for Presidential Election in 1868 j	Number of Seats in the House of Representatives by Apportionment of 1872 k	Number of Electoral Votes in the 1872 Presidential Election l
	National Average	12.7	129,747	170,973	864,614								
1	Kentucky	16.8	39,361	44,442	222,210	10	76,313	2	Dem.	74.5%	13	10	12
2	*Maryland	22.5	28,552	35,078	175,391	11	31,919	7	Dem.	67.1%	21	6	7
3	*Missouri	6.9	23,701	23,614	118,071	13	25,883	18	Rep.	56.9%	14	13	15
4	*Pennsylvania	1.9	9,475	13,059	65,294	15	28,898	26	Rep.	52.2%	2	27	29
5	*Ohio	2.4	6,112	10,643	63,213	16	41,428	23	Rep.	54.0%	3	20	22
6	*New York	1.2	8,167	10,416	52,081	17	10,000	31	Dem.	50.5%	1	23	35
7	*New Jersey	3.4	4,226	6,132	30,658	18	2,880	30	Dem.	50.8%	11	7	9
8	Illinois	1.1	1,271	5,752	28,762	19	51,150	20	Rep.	55.6%	4	19	21
9	*Indiana	1.5	1,805	4,912	24,560	20	9,572	29	Rep.	51.3%	5	13	15
10	*Delaware	18.2	3,604	4,559	22,794	21	3,257	14	Dem.	59.0%	31	1	3
11	*West Virginia	4.1	—	3,596	17,980	22	8,719	15	Rep.	58.9%	26	3	5
12	Kansas	4.7	—	3,422	17,108	23	16,408	5	Rep.	68.9%	27	3	5
13	Michigan	1.0	1,333	2,370	11,849	25	31,481	17	Rep.	56.9%	6	9	11
14	*Connecticut	1.8	1,438	1,934	9,668	26	3,041	27	Rep.	51.5%	20	4	6
15	*California	0.8	681	854	4,272	29	514	33	Rep.	50.2%	18	4	6
16	Nevada	0.8	—	71	357	36	1,162	21	Rep.	55.3%	33	1	3
17	Oregon	0.4	21	69	346	37	164	32	Dem.	50.3%	29	1	3

*State which has an important potential Negro vote.

a U.S., Bureau of the Census, *Negro Population, 1790–1915* (Washington, D.C., 1918), p. 51.

b *The Patterson Daily Press*, March 31, 1870; [Cumberland, Md.] *Civilian and Telegraph*, February 10, 1870; [Burlington, Vt.] *Free Press*, quoted in *Galveston News*, February 16, 1870. The estimate of the Negro vote was usually one-fifth or one-sixth of the total Negro population in each state, according to the census of 1860. Either estimate appears fairly conservative except in the border states. Examples of actual turnout of Negro voters are difficult to come by. In Connecticut the one-fifth estimate of eligible Negro voters was 1,934, but the turnout in 1871 was less (1,438). Yet in California, in 1871, Negro voters numbered 1,400, while the one-fifth estimate was 854. In Maryland 12,000 Negroes cast ballots. The turnout was considerably under the 28,000–35,000 estimate. In West Virginia 2,705 Negro voters in 1870 were less than the estimate of 3,500. An estimate of the potential power of the potential Negro vote based on the majority for Republican presidential candidate Ulysses S. Grant in 1868 constitutes the most conservative calculation, because Grant ran considerably ahead of the Republican state ticket. Grant was stronger than the state Republican candidates and thus state Republican majorities were much slimmer. In Pennsylvania, for example, the state Republican majority ran between 4,000–17,000, while Grant's majority was 28,000. There the potential Negro voters numbered 13,000. In Ohio, Grant's majority was 41,000, but Hayes's majorities ran between 3,000–7,000. In Indiana, Grant carried the state in 1868 by 9,000, but the Republican majority was 961. In Connecticut, Grant carried the state by 3,000, but Republican Governor Marshall Jewell won by 411 votes in 1869 and lost by 1,764 votes in 1870. In 1871, with the help of the Negro vote, Republicans recaptured the governorship by 103 votes. In short, the potential Negro vote could prove more important in state and congressional elections than in presidential elections, at least that of 1868.

c One-fifth of the total Negro population in each state, according to the census of 1870.

d U.S., Bureau of the Census, *Ninth Census: 1870* (3 vols.; Washington, D.C., 1872), I, 5.

e *Ibid.*

f *Tribune Almanac for 1869*, pp. 57–88; Burnham, *Presidential Ballots*, pp. 246–57.

g Fletcher W. Hewes, *Citizen's Atlas of American Politics, 1789–1888, a Series of Colored Maps and Charts* (New York: Charles Scribner's Sons, 1888), p. 14.

h *Ibid.*

i *Ibid.*

j *Ibid.*

k U.S., Congress, House of Representatives, *Biographical Directory of the American Congress, 1774–1949*, 81st Cong., 2nd Sess., 1950, House Doc. 607, p. 45.

l Burnham, *Presidential Ballots*, p. 888.

TABLE 2: CHRONOLOGY OF RATIFICATION OF THE FIFTEENTH AMENDMENT

Rank	State		First Chamber Ratified on		Second Chamber Ratification (Effective Date of Ratification by State)
1	Nevada	Senate	March 1, 1869	Assembly	March 1, 1869
2	West Virginia	House of Delegates	March 2, 1869	Senate	March 3, 1869
3	Louisiana	Senate	Feb. 27, 1869	House of Rep.	March 1, 1869
4	North Carolina	House of Rep.	March 4, 1869	Senate	March 4, 1869
5	Wisconsin	Assembly	March 3, 1869	Senate	March 5, 1869
6	Illinois	Senate	March 5, 1869	House of Rep.	March 5, 1869
7	Michigan	House of Rep.	March 5, 1869	Senate	March 5, 1869
8	Maine	Senate	March 11, 1869	House of Rep.	March 11, 1869
9	South Carolina	Senate	March 6, 1869	House of Rep.	March 11, 1869
10	Massachusetts	House of Rep.	March 9, 1869	Senate	March 12, 1869
11	Arkansas	Senate	March 13, 1869	House of Rep.	March 15, 1869
	[Kentucky rejects March 11 & 12, 1869]				
	[Delaware rejects March 17 & 18, 1869]				
	[Georgia rejects March 18, 1869]				
12	Pennsylvania	Senate	March 11, 1869	House of Rep.	March 25, 1869
13	New York	Assembly	March 17, 1869	Senate	April 14, 1869
14	Connecticut	Senate	May 5, 1869	House of Rep.	May 13, 1869
	[Ohio rejects April 1, 1869; Senate April 30, 1869—later rescinds]				
15	Indiana	Senate	May 13, 1869	House of Rep.	May 14, 1869
16	Florida	Assembly	June 11, 1869	Senate	June 14, 1869
17	New Hampshire	House of Rep.	June 24, 1869	Senate	July 1, 1869
18	Required Virginia	House of Delegates	Oct. 8, 1869	Senate	Oct. 8, 1869
19	Vermont	House of Rep.	Oct. 19, 1869	Senate	Oct. 20, 1869
20	Alabama	Senate	Nov. 15, 1869	House of Rep.	Nov. 16, 1869
	[New York rescinds ratification Jan. 5, 1870]				
21	Missouri	Senate	Jan. 7, 1870	House of Rep.	Jan. 7, 1870
22	Minnesota	Senate	Jan. 12, 1870	House of Rep.	Jan. 13, 1870
23	Required Mississippi	Senate	Jan. 15, 1870	House of Rep.	Jan. 17, 1870
24	Rhode Island	Senate	May 27, 1869	House of Rep.	Jan. 18, 1870
25	Kansas	House of Rep.	Jan. 18, 1870	Senate	Jan. 19, 1870

Rank	State	First Chamber Ratified on		Second Chamber Ratification (Effective Date of Ratification by State)	
26	Ohio	Senate	Jan. 14, 1870	House of Rep.	Jan. 20, 1870
	[earlier rejected]				
27	Iowa	Senate	Jan. 26, 1870	House of Rep.	Jan. 27, 1870
	[California rejects Jan. 27 & 28, 1870]				
28	Required Georgia	Senate	Feb. 2, 1870	House of Rep.	Feb. 2, 1870

[House previously ratified on March 11 & 16, 1869 but Senate rejected on March 18, 1869]

Counting New York and Georgia Fifteenth Amendment is ratified.

[New York rejects Feb. 1 & 7, 1870]

29	Nebraska	Senate	Feb. 17, 1870	House of Rep.	Feb. 17, 1870

Not counting New York or Georgia Fifteenth Amendment is ratified.

30	Required Texas	House of Rep.	Feb. 15, 1870	Senate	Feb. 18, 1870

[Tennessee rejects Nov. 16, 1869 & Feb. 24, 1870]
[Maryland rejects Feb. 4 & 25, 1870]
Proclamation of Ratification—March 30, 1870
[Oregon rejects by both houses on Oct. 26, 1870]
[New Jersey ratifies Feb. 15, 1871]
[Delaware ratifies Feb. 12, 1901]
[Oregon ratifies Feb. 24, 1959]
[California ratifies April 3, 1962]

enough to fight and die for the Union during the war, he was a good enough citizen to vote.[9] The importance and influence of this argument cannot be overestimated.

The individualist ethic was also extremely important. Republicans felt that, like the white man, the black man deserved an equal chance, and this argument for a fair start in the race of life struck a responsive chord among Republican moderates. Anyone who tried to trip the colored man was a coward.[10] Certainly, in 1869 many of these politicians had no doubt who would win the race,[11] but a lot of them were, significantly, conceding equality of opportunity in principle, if not always in practice. Idealism, patriotism, and individualism supported the conclusion that Negro suffrage was just.

On the other hand, probably more important than the appeal to justice was the appeal to expediency. Northern Negroes, politi-

[9] *Ibid.*, pp. 658–59, 787, 818, 840, 864, 909, 940, 942; [Trenton] *Daily State Gazette*, February 2, 1870.

[10] Pennsylvania, *Legislative Record*, 93rd Sess., pp. 788, 842, 863, 940, 942.

[11] *Ibid.*, pp. 842, 942.

TABLE 3: RANK OF THE RATIFYING STATES BY THE PERCENTAGE OF YEA VOTES ON RATIFICATION OF THE FIFTEENTH AMENDMENT

Rank	State	Per Cent of Yea Votes in Both Chambers		
26	Ohio	50	51	[closest vote]
25	New York	53	60	
24	West Virginia	53	62	
24	Pennsylvania	54	61	
23	Indiana	54	63	[figured by per cent of yeas to total membership, which includes bolters]
22	Connecticut	54	70	
21	Wisconsin	57	68	
20	Florida	62	66	
19	Nevada	59	70	
18	Minnesota	65	68	
17	Illinois	65	72	
16	Georgia	70	72	
15	Michigan	73	83	
14	Rhode Island	70	87	
13	Missouri	71	87	
13	New Hampshire	58	100	
12	North Carolina	81	87	
11	Louisiana	86	86	
10	Iowa	87	88	
9	Nebraska	87	91	
8	Texas	87	92	
7	Alabama	82	100	
6	Kansas	86	100	
6	Massachusetts	92	94	
5	South Carolina	94	96	
5	Arkansas	90	100	
4	Vermont	94	100	
3	Virginia	94	100	
2	Maine	96	100	
1	Mississippi	100	100	

SOURCES: State legislative journals are cited in the accounts of ratification by the several states.

The dates of ratification supplement and supersede Francis N. Thorpe, *The Federal and State Constitutions* (Washington, D. C., 1909), I, 35; U. S., Congress, Senate, *Ratification of the Constitution and Amendments by the States*, 71st Cong., 3rd Sess. (1931), Sen. Doc. 2408; U. S., Congress, Senate, *The Constitution of the United States of America* . . . , 82nd Cong., 2nd Sess. (1953); U. S., Congress, Senate, *The Constitution of the United States*, 87th Cong., 1st Sess. (1961), Sen. Doc. 49, pp. 31, 45.

cians proclaimed, were more educated and less numerous than
southern Negroes and would therefore cause less trouble. That
the ballot would be beneficial for the Negro, the country, and
the party was another major theme. Republican Governor John
M. Palmer of Illinois said in January, 1870, that officials and
politicians would not worry about the interest and rights of
Negroes who were without the franchise. " But concede to the
colored citizen the right to vote," he noted, " and suddenly all is
changed. The governor, members of Congress and of the legislature suddenly discover your value. They become polite to your
person and thoughtful of your interests, for they want your good
will and your vote." [12] Similarly, the radical idealist Wendell
Phillips answered abolitionist objections to the powers and provisions of the Amendment by arguing that it " contains within
itself the cure for all its own defects. A man with a ballot in
his hand is the master of the situation. He defines all his other
rights. What is not already given him, he takes. . . . The Ballot
is opportunity, education, fair play, right to office, and elbow
room." [13] In short, a voteless citizen was a helpless citizen, but
the voting Negro could defend himself and protect his interests.

Politicians remarked that the ballot for the northern Negro
would help the Republican party stay in power, thereby preserving
the fruits of war and promoting the well-being of the country.
The Pennsylvania Senate Committee on Federal Relations epito-
mized Republican arguments, characterizing the Amendment as
" an act of simple justice, which is, at the same time, one of the
highest expediency and of the most considerate statesmanship." [14]

Underlying all these Republican arguments was an almost
frantic sense of anticipation evoked by the fight for ratification.
Some Republicans cherished utopian expectations that a new era
for the Negro would dawn with the ratification of the Amendment, that prejudice and discrimination would disappear. They
took at face value what few politicians said. More important,
they conceived of the Amendment as marking an end to the problems of Reconstruction for the white man. Utopia meant the

[12] John M. Palmer, *Personal Recollections of John M. Palmer: The Story of an
Earnest Life* (Cincinnati, Ohio: Robert Clarke Co., 1901), p. 330.
[13] [New York] *National Anti-Slavery Standard*, March 20, 1869.
[14] Commonwealth of Pennsylvania, *Journal of the Senate*, 93rd Sess. (1869),
p. 511.

fulfillment of Grant's promise of peace, the price of which was
Negro suffrage and something more. Once the Negro had political
equality, he would then no longer comprise an element of mischief
in American politics, said the editor of the Wheeling *Daily Intelligencer*.[15] The Negro would be put out of politics, declared
Harper's Weekly.[16] The government would no longer concern
itself with the Negro, argued the New York *Times*.[17] Rather,
the Negro would depend on his own self-reliance and self-educa-
tion, *The Nation* argued.[18] In much of this sort of reasoning it
was tacitly assumed that once he had the vote, the Negro would
stay in his place and forget social equality.[19] Though the roots of
laissez-faire government and the ethic of individualism run deep
in this thinking, the emphasis on the passivity rather than the
activity of the Negro in politics and society, combined with the
stark negativism toward the Negro as an individual and as a race,
suggested prejudice and panic at the taproot. The difference
between the treatment and attitude toward the Negro in the North
and the South was aptly stated by Thomas Carlyle, who claimed
that the southerner said to the Negro " ' God bless you! and be a
slave,' while the northerner said, ' God damn you! and be
free.' " [20]

Democrats attacked the powers and provisions of the Amendment, the method and validity of ratification, and the expediency
and wisdom of Negro suffrage. The Amendment was declared
unconstitutional, because it deprived the states of their right to
regulate elections and set qualifications for suffrage. It was also
unconstitutional, they argued, because it went beyond the amending power by creating new powers not originally delegated to the
federal government. Federal intervention and ultimate control
of not only federal but state elections would result.[21] The method
of ratification was also rejected, because the Amendment was not

[15] Wheeling *Daily Intelligencer*, March 1, 1869.
[16] *Harper's Weekly*, XIII (May 1, 1869), 274.
[17] The New York *Times*, April 1, 1870.
[18] *Ibid.; The Nation*, February 18, 1869.
[19] *The Nation*, March 11, 1869.
[20] Sarah Norton and M. A. DeWolfe Howe (eds.), *Letters of Charles Eliot
Norton with Biographical Comment* (2 vols.; Boston, Mass.: Houghton Mifflin
Co., 1913), I, 338.
[21] Pennsylvania, *Legislative Record*, 93rd Sess., pp. 961–64; the Detroit *Free
Press*, March 6, 1869; the New York *Herald*, September 23, 1869; Rochester *Daily
Union and Advertiser*, February 27, 1869.

to be submitted for approval to state conventions, state referendums, or state legislatures elected with instructions on the
question.[22] Instead, Democrats claimed, ratification was a political
trick that broke a party pledge and defied public opinion in forcing
Negro suffrage on the North.[23] Ratification was not only immoral,
it was also illegal. Required, irregular, and unpopular ratification
would be invalid.[24] Negro suffrage was attacked outright. Negroes
were illiterate and inferior [25] and should not be allowed to vote,
as Reconstruction in the South had demonstrated. If Negroes
voted, politics would be corrupted, intermarriage of the races
occur, and an outbreak of race wars commence.[26] In short, the
Amendment was wicked, ratification was a farce, and the ballot
for the Negro meant political chaos.

The Democrats repeated their liturgy without conviction or
enthusiasm. State rights mattered, but all this had been said too
often before. Democrats sounded discouraged and seemed pessi-
mistic, and their arguments about broken Republican campaign
promises sounded more like jealousy than indignation. They, in
fact, argued for a rigid constitutional control, for a Constitution
that did not provide for its own amendment, and for a political
order that could not cope with new times and new problems.
Resorting to solemn nonsense, Democrats asserted that if the
inferior "nigger" voted, he would take over the country; that
race war would come just as surely as miscegenation; and that
whites should prevent blacks from voting in order to save whites
from such vices as the purchase of Negro votes. Such double talk
was not a Democratic monopoly, but the Democrats relied upon it
heavily.

The specific intent of the framers and supporters of the Amendment as understood by state legislators and newspapermen was
clearly expressed and widely shared. Democrats argued boldly,
with the tacit consent of many Republicans, that the primary

[22] Pennsylvania, *Journal of the Senate*, 93rd Sess., pp. 513–17, 540; State of
New York, *Journal of the Assembly*, 92nd Sess. (1869), I, 543–44.

[23] Pennsylvania, *Legislative Record*, 93rd Sess., pp. 664, 926; Rochester *Daily
Union and Advertiser*, February 27, 1869; State of New Jersey, *Documents*, 94th
Sess. (1870), pp. 23–26.

[24] Rochester *Daily Union and Advertiser*, March 31, 1870; [New York] *The
World*, April 3, 1870.

[25] Pennsylvania, *Legislative Record*, 93rd Sess., pp. 842, 942.

[26] *Ibid.*, pp. 924–27, 964.

object of the Fifteenth Amendment was the enfranchisement of the Negro in the North. Republicans needed, and wanted, Negro voters in order to keep the North Republican. Northerners and southerners of both parties recognized that the practical effect of the Amendment was the substantial expansion of the northern Negro vote.[27] Politicians grasped the political advantage of the vote and calculated carefully its political repercussions.[28]

A consensus of some sort existed in the Republican press, and was less precisely expressed by Republican legislators. In general, the Amendment was considered to mean what it said. Though the primary power to determine the right and exercise of suffrage remained with the states, that power was not unlimited, since it was restricted by the express restraint contained in the prohibition of racial tests for suffrage under the first section of the Fifteenth Amendment. In other words, the color bar was outlawed, but state jurisdiction over elections and qualifications remained. It was generally acknowledged by many Republican editors and legislators that states could still set literacy and property tests for suffrage, providing these were impartial in their object and in their administration. Poll taxes and literacy tests would not, therefore, be outlawed by the Fifteenth Amendment.

This Republican consensus was spelled out in a series of excellent editorials in the New York *Times*, but the fundamental position was also endorsed by more radical newspapers. Generally, Republicans were glad that the Amendment did not ban property and literacy tests, nor enfranchise Chinese or women, nor guarantee the right of the Negro to hold office. Generally, too, they were relieved that Congress had recognized that the object of the Fifteenth Amendment could be secured only by amending the Constitution, not simply by passing a law. Republicans were also pleased that the Amendment was prohibitive in form, not affirmative, and that it did not confer suffrage by federal authority.[29] In short, a Republican consensus, more conservative in the thirty-seven states than in Congress, accepted the Fifteenth Amendment

[27] [New York] *The World*, March 18, 1869; [New York] *National Anti-Slavery Standard*, June 26, 1869.

[28] Pennsylvania, *Legislative Record*, 93rd Sess., pp. 656, 658, 661, 863, 895, 907–8, 962–65, 981, 1331.

[29] New York *Tribune*, February 27, 1869; the New York *Herald*, February 27, 1869; the New York *Times*, March 8, 16, 1869; the Chicago *Tribune*, March 1, 9, 1869; [Springfield] Illinois *Daily State Journal*, March 1, 1869.

because its powers, provisions, and objectives were fairly moderate. Ratification would be secured because the framers recognized what the political traffic would bear. A moderate Amendment was the safest, swiftest, and surest road to ratification.

When the ratification debate turned to the second section of the Amendment, a thick fog obscured a clear understanding of federal powers. A majority of Democrats, but also some prominent Republicans, magnified the nature and extent of congressional powers of enforcement by virtue of the second section of the Amendment, though most Republicans minimized jurisdiction.[30] This bipartisan anxiety was rooted in the fear that there would be no judicial remedy for the undesirable exercise of legislative power under the second section. Opponents feared that Congress would set suffrage qualifications, confer or deny the exercise of suffrage, and intervene in the conduct of state and local elections. But if there were men sincerely concerned about state rights, there also appeared to be corrupt politicians who were worried about federal inspection of fraudulent elections, and even larger numbers of Republicans and Democrats who naturally argued the question solely for partisan advantage. In much of the ratification debate the politician, as Learned Hand wrote in another connection, construed words as " empty vessels into which he can pour nearly anything he will."

[30] The New York *Herald*, September 23, 1869, March 22, 1869; Pennsylvania, *Legislative Record*, 93rd Sess., pp. 664, 785, 907, 9251; Salmon P. Chase to William M. Byrd, April 3, 1869, Letterbook, Salmon P. Chase MSS, Library of Congress; Adams, *North American Review*, CVIII, 613.

CHAPTER IV

SOUTHERN RECEPTION

To Republican sponsors of ratification the southern states presented a field to be exploited rather than a hurdle to be cleared. Governed chiefly by radical Republican régimes and saddled with Negro suffrage by the Reconstruction acts, southern legislatures could be counted on to ratify the Amendment, and the promise was borne out by performance.

The Fifteenth Amendment provoked no bitter, prolonged, and close fights in the legislatures of the deep South. The percentage of affirmative votes for ratification among southern legislators was higher than that by state legislators outside the South,[1] although ratification was required by Congress as a condition of representation in Congress for the states of Mississippi, Virginia, Texas, and Georgia. The Amendment was passed unanimously by both chambers in Mississippi and by one chamber in Virginia, Arkansas, and Alabama. In Louisiana ratification was carried out without fuss, but no conservative voted affirmatively, as was the case in most southern states. Though the Amendment was duly ratified in Florida, the extent of support was unusually low for the South and reflected a strict party division. One Texan newspaper declared that ratification took place " without scarcely rippling the gently flowing current of Reconstruction," [2] helped along by many conservative absentees. In South Carolina it was a formality, but again with most conservatives absent. There was more opposition in North Carolina, where conservatives launched a filibuster but then split on the final voting.

[1] U. S. Congress, Senate, *Ratification of the Constitution and Amendments by the States*, 71st Cong., 3rd Sess. (1931), Sen. Doc. 240, p. 8; Republican Congressional Committee, *Suffrage and Civil Rights: The Record of the Democracy on the XVth Amendment* . . . (1872), pp. 2–4. See above, Table 2, p. 84.

[2] San Antonio *Express*, February 24, 1870.

The reason for easy ratification went beyond Republican domination of most southern legislatures. By 1869 Negro suffrage was accepted by many white southerners as a fixed fact that could not and, less frequently, should not be changed. White southerners from every political faction believed that the Fifteenth Amendment did not have a practical effect in the South, where Negroes already voted.[3] They felt that the object of the Amendment was the enfranchisement of the Negro in the border states and in the North and West.[4] There were some instances, however, when both friends and enemies of the Amendment argued that ratification would guarantee Negro suffrage permanently in the South by ensuring against local prejudice and against any future attempts to repeal the Negro suffrage provision in the state constitutions or by federal control of state elections. Thus Republican Governor William W. Holden of North Carolina urged ratification primarily because a guarantee of Negro suffrage would be placed in the federal constitution, " where no future change or convulsion can destroy it." [5] But to most white southerners the Amendment appeared irrelevant.

Southern Republicans were generally glad to do their duty for the cause of Negro suffrage and promote partisan interests, though

[3] The thrust of the debate in the Arkansas legislature amounted to the observation that the Amendment would not directly affect Arkansas ([Little Rock] *Morning Republican*, March 16, 1869; [Little Rock] *Daily Arkansas Gazette*, March 16, 1869). In Alabama one radical newspaper observed that the Amendment did not primarily concern Alabama ([Montgomery] Alabama *State Journal*, March 10, 1869). A Democratic newspaper agreed and observed, " As to the voting clause, we of the South have no immediate practical concern in this matter" (Mobile *Daily Register*, 4 March 1869). In Florida a conservative minority report of the Committee on the Judiciary conceded that ratification would not affect suffrage in Florida (Florida, *Journal of the Assembly*, Ext. Sess. (June, 1869), pp. 17–19). The same opinion was also shared in Texas (San Antonio *Express*, March 3, 1869; [Galveston] *Flake's Bulletin*, April 21, 1869). South Carolina newspapers hinted or stated that the South was not vitally concerned with the Fifteenth Amendment (the Charleston *Daily News*, March 2, 1869; the Charleston *Daily Courier*, April 4, 1869; [Charleston] *The Daily Republican*, March 31, 1870). It was also dismissed as irrelevant by Georgia newspapers ([Atlanta] *The Daily New Era*, March 6, 1869; the Savannah *Daily Republican*, March 24, 1869; [Augusta] *Daily Press*, March 3, 1869).

[4] [Galveston] *Flake's Bulletin*, March 10, April 21, 1869; Galveston *News*, April 1, 1870; the Charleston *Daily Courier*, April 4, 1870; the Charleston *Daily News*, March 2, 1869.

[5] North Carolina, *Journal of the House of Representatives*, 1868–69 Sess., pp. 343–45. See also the speech of Representative Joseph Brooks, March 15, 1869, in [Little Rock] *Morning Republican*, March 16, 1869.

a few of them voted against the Amendment and some preferred to be absent when roll calls began.[6] In comparison with the voting pattern in other sections, southern Republicans appeared slightly less cohesive, but the party's overwhelming control of the legislatures combined with bipartisan support and absences to produce high percentages of legislative support for the Amendment.

While Republican support was substantial enough for every Republican legislature in the South to ratify, there was an unmistakable undercurrent of discontent. Southern Republicans had shown in Congress how disenchanted they were with the provisions of the Amendment. By the time of the fight for ratification this frigidity had melted somewhat, but it had not disappeared. Southern Republicans still considered the Amendment defective and impotent. Those politicians who appointed Negro officials and needed Negro votes remained unhappy that the Amendment did not explicitly guarantee the right of the Negro to hold office, nor did it ban poll taxes and literacy tests. The Montgomery *State Journal* concluded: " We will take the Fifteenth Amendment, not because it is just as we would have had it, but because it is good as far as it goes. . . ."[7] In rare instances southern Republicans even considered the Amendment too strong and too dangerous because of potentially greater federal powers,[8] but a majority of them accepted, where they did not applaud, ratification.

Southern Democrats and conservatives were more seriously divided. Democrats were afraid of antagonizing Negro voters. In states with a high percentage of Negroes among the population, such as Louisiana and South Carolina, most Democrats or conservatives in the state legislatures were absent on the critical vote. Texas, Mississippi, Virginia, and Georgia conservatives in the 1869 vote supported ratification as a necessary, if unpleasant, step toward readmission to Congress. In these states the Democratic parties had a very different interest in the Amendment than

---

[6] See below, Table 4, p. 96.

[7] [Montgomery] Alabama *State Journal*, March 10, 1869.

[8] *Daily Richmond Whig*, March 2, 1869. There were rare instances in which Republicans in the South opposed the Amendment because it was too strong. Senator John C. Ray of Arkansas voted against it because he felt that Congress, under the second section of the Amendment, could legislate on state suffrage qualifications. ([Little Rock] *Morning Republican*, March 16, 1869.) Racial prejudice appeared strong enough in some areas for Republicans to be less than enchanted by Negro suffrage.

did the national party. Because the conservative state parties were relatively weak, out of power, and without national patronage, local party interests supporting ratification won out over national Democratic interests opposing ratification, particularly in Texas and Mississippi and less so in Louisiana and South Carolina. But many unrepentant conservatives opposed Negro suffrage outright or had nothing to do with the Fifteenth Amendment. A majority of conservatives in states that had already regained representation in Congress opposed ratification, as in Florida, North Carolina, and Georgia in the 1870 vote.[9]

The arguments against ratification were not new. Southern conservatives rallied around the banner of state rights. The Amendment, they objected, was dangerous because the federal government would henceforth set suffrage qualifications; states would be deprived of their rights. Federal intervention and Republican power would be increased at the expense of the states.[10] Ratification was criticized because it was required of four states and secured by unpopular régimes in others.[11] Though Negro suffrage was attacked less often,[12] friends of universal suffrage were labeled cowards and traitors.[13]

A few southern conservative spokesmen actually saw advantages that would accrue to their party from the Amendment. One Alabama newspaper hinted that force and bribery would bring Negro voters into the Democratic camp.[14] A Texas paper predicted that the Amendment might become a dead letter because Congress would prove reluctant to compel obedience through the use of the army. Moreover, the Democratic border states might obstruct its enforcement.[15] Some newspapers hoped that the Negro question would fade away, while others predicted that under the

[9] See below, Table 4, p. 96.

[10] Galveston *News*, February 16, 1870; New Orleans *Commercial Bulletin*, March 6, 1869; Florida, *Journal of the Senate*, Ext. Sess. (June, 1869), pp. 29–30; Florida, *Journal of the Assembly*, Ext. Sess. (June, 1869), pp. 17–19; the Charleston *Daily Courier*, March 19, 1869; South Carolina, *Journal of the House of Representatives*, 1868 Sess., pp. 516–17; Savannah *Daily Republican*, March 24, 1869; [Macon] *Telegraph*, quoted in [Augusta] *Daily Press*, March 4, 1869.

[11] Mobile *Daily Register*, April 2, 1870; Savannah *Morning News*, February 2, 3, April 2, 1870; [Milledgeville] *Federal Union*, February 8, 1870.

[12] [Philadelphia] *The Age*, March 24, 1869.

[13] [Milledgeville] *Federal Union*, March 16, 1869; [Augusta] *Daily Press*, March 19, 1869.

[14] Mobile *Daily Register*, April 5, 1870.

[15] [Galveston] *Flake's Bulletin*, February 23, 1870.

TABLE 4: RATIFICATION OF THE FIFTEENTH AMENDMENT BY STATES OF THE FORMER CONFEDERACY

Rank by Southern State by Per Cent of Yeas	HOUSE					SENATE				
	Yes	No	Absences	Per Cent of Vote	Date	Yes	No	Absences	Per Cent of Vote	Date
Mississippi	62 Rep. / 15 Con. (77)	0	20 Rep. / 10 Con. (30)	100	Jan. 17, 1870 a	23 Rep. / 5 Con. (28)	0	3 Rep. / 2 Con. (5)	95	Jan. 15, 1870 b
[Required] Virginia	39 Rep. / 93 Con. (132)	0	3 Con. / 2 Rep. (5)	100	Oct. 8, 1869 c	12 Rep. / 28 Con. (40)	1 Rep. (1)	1 Con. (1)	95	Oct. 8, 1869 d
[Required] South Carolina	87 Rep. / 1 Con. (88)	3 Con. (3)	20 Rep. / 9 Con. (29)	96	Mar. 11, 1869 e	17 Rep. / 1 Con. (18)	1 Con. (1)	8 Rep. / 4 Con. (12)	94	Mar. 6, 1869 f
Arkansas	52 Rep. / 1 Con. (53)	0	27 Rep. (27)	100	Mar. 15, 1869 g	19 Rep. (19)	1 Con. / 2 Rep. (3)	1 Con. (1)	90	Mar. 13, 1869 h
Alabama	apparently 53 Rep.; mostly Rep. (67)	Probably all Con. (15)	13 Rep. / 5 Con. (18)	82	Nov. 15, 1869 i	all Rep. / 17 Rep. (24)	0	8 Rep. / 1 Con. (9)	100	Nov. 15, 1869 j
Texas	53 Rep. / 16 Con. (69)	10 Con. (10)	14 Con. (14)	87	Feb. 15, 1869 k	7 Rep. / 18 Rep. (24)	2 Con. / 2 Rep. (4)	4 Con. / 4 Rep. (4)	92	Feb. 18, 1870 l
[Required] Louisiana	59 Rep. (59)	9 Con. (9)	16 Rep. / 17 Rep. (33)	86	Mar. 1, 1869 m	18 Rep. (18)	1 Con. (3)	11 Con. / 4 Rep. (15)	86	Feb. 27, 1869 n
North Carolina	75 Rep. / 12 Con. (87)	20 Con. (20)	7 Rep. / 6 Con. (13)	81	Mar. 4, 1869 o	37 Rep. / 3 Con. (40)	6 Con. (6)	4 Rep. (4)	87	Mar. 4, 1869 p
Georgia [Required]	70 Rep. / 12 Con. (75)	29 Con. (29)	6 Con. / not known	72	Feb. 2, 1870 q	3 Con. / 24 Rep. (24)	10 Con. (10)	not known	70	Feb. 2, 1870 r
Florida	26 Rep. / 5 Con. (26)	13 Con. (13)	not known	66	June 11, 1869 s	13 Rep. (13)	8 Con. (8)	not known	62	June 14, 1869 t

Rep.: Republican Con.: Conservative or Democratic

a Mississippi, *Journal of the House of Representatives*, Reg. Sess. (1870), p. 26; E. McPherson, pp. 561–62; *Tribune Almanac for 1870*, p. 59.

b Mississippi, *Journal of the Senate*, Reg. Sess. (1870), p. 19; E. McPherson, pp. 558–59; *Tribune Almanac for 1870*, p. 65.

c Virginia, *Journal of the House of Delegates*, Reg. Sess. (1869), p. 42; E. McPherson, pp. 561–62; *Tribune Almanac for 1870*, p. 59.

d Virginia, *Journal of the Senate*, Reg. Sess., p. 32; E. McPherson, p. 561; *Tribune Almanac for 1870*, p. 59.

e South Carolina, *Journal of the House of Representatives*, 1868 Sess., pp. 516–17; E. McPherson, pp. 497–98.

f South Carolina, *Journal of the Senate*, 1868 Sess., p. 418; E. McPherson, p. 497; *Tribune Almanac for 1869*, p. 77.

g Arkansas, *Journal of the House of Representatives*, 17th Sess. (1869), pp. 651, 658; E. McPherson, p. 488; *Tribune Almanac for 1869*, p. 84.

h Arkansas, *Journal of the Senate*, 17th Sess. (1869), p. 563; E. McPherson, p. 488; *Tribune Almanac for 1869*, p. 84.

i Alabama, *Journal of the House of Representatives*, 1869–70 Sess., p. 31; E. McPherson, p. 557; *Tribune Almanac for 1870*, p. 59.

j Alabama, *Journal of the Senate*, 1869–70 Sess., pp. 28–29; E. McPherson, p. 557; *Tribune Almanac for 1870*, p. 59.

k Texas, *Journal of the House of Representatives*, Prov. Sess. (1870), p. 32; E. McPherson, p. 560; *Tribune Almanac for 1870*, p. 64.

l Texas, *Journal of the Senate*, Prov. Sess. (1870), p. 30; E. McPherson, p. 560; *Tribune for 1870*, p. 64.

m Louisiana, *Journal of the House of Representatives*, 1869 Sess., p. 248; *Debates of the House of Representatives*, 1869 Sess., p. 430; E. McPherson, p. 492; *Tribune Almanac for 1869*, p. 80.

n Louisiana, *Journal of the Senate*, 1869 Sess., p. 192; E. McPherson, p. 492; *Tribune Almanac for 1869*, p. 80.

o North Carolina, *Journal of the House of Representatives*, 1868–69 Sess., pp. 346–47; E. McPherson, p. 496; *Tribune Almanac for 1869*, p. 76.

p North Carolina, *Journal of the Senate*, 1868–69 Sess., pp. 401–2; E. McPherson, p. 496; *Tribune Almanac for 1869*, p. 76.

q Georgia, *Journal of the House of Representatives*, Ann. Sess. (January, 1870), pp. 76–77; E. McPherson, p. 447.

r Georgia, *Journal of the Senate*, Ann. Sess. (January, 1870), I, 74; E. McPherson, p. 557.

s Florida, *Journal of the Assembly*, Ext. Sess. (June, 1869), pp. 33–34; E. McPherson, p. 489.

t Florida, *Journal of the Senate*, Ext. Sess. (June, 1869), pp. 33–34; E. McPherson, p. 489.

Amendment's provision states could still exclude Negroes from office and deny any person the vote because of property, tax, education, language, nativity, and religion. The *Daily Richmond Whig* concluded that there were " loopholes through which a coach and four horses can be driven." [16]

Four southern states were required to ratify the Fifteenth Amendment. Only a month after it was submitted to the states, the Forty-first Congress passed acts that set the conditions under which these states would be readmitted to the Union and their representatives seated in Congress. The first act concerned Virginia, Mississippi, and Texas. Timing was important. Indiana Democrats had bolted the legislature, and friends of the Amendment were worried about the chances of its adoption, because rejection by Indiana and Ohio might defeat the ratification. At this juncture Senator Morton introduced, on April 9, 1869, an amendment to the Reconstruction bill for Virginia, Mississippi, and Texas, which would require these states to ratify as a condition for readmission.[17] His proposal created a storm of protest.

Senator Lyman Trumbull (Republican, Illinois) objected to the proposal because the terms of readmission had been laid down in the Reconstruction acts of 1867 and 1868. To impose a new condition now would be a breach of faith with southerners. When would this sort of thing stop? Would each future Congress set a new condition? Trumbull supported the Fifteenth Amendment, but he questioned the need to require ratification when these states would ratify in any event.[18] Republican Roscoe Conkling of New York agreed with Trumbull. Democrat Allen G. Thurman of Ohio, who opposed the Fifteenth Amendment, also opposed Morton's proposal, declaring that Congress could propose an amendment to the Constitution but could not coerce a state into ratifying it. Thurman stressed that Morton's amendment was designed to force Negro suffrage on the North by coercing Virginia, Mississippi, and Texas into ratification.[19]

Morton bluntly answered the charges. Because the three states had not yet complied with the original conditions required, he dismissed the charge of a broken promise. He felt that it was

[16] *Daily Richmond Whig*, March 2, 1869.
[17] *Globe*, 41st Cong., 1st Sess. (1869), p. 653.
[18] *Ibid.*, pp. 653–54.
[19] *Ibid.*, pp. 654–55.

the right of Congress " to propose as many conditions as we see fit " as long as they were " proper and just in themselves." [20] But Morton quickly abandoned the shaky ground of principle for the hard rock of expediency. He emphasized that southerners could not object to ratification of the Fifteenth Amendment because Negro suffrage was already required in their state constitutions. More important, he said, Democrats, by making sure that Virginia, Texas, and Mississippi would not ratify the Amendment, were trying to keep the Negro issue alive in order to hurt Republicans in the elections of 1870 and 1872. The only way to defeat such a plan was to make sure that the three southern states ratified the Amendment and thus undercut the Democratic bolt in the Indiana legislature. The Negro issue would be ended and Negro suffrage guaranteed. Morton concluded that the Amendment was of " vast importance" to both the Republican party and the country, and was " right, proper, and necessary." [21] Every friend of the Amendment ought to support his proposal.

Morton's powerful speech made sense to practical politicians. The Senate accepted his proposal, circumvented the wishes of President Grant, who had not requested the condition of required ratification by the three states, and in effect overruled the Judiciary Committee, which had previously rejected Morton's plan. Actually, the Senate vote on April 9, 1869, badly split Republican ranks, with thirty Senators voting " yes," twenty " no," [22] and Morton's proposal was accepted by the House of Representatives on the same day.[23]

Northern reaction to Morton's requirement divided along party lines. Democratic organs were unfriendly. The Washington *National Intelligencer* denounced Morton's scheme as forcing the " odious" Fifteenth Amendment on an unwilling North; the proposition amounted to a " call upon the South to prescribe the people of the North." [24] A reporter for the New York *World* observed that " without this enforced ratification its defeat is likely." [25] The same reporter asserted that northern Republican

[20] *Ibid.*
[21] *Ibid.*
[22] *Ibid.*, p. 656. There were 16 absent.
[23] *Ibid.*, p. 700. The vote on April 9, 1869, was 107 "yes," 30 "no," and 55 not voting.
[24] [Washington] *Daily National Intelligencer*, April 10, 1869.
[25] [New York] *The World*, April 10, 1869.

politicians favored Morton's proposal because it would circumvent rejection of the Amendment by Ohio and Indiana, while southern Republicans supported it because they hoped it would defeat ratification of the Amendment by Mississippi, Virginia, and Texas. Readmission to Congress would then be delayed and these politicians would be assured of continued power and prolonged plunder. The Washington *National Republican* regarded the Morton plan as " wise and proper," [26] for there would be more trouble in the North over ratification than in the South. While accepting it, the New York *Tribune* regarded the proposal as unnecessary, because the Amendment would be ratified without the unreconstructed states.[27] The New York *Herald* considered approval of Morton's plan a personal victory for Morton, because the Senate Judiciary Committee had turned down the idea before and some influential minds had objected to the proposal.[28]

The New York *Times* predicted that Mississippi, Virginia, and Texas would ratify the Fifteenth Amendment, because southerners in general should consider ratification a good opportunity to punish the North for imposing Negro suffrage in the first place. But the *Times* was disturbed about coercing these three states into voting for the Amendment since " without such freedom of action all pretense of a vote is sheer mockery." [29] The object of Morton's proposal was to gain universal Southern assent in order to overcome probable opposition to ratification by unreliable Ohio, Indiana, New York, and Democratic states. Though this reckless device might secure the adoption of the Amendment, the newspaper predicted, it would undermine it and ultimately hurt the Republican party.

Southerners grasped the object of Morton's plan. Observing that most southern papers regarded the requirement of ratification as an additional burden upon the South, *Flake's Bulletin* of Galveston disagreed, finding that ratification of the Fifteenth Amendment could not make any difference, because Negro suffrage was an established fact and the South could not dismiss it. But Negro suffrage " is not an established fact at the North. It is not an established fact in Indiana, nor can it be, save through the agency

[26] [Washington] *The National Republican*, April 10, 15, 1869.
[27] New York *Tribune*, April 10, 1869.
[28] The New York *Herald*, April 10, 1869.
[29] The New York *Times*, April 12, 1869.

of the Southern States. It is for the purpose of coercing the North and fastening negro suffrage upon them, that this proviso was inserted." [30] A Virginia newspaper agreed: " It is the old game of the monkey using the cat to draw the chestnut from the fire. These Amendmenters need us sadly in order to get the fifteenth from its unsafe incubation and settle the matter." [31]

Mississippi, Virginia, and Texas complied with the congressional requirement. Only in Georgia was there a real controversy before ratification. Georgia Republicans were disenchanted because the Amendment lacked an officeholding provision. More important, they wanted to overthrow conservative control of the state legislature. Republicans reasoned that if the Fifteenth Amendment were rejected by the legislature, then Congress would become so infuriated as to restore the provisional government, oust some conservatives from the legislature, and restore radical Republican control. Under the leadership of Governor Rufus B. Bullock, Republicans tried to sabotage ratification. First Bullock tried to goad extreme conservatives into opposition to the Amendment by declaring that the Fifteenth Amendment guaranteed Negro officeholding, as it clearly did not. Conservatives were antagonized by Bullock's assertion, because they had dismissed all Negro members from the legislature.[32] Then by the adroit use of patronage for the state roads, Bullock persuaded many Republicans to absent themselves from voting on the ratification or to oppose it. Despite this attempt at sabotage, the House of Representatives ratified the Amendment on March 16, 1869. Ultimately, ratification was defeated only by the Republican presiding officer of the Senate, a good friend of Bullock's, who broke a tie vote on March 17 and cast his vote for postponement and virtual rejection. Thirteen of the seventeen votes for postponement were cast by extremist Republicans. Later the Senate rejected the Amendment on March 18.[33] Governor Bullock subsequently admitted that

[30] [Galveston] *Flake's Bulletin*, April 21, 1869.

[31] [Salem] *Roanoke Times*, April 17, 1869.

[32] Message of Governor Rufus B. Bullock, March 9, 1869, in Georgia, *Journal of the Senate*, Ann. Sess. (1869), pp. 653–57.

[33] *Ibid.*, pp. 794–806; Georgia, *Journal of the House of Representatives*, Ann. Sess. (1869), pp. 665–66. The maneuvers by Bullock, and Republican sabotage, were clearly understood by Georgians; see [Augusta] *Daily Press*, March 12–19, 29, 1869; [Atlanta] *The Daily New Era*, March 11, 19, 23, 26, 1869; I. W. Avery, *The History of the State of Georgia* (New York: Brown & Derby, 1881), pp. 410–43.

Republicans had killed the Amendment in the Republican-controlled Senate, while conservatives had accepted it in the conservative-dominated House.[34] Radical Republicans, who wanted to regain power and were unhappy that the Amendment failed to provide for Negro officeholding and wanted to ban literacy tests, had joined forces with extreme conservatives, who wanted no federal amendment concerning Negro suffrage.

In December, 1869, Congress set new conditions for the readmission of Georgia. At the time, the chances of national ratification appeared bleak, and Georgia's vote might have decided the fate of the Fifteenth Amendment. Again, Senator Morton came to the rescue. He offered, on December 16, 1869, a motion requiring Georgia to ratify the Fifteenth Amendment as a condition for readmission to the Union.[35]

Objections, similar to those made to Morton's previous proposal, were raised, notably by Senator Matthew H. Carpenter of Wisconsin, who favored the Fifteenth Amendment but not the required ratification.[36] Most Republican senators agreed that Georgia should not be readmitted to Congress until she had ratified the Amendment, but there was sincere disagreement among Republicans as to whether ratification by Georgia should be required in law or in fact.

In a powerful reply Morton contended that the fate of the Amendment was at stake. He argued that unless his motion was adopted, Georgia would in effect be told that she would not have to ratify when in fact she would.[37] If Congress required ratification by Georgia, then Democratic opposition in the Ohio legislature would collapse; Rhode Island would ratify; New York would not rescind its ratification; and Democrats everywhere would accept Negro suffrage and recruit Negro voters. Morton concluded that " when the ratification hangs on the vote of one single State, when we have come within just one State of securing this amendment, and to secure that we have got to do just what we have done before, now to halt, now to fall back would be regarded by the world as cowardice, would be regarded as a confession,

[34] *Globe*, 41st Cong., 2nd Sess., pp. 284–85.
[35] *Ibid.*, p. 165.
[36] *Ibid.*
[37] *Ibid.*, pp. 166, 209.

would be an abandonment of this amendment." [38] Congress agreed and adopted his requirement.[39]

Under the act passed by Congress, Governor Bullock called a session of the legislature and authorized all members elected in 1868, including Negro members who had been expelled, to attend the session. Some conservative legislators were declared ineligible under the jurisdiction of a military board, since they did not meet the requirements of the test oath, and they were ejected. Bullock Republicans were accepted as members of the legislature, and strong Republican majorities were achieved. Then, on February 2, 1870, the Georgia legislature ratified. The percentage of support, however, was unusually low for a southern state. Although Bullock's Republicans had caused initial defeat of ratification, they used that defeat as an excuse to oust conservatives from the legislature. Conservatives then opposed ratification in 1870.

The ratification by Georgia on February 2, 1870, marked success for the Fifteenth Amendment. It became law; the rough road of ratification had been traversed. This could not have been accomplished without the assent of the South for without Virginia and possibly Mississippi and Georgia, it would not have received the required number of twenty-eight assents. In other words, without the resourceful and persistent leadership of Senator Oliver P. Morton, there would have been no Fifteenth Amendment.

In summary, the Fifteenth Amendment caused few sharp controveries in the South. There, the issue of Negro suffrage appeared settled in 1869, for to most southern conservatives Negro suffrage was a necessary evil and to southern Republicans an indispensable need. Many newspapers and legislators observed that the North, not the South, was the primary object of the Amendment. Notable

[38] *Ibid.*, p. 209.

[39] *Ibid.*, pp. 224, 293. The vote in the Senate on December 17, 1869, was 38 "yes," 15 "no," and 12 absent. That in the House of Representatives on December 21, 1869, was 121 "yes," 51 "no," and 39 not voting. The vote in the Senate was more partisan than that on Morton's proposal for Mississippi, Virginia, and Texas. Many conservative Republican opponents of the earlier Morton proposal in April were absent for the December vote. Probably the need of Georgia's ratification, the precedence of required ratification, and the disgust with Georgia's expulsion of Negro legislators influenced voting and caused less opposition. The intent of Morton's proposal was grasped by the press; see [Washington] *Daily National Intelligencer*, December 15, 17, 1869. Significantly, the *Times*, which earlier in April had opposed required ratification for Mississippi, Texas, and Virginia, endorsed required ratification for Georga (the New York *Times*, November 20, 1869).

too was the division among Democrats and the latent discontent of Republicans with regard to it. Democrats were split over bidding for Negro votes. Republicans were angry because the Amendment was not sufficiently comprehensive and was designed primarily to help Republicans in the North, not aid Republicans in the South. The very moderation of the Fifteenth Amendment appealed to some Democrats and annoyed some Republicans. Negro officeholding was not guaranteed; suffrage qualifications remained with the states to set and administer; suffrage was qualified and impartial, not universal and absolute. But southern Republicans had no real alternative. They recognized that the pending Amendment, however imperfect, was a step in the right direction.

CHAPTER V

BORDER STATE OPPOSITION

The border states were generally Democratic, extremely conservative, and violently opposed to Negro suffrage. Border state
Democrats had reason to oppose it, because Negro voting might
change the balance of power in some states.[1] Republicans wanted

TABLE 5: THE BORDER STATES AND THE POTENTIAL NEGRO VOTE

State	Negroes Per Cent in Population [a]	Number of Negroes [b]	Potential Negro Vote [c]	Democratic Presidential Majority 1868 [d]	Seats in the House of Representatives, 1872 [e]
Maryland	22.5	175,391	35,078	31,919	6
Delaware	18.2	22,794	4,559	3,257	1
Kentucky	16.8	222,210	44,442	76,313	10
Missouri	6.9	118,071	23,614	25,883 Rep.	13
West Virginia	4.1	17,980	3,596	8,719 Rep.	3

[a] U. S. Bureau of the Census, *Negro Population, 1790–1915*.
[b] U. S. Bureau of the Census, *Ninth Census*, I, 5.
[c] The potential Negro vote is estimated at one-fifth of the Negro population.
During the ratification fight newspapers used the figure of one-fifth or one-sixth.
In some elections analyzed after Negroes began voting the figure of one-fifth seems
most accurate. ([Cumberland, Md.] *Civilian and Telegraph*, February 10, 1870;
Galveston *News*, April 1, 1870; the Patterson *Daily Press*, March 31, 1870.)
[d] *Tribune Almanac for 1869*, pp. 67, 68, 83, 85.
[e] *Tribune Almanac for 1872*, p. 56.

Negro voting, but in some states the lure of political success was
so tempered by fears of the political risk in being champions of
Negro suffrage that Republican efforts were paralyzed. The
expected pattern of rejection was realized.

[1] A potential 35,000 Negro voters in Maryland might have overcome a Democratic
presidential majority of 32,000 in 1868. In Delaware 4,500 potential recruits for
the Republicans might have offset a 3,000 Democratic presidential majority. Negro
voters might have kept West Virginia and Missouri Republican; in Kentucky and
Tennessee, they might have kept the Republican party alive.

105

In West Virginia and Missouri, where whites who had favored the Confederacy were prescribed, Republicans had retained power. Some of them hoped that Negro voting would help to preserve Republican control of their states and secure domination of the other border states. But fear of endorsing ratification was so great and prejudice against Negro voting so real, even among white Republicans, that the Republican choice was an agonizing one. No better example of such a dilemma could be found than in West Virginia.

It was vital that ratification be settled by the pending session of the West Virginia legislature, for otherwise it would be postponed to the session of January, 1870. Republicans worried that the issue would plague their campaign and cause much mischief, observed the Wheeling *Daily Intelligencer*.[2] During congressional passage of the Amendment one West Virginia Senator had written United States Senator Waitman T. Willey that potential trouble must be prevented, " for another legislature elected upon this issue will probably repudiate and reject it." [3] He hoped that an amendment could be passed by Congress in time for the present legislature to act upon it. Clearly, Republican legislators up for re-election did not want the issue still alive, but apparently hoped that immediate action would eliminate it, since people might forget ratification when election time rolled around. In short, ratification was a great gamble.

Some Republicans were not willing to take the risk, joining Democrats on March 2, 1869, in the House of Delegates to shelve ratification. The vote, however, was close: twenty to twenty-one.[4] The House then adjourned for lunch. It must have been a frantic lunch hour for supporters of the Amendment, because the House in the afternoon reversed itself by a large margin. Consideration was secured, because four delegates—two Republicans and two Democrats—voted to reconsider the morning's decision.[5] Apparently, since all four opposed the Amendment, they felt that ratification would be defeated and hoped to embarrass the supporters

[2] The Wheeling *Daily Intelligencer*, March 4, 1869.
[3] Joseph T. Hoke to Waitman T. Willey, February 19, 1869, Waitman T. Willey MSS, West Virginia University. Hoke was Republican President of the West Virginia Senate. See also W. O. Wright to Charles Sumner, February 7, 1869, Sumner MSS. Wright was a member of the House of Delegates.
[4] West Virginia, *Journal of the House of Delegates*, 7th Sess. (1869), p. 210.
[5] *Ibid.*, p. 217. The vote to consider the Amendment was 27 " yes " to 17 " no."

of the Amendment by a roll-call vote. Contrary to their expectations, the Amendment then passed the House by a close vote of twenty-two " yes " to nineteen " no." All ten Democrats present voted against the Amendment, and nine out of thirty-one Republicans present also opposed it.[6] Passage was secured by a solid core of supporters, the absence of four opponents of the Amendment, the switch of one Republican legislator from opposition to assent, and the appearance of an additional Republican supporter. Great party pressure was apparently applied to wavering Republican legislators. The vote also indicated a traditional pattern of West Virginia politics. With the exception of one county, no delegate from areas formerly pro-Confederate voted to ratify. Thus delegates from southern, eastern, and interior sections of the state, along with those from the eastern Panhandle, opposed ratification or were absent. Those from Unionist counties of the western section along the Ohio River, northern West Virginia, and the northern Panhandle generally supported the Amendment, though there were some bitter opponents. Disagreement among the Unionists was not surprising, for during the war many West Virginians stood by the Union but remained strongly anti-Negro, and some had opposed emancipation while other Unionists endorsed it.[7]

In the Senate enough Republicans agreed to pass the Amendment. The vote on adoption was 10 " yes " to six " no," with a critical absence of six Republicans. The opposition consisted of three Republicans and all three Democrats.[8] After the voting was completed the three Republicans who had opposed ratification announced that they would co-operate with their Republican colleagues and defend ratification. These Senators either opposed the Amendment sincerely or wanted to avoid defeat in a future election. But it would appear that they wanted to share the benefits of the Negro vote or had, under party pressure, publicly repented their opposition to ratification. In any case, the incident illustrated how sensitive were the nerves of Republican politicians in the border states.

[6] *Ibid.*, p. 218; E. McPherson, p. 498. On the final vote 31 Republicans voted, with 10 Republicans and 5 Democrats absent.

[7] Charles H. Ambler, *A History of West Virginia* (New York: Prentice-Hall, 1933), p. 367.

[8] West Virginia, *Journal of the Senate*, 7th Sess. (1869), p. 175; E. McPherson, p. 498.

The qualified and reluctant support given the Amendment by West Virginia Republicans indicated how unpopular Negro suffrage was. Yet some Republicans felt that Negro voting would prevent Republican state defeat.[9] Though many practical West Virginia Republicans were probably aware that the Fifteenth Amendment would weaken their state party, they perhaps supported it under pressure from Washington, realizing that only through ratification could national party victories be attained and federal patronage awarded. The clear conflict of interest between the state and the national organization appeared important. If Republican majorities were only four to eight thousand, clearly enfranchising two to three thousand Negro voters could not possibly offset fifteen to twenty-five thousand disfranchised Confederate Democratic votes.[10] Subsequent events indicated a disastrous reaction to Republican championing of Negro voting, for the fall election of 1869 went badly, as Democrats in eastern and western counties became aggressive, while Republicans in northern and western counties grew more conservative. In 1870, Democrats recaptured the state legislature and governorship to seal the fate of the Republicans.[11]

Perhaps the same sort of pressures were felt by Missouri Republicans, who also held unsure power and secured ratification. In fact, Missouri Republicans were in such a hurry to ram through ratification on March 1, 1869, that, by omitting the second section of the Amendment, they ratified the wrong version. The Jefferson City *Times* was not amused by this performance which made Missouri Republicans the laughing stock of the country. The newspaper observed, "We lose all patience when we reflect that we have to fight such desperate political battles, to have the advantages of victory frittered away by the incapacity of our men. How long, Oh Lord!"[12] The damage was finally repaired on January 7, 1870, but the Negro vote was not enough to keep regular Republicans from being defeated by liberal Republicans.

[9] The Wheeling *Daily Intelligencer*, March 1, 1869.

[10] *Ibid.; Tribune Almanac for 1869*, p. 68; Charles H. Ambler, "Disfranchisement in West Virginia," *Yale Review*, XIV (May, 1905), 54–55.

[11] Ambler, *History*, p. 367. Senator Willey attributed defeat to hostility to Negro suffrage. Diary, October 26, 1870, Willey MSS, reproduced in a letter from David Rothman.

[12] [Jefferson City] *Times*, quoted in [Trenton, N. J.] *Daily State Gazette*, March 30, 1869.

The latter were in turn ejected by Democrats, who regained complete control by 1872.[13]

The much weaker Republicans in Tennessee and Kentucky appeared similarly divided over Negro suffrage and could not prevent rejection; at best the Negro vote would guarantee only the maintenance of a minority party. In Delaware and Maryland, Republicans were weak but had a chance to make a comeback, if not to prevent rejection of the Amendment. Republicans there honestly felt that the Amendment would do them much good. Both state parties had advocated a federal suffrage amendment during the presidential campaign of 1868.[14] And after the Amendment came into force, the Republicans went on the offensive and tried to win the loyalty of the Negro voter.[15] But the turnout of Negroes was poor, partially because they were intimidated or bribed by Democrats. What was worse, white Republicans became alienated because of Negro voting and either stayed away from the polls or voted with the Democrats.[16] Thus the Fifteenth Amendment proved to be the grand illusion of border state Republicans.

Unlike southern Democrats, who had to live with Negro voters, border state Democrats could fight the Fifteenth Amendment in order to prevent Negroes from becoming voters. They were therefore highly cohesive in their voting against ratification. Unlike middle Atlantic Democrats, they openly questioned the desirability of Negro suffrage, and the Negro inferiority issue was proclaimed. The Amendment, declared Delaware Democrats, would establish an unnatural equality between the races.[17] Negroes were inferior and could not be allowed to vote, argued the Governor of Mary-

[13] Missouri, *Journal of the House of Representatives*, 25th Sess. (1869), pp. 605–6; 25th Adj. Sess. (1870), p. 57; *Journal of the Senate*, 25th Sess. (1869), p. 434; 25th Adj. Sess. (1870), p. 35. Republicans were not bashful when they told Negroes how Republicans had supported ratification and thus deserved Negro support ([St. Louis] *The Missouri Democrat*, April 1, 1870).

[14] Wilmington *Daily Commercial*, March 1, 31, 1869.

[15] Wilmington *Daily Commercial*, March 31, April 1, 1870; [Cumberland] *Civilian and Telegraph*, April 7, 1870; [Baltimore] *American and Commercial Advertiser*, April 1, 1870.

[16] [Cumberland] *Civilian and Telegraph*, November 10, 17, 1870; *Tribune Almanac for 1871*, p. 63; [Baltimore] *American and Commercial Advertiser*, November 10, 1870; [Baltimore] *Sun*, November 10, 1870; John A. Munroe, " The Negro in Delaware," *The South Atlantic Quarterly*, LVI (Autumn, 1957), 437.

[17] Delaware, *Journal of the House of Representatives*, 1869 Sess., p. 556.

land.[18] The issue of state rights was also rehearsed.[19] Though such arguments were believed, underlying them all was perhaps the fear of losing power.

Worrying about future Negro voting, Democrats rejected the Fifteenth Amendment in the border state legislatures they controlled. First Kentucky, even with some Republican support, rejected ratification during March, 1869, followed by Delaware. In contrast, Tennessee conservatives marked time until late February, 1870, after actual ratification by the required number of states had been secured. Rejection then occurred the day following the adoption of a new state constitution guaranteeing Negro suffrage. Apparently Tennessee conservatives were willing to fight enforcement of the Amendment (by poll tax) and show their disapproval of federally imposed Negro suffrage (by rejection of ratification), but they shied away from repudiating outright Negro suffrage and bringing down the wrath of Congress upon their state. Thus Tennessee did not appear as self-confidently conservative as Kentucky or Delaware Democrats. Maryland, with agonizing indecision, followed Tennessee by one day, on February 25, five days before the Amendment was proclaimed. It is not clear why Maryland delayed in acting and then rejected when there was no good cause to be served by it, but some Democrats did avoid the vote.[20]

Once Negro suffrage came or was about to come, however, even border state Democrats reacted as good politicians. Kentucky Democrats tried mainly to recruit more white voters and keep Negroes out of their party and away from the polls. Tennessee, and particularly Delaware, Democrats resorted to wholesale fraud.[21] Those from West Virginia, somewhat perplexed, asked advice of Willard Saulsbury, the United States Senator from Dela-

[18] Maryland, *Journal of the Senate*, 1870 Sess., Doc. A, pp. 61–70.
[19] *Ibid*.; Kentucky, *Journal of the House of Representatives*, Adj. Sess. (1869), pp. 746–48.
[20] Kentucky, *Journal of the House of Representatives*, Adj. Sess. (1869), pp. 746–48; *Journal of the Senate*, Adj. Sess. (1869), p. 628. Delaware, *Journal of the Senate*, 1869 Sess., p. 410; *Journal of the House of Representatives*, 1869 Sess., p. 557. Tennessee, *Journal of the House of Representatives*, 36th Gen. Assembly, 1st Sess. (1869–70), I, 193; *Journal of the Senate*, 36th Gen. Assembly, 1st Sess. (1869–70), p. 443. Maryland, *Journal of the House of Delegates*, 1870 Sess., pp. 268–69; *Journal of the Senate*, 1870 Sess., pp. 291, 309, 316; E. McPherson, pp. 491–92. [Baltimore] *American and Commercial Advertiser*, January 5, February 5, 1870.
[21] Munroe, *South Atlantic Quarterly*, LVI.

ware, who suggested that the politicians not try to recruit Negro votes, because time was "too short to pull the wool over their eyes." [22] Instead it would be better to howl "nigger" and to brag about the white man's Democratic party.

No better illustration of the dilemma of border state Democrats can be found than in Maryland. During February and March, 1870, a fierce controversy raged within the Maryland Democratic party over what to do about the Negro vote. One camp of Democratic diehards wanted nothing to do with the Negro voter. The Frederick *Union* preached: "Let those who will, chameleon-like, change their colors for the sake of patronage, office, and power, *we* cannot and will not. We cannot give the lie to all that we have hitherto said and written on this subject, by courting the negro vote. . . ." [23] Another conservative newspaper concluded that the Fifteenth Amendment must be opposed because it was "conceived in iniquity, born in villainy and carried out in fraud." [24] The diehard camp felt that the Amendment should be tested in the courts or ignored by Democratic voting registrars. [25]

Many Democratic newspapers, however, endorsed the opposite course of action. Negro voters should be accepted as an unpleasant fact; [26] Democrats should solicit Negro votes by favor, whiskey, and, if necessary, intimidation. [27] Democrats were urged to beat Republicans by playing their own game of bidding for the Negro vote. If Democrats did nothing, they would commit political suicide; divide the Negro vote and rule Maryland was the answer.

The explosive issue was resolved at an emergency meeting of the Democratic-Conservative State Central Committee, which convened at Annapolis while the legislature was still in session. In a dramatic about-face the committee extended political recognition to Maryland Negroes. The legislature followed orders and

[22] Letter of Willard Saulsbury published in [Kingwood] *Preston County Journal*, May 14, 1870.
[23] Frederick *Union,* quoted in [Baltimore] *American and Commercial Advertiser,* March 29, 1870.
[24] Rockville *Sentinel,* quoted in *ibid.,* February 26, 1870.
[25] *Ibid.*; the Baltimore *Gazette,* March 29, 30, 1870.
[26] [Baltimore] *Sun,* February 4, March 31, 1870; [Westminster] *Democratic Advocate* and [Hagerstown] *Mail,* quoted in [Baltimore] *American and Commercial Advertiser,* February 26, 1870; [Cecil] *Democrat* and [Annapolis] *Republican,* quoted in *ibid.,* March 29, 1870.
[27] [Centreville] *Observer* and [Easton] *Star,* quoted in [Baltimore] *American and Commercial Advertiser,* March 29, 1870.

enacted a new registration law that allowed the Negro to vote. Maryland Democrats did not want the federal government to force Negro suffrage on their state, and there was no reason to antagonize further the Negro vote there. But in practice Maryland Democrats acted like most border state Democrats, and by various schemes the Negro vote was successfully neutralized. In the border states, where public opinion tolerated governmental and personal fraud, the Fifteenth Amendment became a dead letter.

CHAPTER VI

MIDDLE ATLANTIC COMPROMISE

Ratification was difficult in the middle Atlantic states. In Connecticut, New York, New Jersey, Pennsylvania, as well as in the older middle western states of Ohio and Indiana, the controversy was greatest, the party division closest,[1] and the stakes highest.

Politicians of both parties recognized the practical effect of the enfranchisement of the Negro in the North. In New Jersey 4,200 potential Negro voters might well overturn an 1868 Democratic presidential majority of 2,800.[2] Democratic legislators charged that Republicans were interested not in the welfare of the Negro but in that of the Republican party. Democratic Speaker of the New Jersey House of Representatives, Leon Abbott, contended that Republicans in their Reconstruction acts had changed the whole political complexion of states in the South and " now propose to do it in the North by this amendment." [3]

In Pennsylvania, legislators grasped the fundamental importance of 10,000 to 15,000 potential Negro voters.[4] Democrats argued

[1] In Pennsylvania, Republican state candidates usually received between 49.6 per cent and 52.6 per cent of the vote. In New York as well as in Connecticut, Democrats and Republicans played musical chairs for the governorships. In presidential contests in New York the winner always received less than 55 per cent of the total vote.

[2] In 1870 there were 30,658 Negroes in New Jersey. One-fifth of them (4,226) would probably be eligible for suffrage. The Democratic presidential majority in New Jersey in 1868 was a mere 2,880. (Bureau of the Census, *Ninth Census*, I, 5; *Tribune Almanac for 1869*, p. 65.)

[3] [Trenton] *Daily State Gazette*, February 2, 1870.

[4] Pennsylvania, *The Legislative Record*, 93rd Sess., pp. 656, 661, 895, 981. Generally, the figure referred to in debate and in the press was a potential Negro vote of 15,000. One-fifth of the Negro population of 65,294 would be 13,059. Another press estimate in 1870 was 9,475. Republican majorities could be affected by the Negro vote as follows: election of 1868 for Auditor General, Republican majority of 9,677; election of 1869 for Governor, 4,596. Although Grant received in 1868 a majority of 28,898, the vote was shaky, considering the total vote cast.

113

that the Republican ticket had carried the state by only 9,000 votes in 1868 and therefore needed more votes to stay in power,[5] concluding that the " proposition is born of the necessities of the Republican party," [6] to exploit the potential Negro vote in the North. Recognition of the partisan character of the Fifteenth Amendment generated a partisan response.[7]

The intent and effect of the Amendment were grasped by newspapers with different political outlooks. The *National Anti-Slavery Standard*, the abolitionist organ, predicted that " with the hundreds of thousands of colored citizens enfranchised in the Border and Northern States the balance of power is in favor of Radicalism and against Northern Negro-hating copperheads and rebel allies." [8] The Democratic New York *World*, which agreed with the *Standard* about the practical effect of ratification, believed that " in a very close contest, the Negro vote should be sufficient to turn the scale in several of the Northern States." [9] It thought that the Negro vote might help win the October elections in Pennsylvania and might decide the presidential contest of 1872. Grant, declared the *World*, cared nothing about the political rights of Negroes, but he did care everything about their votes. The paper concluded with an exhortation to bury the Amendment, because " there is nothing which the Democratic party can do which will conduce more to its success in 1872 than the defeat of this Fifteenth Amendment." [10]

Later in 1870 the *World* elaborated its position in two brilliant editorials. The paper felt that the Fifteenth Amendment was a party measure: " Its sole purpose was to strengthen the Republican party in the Northern States." [11] Republican leaders saw that the Negro vote was becoming increasingly undependable in the South.

The Negro vote would help keep Philadelphia Republican. (Bureau of the Census, *Ninth Census*, I, 5, 58–59; the Patterson *Daily Press*, March 31, 1870; *Tribune Almanac for 1869*, p. 66; *Tribune Almanac for 1870*, p. 57; Burnham, *Presidential Ballots*, pp. 101, 249. The importance of the Negro vote has been stressed by John W. Huston, in " The Ratification of the 13th, 14th, and 15th Amendments to the United States Constitution by the State of Pennsylvania " (M. A. dissertation, Dept. of History, University of Pittsburgh, 1950), pp. 101, 121.

[5] Pennsylvania, *The Legislative Record*, 93rd Sess., p. 669.

[6] *Ibid.*, p. 674.

[7] *Ibid.*, p. 668.

[8] [New York] *National Anti-Slavery Standard*, March 6, 1869.

[9] [New York] *The World*, March 18, 1869.

[10] *Ibid.*

[11] *Ibid.*, April 1, 1870.

Once the army was withdrawn, the Freedmen's Bureau shut down, and political activity of southern whites resumed, Negroes would start voting Democratic, because the "natural ascendancy of intelligence over ignorance, and of property over poverty, would prevail." [12] With freedom of action for the whites, the South would become solidly Democratic. Republicans, therefore, must turn to the North to strengthen the party there. Thus the "whole effect of this Fifteenth Amendment is merely to confer the ballot upon the Negroes scattered through the Northern States. . . ." [13] Republican leaders "calculated that the Negro vote in the doubtful Northern states would be sufficient to maintain the Republican ascendancy in those states and, through them, in the politics of the country. It was with this in view that they judged the Fifteenth Amendment essential to the success of their party." [14] The Amendment, therefore, was pure party expediency; [15] it was a "trick of desperate political gamesters. . . ." [16]

Because of the importance of the Negro vote, the Democrats strongly opposed the Amendment. With cohesive support, New Jersey Democratic legislators rejected it in January, 1870. [17] New York Democrats vigorously but unsuccessfully fought ratification in March and April, 1869, and tried to rescind it during January, 1870. [18] Those in Pennsylvania fought hard against ratification

[12] *Ibid.*

[13] *Ibid.*, March 31, 1870.

[14] *Ibid.*, April 1, 1870.

[15] *Ibid.*, January 7, 1870.

[16] *Ibid.*, April 1, 1870.

[17] In a vote along party lines the New Jersey Assembly rejected the Amendment on February 1, 1870 (New Jersey, *Minutes of the General Assembly*, 94th Sess., 1870, pp. 185–86; E. McPherson, pp. 559–60). The New Jersey Senate rather tardily rejected the Amendment on February 7, 1870, also by strict party vote (New Jersey, *Journal of the Senate*, 94th Sess., 1870, p. 323).

[18] In 1869 the legislature under Republican control ratified the Amendment along straight party lines. On March 17, 1869, the Assembly ratified, and on April 14, 1869, the Senate ratified. (New York, *Journal of the Assembly*, 92nd Sess., I, 544–45; E. McPherson, pp. 495–96; New York, *Journal of the Senate*, 92nd Sess., 1869, p. 590.) The election of 1869 brought Democrats into control of the legislature. On January 5, 1870, Democrats voted to rescind ratification in the new legislature by a party vote, with the exception of Jay A. Pease, upstate Democratic assemblyman, whose closely divided Republican county of Lewis had approved Negro suffrage in the state referendum. (New York, *Journal of the Senate*, 93rd Sess., 1870, p. 30; E. McPherson, p. 562; New York *Journal of the Assembly*, 93rd Sess., 1870, I, 44; *Tribune Almanac for 1870*, p. 53.) For an account of the New York rejection, see Sylvia Cohn, "The Reaction of New York and Ohio to the Ratification of the Fifteenth Amendment" (M. A. dissertation, Dept. of History, University of Chicago, 1944).

during March, 1869, but they were in the minority in the legislature.[19]

Democratic opposition was shrewdly resilient as well. What was striking about Democrats in the middle Atlantic states was their tendency to be milder and lower-keyed in their opposition than were those in the border states, on the Pacific coast, and along the Ohio River. New York Democrats, such as Peter B. Sweeny, argued against the Fifteenth Amendment because of their opposition not to Negro enfranchisement but to federal control of suffrage.[20] Tammany had much to lose if it ever lost control of election inspectors and canvassers or had to endure federal inspection of elections.[21]

Democrats were unwilling to accept Negro suffrage and to give Republicans an advantage without a fight. But once ratification appeared certain and Negro voting became inevitable, they knew that such voting would be permanent in the North. This acceptance contrasted sharply with the attitude of some border state Democrats. Those in the middle Atlantic states, therefore, acted as practical politicians but talked like disinterested diplomats.

[19] Pennsylvania, *The Legislative Record*, 93rd Sess., pp. 669, 670, 674, 785, 842, 844–45, 863, 895, 907–8, 909, 925–26, 962, 981. Republicans finally ratified after extensive debate. On March 11, 1869, the Senate approved, and on March 25, 1869, the House of Representatives followed. Both votes were strictly partisan. (Pennsylvania, *Journal of the Senate*, 93rd Sess., p. 570; E. McPherson, p. 497; Pennsylvania, *Journal of the House of Representatives*, 93rd Sess., 1869, pp. 767–68.)

[20] The New York *Herald*, November 26, 1869; January 6, 1870; the New York *Times*, January 6, 1870.

[21] The New York *Herald*, January 4, 1870. New York City election frauds were very much on the minds of New York Republicans, who felt that Tammany had stolen the presidential victory in 1868 (U. S. Congress, Senate, 40th Cong., 3rd Sess., 1868, Sen. Mis. Doc. 4, *Memorial of a Committee of the Union League Club of the City of New York*, pp. 1–18). One primary object of the Enforcement Act of February 28, 1871, was to stamp out election frauds in Democratic urban strongholds. The bulk of federal expenditures under the Enforcement acts was in the North. For example, almost half the cost of policing elections was for New York City elections. There was a higher ratio of convictions to acquittals in the North. (Robert A. Horn, "National Control of Congressional Elections," Ph. D. dissertation, Dept. of Politics, Princeton University, 1942, pp. 143, 154–55, 183–87, 232–34; see also *Record*, 51st Cong., 2nd Sess., 1890, p. 680.) Everette Swinney, doctoral candidate at the University of Texas and currently at work on a history of the enforcement of the Fifteenth Amendment, writes that the Horn dissertation provides a needed corrective to the traditional interpretation which emphasized exclusively the South as the objective of the Enforcement acts. But Swinney points out that Horn has somewhat overstated his case by discounting the obvious intent and practical result of the acts: to suppress the Ku Klux Klan in the South in the early 1870's. (Letter from Everette Swinney, October 13, 1962.)

A good example of Democratic tactics was found in New Jersey. Democratic Governor Theodore F. Randolph, in his two messages to the New Jersey legislature, was moderate in his argument, temperate in his expression, and apparently flexible in his outlook. Both prudent and pragmatic, Governor Randolph advocated rejection of the Amendment as a good Democrat and acquiesced in Negro enfranchisement as a realistic politician who would not antagonize Negro voters. He recommended that the federal Supreme Court might rule unfavorably upon the Amendment, but counseled acceptance of its verdict no matter what it would be. He also left the door open for some sort of education test for a qualified Negro suffrage.[22] Republican newspapers commended his conciliatory tone and liberal views. The Paterson *Daily Press* observed that Randolph followed the party line but that his first message was " in marked contrast to the positive, muscular, sledge-hammer style of opposition usually indulged in by Democratic champions." [23]

Once the Amendment was in force, New Jersey Democrats altered their course. The Democratic Newark *Daily Journal* suggested " withdrawing gracefully from a fruitless conflict with Federal authorities." [24] The moderate policy of Governor Randolph fitted in well with an accommodation to the Negro vote. With Republicans controlling the legislature in 1871, Randolph, in a generally statesmanlike message, urged compliance with the Fifteenth Amendment.[25] The new departure of the New Jersey Democrats was taking shape.

The mild tone of Democrats was shared by the middle Atlantic Republicans. They had dodged the Negro suffrage issue long enough to know the ropes well. Pennsylvania Republicans in the legislature had voted down Negro suffrage in 1868. Many Republicans were very reluctant to take a stand on the Amendment or preferred to postpone the embarrassing business.[26] Republican newspapers battled the caution of Pennsylvania legislators, who

[22] New Jersey, *Documents*, 93rd Sess. (1869), pp. 1295–96; New Jersey, *Documents*, 94th Sess., pp. 23–26.
[23] The Paterson *Daily Press*, March 25, 1869; January 11, 1870. [Trenton] *Daily State Gazette*, January 12, 15, 18, 1870.
[24] Quoted in the Paterson *Daily Press*, February 10, 1870.
[25] New Jersey, *Documents*, 95th Sess. (1871), pp. 19–20.
[26] *The Miner's Journal and Pottsville General Advertiser*, March 13, 1869; *New York Weekly Journal of Commerce*, March 25, 1869.

were sternly told to " face the music "[27] and do their duty. Opposition to Negro suffrage was formidable even among Republicans and particularly in the mining counties.

New York Republicans were also cautious. They had postponed for two years a state referendum on full Negro suffrage for fear it would hurt their party. When the referendum was held, Republicans did not fight vigorously for its adoption, hoping the Fifteenth Amendment would solve their awkward problem. They endorsed ratification of the federal amendment but were silent about the state referendum.[28] Like Democrats, they showed a healthy sense of self-preservation,[29] trying to avoid defeats because of the unpopularity of Negro suffrage, while eagerly anticipating benefit from the enfranchised Negro.

Strong opposition to Negro suffrage was complicated by the trouble brewing among friends of equal rights. Women suffragettes raised the question of whose rights came first. Susan B. Anthony and Elisabeth Cady Stanton insisted that women were being neglected. The showdown between supporters and opponents of the Amendment came at the annual meeting of the American Equal Rights Association in New York City early in May, 1869. The delegates refused to endorse ratification of the Fifteenth Amendment and virtually expelled Frederick Douglass and all supporters of the Amendment. The Association disbanded and two rival women's groups were set up to fight each other in behalf of women's suffrage. Miss Anthony and Mrs. Stanton organized the National Women Suffrage Association, soon announcing that Negroes should not vote until women did, that impartial not universal suffrage should be endorsed, and that opposition to the Amendment and co-operation with the Democrats should be encouraged. Lucy Stone, who had fought Negro suffrage before, organized a rival group, the American Woman's Suffrage Association, which would not compromise its principle of expanded impartial suffrage by opposition to Negro suffrage and preoccupation with women's suffrage alone.[30]

[27] [Philadelphia] *The Press*, March 10, 1869. The newspaper declared that any Republican who flinched from ignorance or timidity, bribery or cowardice, was no Republican at heart and was unfit to represent a Pennsylvania constituency.

[28] *Annual Cyclopedia for 1869*, p. 489; the New York *Herald*, November 1, 1869.

[29] The New York *Herald*, March 31, 1870.

[30] Hartford *Daily Courant*, May 14, 1869; Lucy Stone to Benjamin F. Wade, August 17, 1869, Benjamin F. Wade MSS, Library of Congress; Robert E. Riegel,

Special interest groups tried to spur Republicans into greater activity and stir broader sympathies. Negroes in Pennsylvania, for example, organized to use the ballot once they got it. The Pennsylvania State Equal Rights League endorsed the Amendment, and its president, William Nesbit, termed it " our political redemption," which would bring " incentives and opportunities." [31] President Nesbit urged that the organization become a political one, aligned with the Republicans, by which the " power of the colored voters of the state of Pennsylvania can be used as a unit." [32] The proposal was opposed by one Negro from Pittsburgh, who felt that " the Republican party had done the Negro good but they were doing themselves good at the same time." [33]

One Negro asked a Republican county chairman for money to keep the league going, since it was a political organization that could get out the Negro vote for the Republicans. The Negro concluded " with a long mouth that the Democrats with guile, money and influence were making overtures to colored men for support. That unless we were active, vigilant, we were not so sure they would not get some votes amongst us." [34] The Republican promised money, since the incentives were clear, the opportunities great, the mutual interests real. Republicans were to reap a rich harvest.[35]

The fight for ratification in Connecticut illustrated the middle Atlantic pattern of shifting Democratic tactics, with their alternate bullying and wooing of the potential Negro voter, and compro-

" The Split of the Feminist Movement in 1869," *Mississippi Valley Historical Review*, XLIX (December, 1962), 485–96.

[31] Manuscript Minutes of the Executive Board of the Pennsylvania State Equal Rights League, 1864–72, Leon Gardiner Collection of Negro History, Historical Society of Pennsylvania.

[32] *Ibid.*

[33] *Ibid.*

[34] W. A. Lavalette to Jacob C. White, Jr., July 13, 1869, *ibid.*

[35] In the 1871 election the full power of the Negro vote was brought to bear. Republicans recaptured the state Senate. See *Tribune Almanac for 1872*, p. 59; Alexander K. McClure, *Old Time Notes of Pennsylvania* (2 vols., Philadelphia, Pa.: John C. Winston Co., 1905), II, 284; *The Nation*, May 5, 1870. Despite two murders in Philadelphia Negroes benefited from the suffrage. See W. E. Burghardt DuBois, *The Philadelphia Negro: A Social Study* ("Publications of the University of Pennsylvania: Studies in Political Economy and Public Law," No. 14 [Philadelphia, Pa.: Ginn, 1899]), pp. 40–42, 372–85. In the fall elections of 1870, Republicans captured both chambers of the legislature in New Jersey (*Tribune Almanac for 1871*, p. 57). New Jersey Republicans had looked forward to the delivery of the Negro vote ([Trenton] *Daily State Gazette*, April 1, 1870).

mising Republican tactics, with their support for ratification and fear of its consequences. Connecticut, like the middle Atlantic states and unlike the other New England states, prohibited Negro suffrage, though the Negro vote could decide closely contested elections. The state was true to her sobriquet, " The Land of Steady Habits," for Connecticut Yankees were conservative in their politics and rigid in their prejudices. A Democrat sat in the Governor's chair and the Republican majority for Grant in 1868 was quite narrow. Voters in the Nutmeg State had defeated Negro suffrage in 1865 by a substantial margin. Anti-Negro sentiment, especially in western Connecticut, was strong enough to intimidate Republicans and galvanize Democrats. The Hartford *Daily Courant* scarcely exaggerated when its editor observed that " bigotry and prejudices . . . have lingered longer and fought harder in Connecticut than in any other New England state." [36] Republicans, wanting to avoid " political quicksand," [37] tried not to make the state election in April, 1869, a virtual referendum on the Fifteenth Amendment. Democrats wanted to exploit the Negro issue.[38]

Republicans would have to be careful; some equivocation was needed to please their factions and dull the Democratic axe. The platform to be adopted at the Republican state convention on February 3, 1869, would have to be strong enough to pacify the radicals, but not offensive enough to incur the displeasure of the moderates. The latter, in control of the party and the convention, adopted a platform stating that " conditions of suffrage should apply impartially." [39] But the plank did not specifically mention Connecticut and avoided reference to the federal suffrage amendment then pending in Congress. Before the plank was adopted, radical Republicans tried to substitute an unequivocal endorsement of impartial suffrage in Connecticut. The moderates, however, rejected the proposal by a vote of two to one.[40] The

[36] Hartford *Daily Courant*, April 2, 1869; Providence *Morning Herald*, March 12, 1869.

[37] William J. Niven, Jr., " The Time of the Whirlwind: A Study in the Political, Social and Economic History of Connecticut from 1861 to 1875," (Ph. D. dissertation, Dept. of History, Columbia University, 1954), p. 244.

[38] *Ibid.*, pp. 393–94.

[39] Hartford *Daily Courant*, February 4, 1869.

[40] New Haven *Register*, February 5, 1869; Niven, " Time of Whirlwind," pp. 393–94; Hartford *Daily Courant*, February 4, 1869. The paper glibly played down the fight.

plank adopted would not alienate the radicals, who had nowhere else to go; it would secure future allegiance of Connecticut Negroes by support of impartial suffrage; but at the same time, to please the moderates, it obscured the practical application to Connecticut.

For the Connecticut Democrats it was important to mollify the Irish, who were fed up with the old-line Yankee control of the party organization and leadership.[41] In New Haven, where the largest Negro population of the state lived,[42] and where Irish Democrats were concentrated in large numbers, the party tried to whip up support by employing the bugbear of Negro supremacy in politics and Negro competition in the marketplace.[43] Conservative Democrats defended the rights of states.[44] Yet prejudice and principle could not be carried too far. Negroes might be voters soon and potential recruits for the Democrats. It would also be prudent not to embarrass some Democratic candidates who had favored Negro suffrage in the past.[45] Thus, although in both the state and congressional conventions Democrats opposed the Fifteenth Amendment and demanded that no federal action be taken unless the states requested it,[46] they, significantly, did not oppose the principle of impartial suffrage. Democrats, then, were too crafty and Republicans too frightened to nail a solid suffrage plank to the party platforms.

Republicans attacked the Democratic position. The *Courant* called their state platform an " intentional equivocation," observing that the Democrats " intentionally refrained from declaring their opposition to the general principles of impartial suffrage," [47] because they needed Negro votes in the South and elsewhere. David R. Locke, the Republican journalist and humorist, ridiculed the Democratic position by having his comic creation, Petroleum V. Nasby, try to make a stump speech in Connecticut. The party leaders told him not to mention the Negro suffrage issue, because Democrats dodged that. " Nasby " replied that as a good Democrat, when he was deprived of the Negro suffrage

[41] Niven, " Time of Whirlwind," p. 561.
[42] Bureau of the Census, *Ninth Census*, I, 17.
[43] Bangor *Daily Whig and Courier*, March 13, 1869.
[44] Niven, " Time of Whirlwind," pp. 255, 288–89.
[45] Hartford *Daily Courant*, February 25, March 22, 1869.
[46] *Ibid.*, January 28, February 25, 1869.
[47] *Ibid.*, and February 4, 1869.

issue, he felt he was at sea without chart or compass, and concluded that Connecticut Democrats were nothing but dodgers trying to please everybody and offend nobody.[48]

During the campaign Democrats tried to profit from the Negro issue. The temporary chairman of the Democratic Congressional Convention, E. N. Lull, stated that "there is but one issue today and this is negro suffrage." [49] He told fellow Democrats that the issue could not be evaded any more, naturally overlooking the fact that both parties in their platforms were trying to do just that. The next legislature, he continued, would decide, and he felt sure that the "temper of Connecticut will reject it." [50] While Democratic editorials and resolutions all over the state emphasized the Negro issue, Democratic politicians echoed the state rights issue, which buttressed the Negro supremacy argument.[51]

Republicans, angry with Democratic howling, appeared disturbed. The *Courant* observed that "Democracy without the nigger is worse than a skillet without a handle." [52] Still, Republicans were compelled to face the Negro suffrage issue. Radicals wanted the issue to be open,[53] but more moderate Republicans preferred to side-step the question.[54]

Republicans emphasized the justice of impartiality rather than the need of favoring the Negro.[55] Most significant was the virtual omission of arguments about the Negro vote in Connecticut. The *Courant*, for example, published editorials on the Amendment twenty-five times during the campaign but only once explicitly mentioned the Negro vote.[56] Clearly, Republicans needed and wanted it, but the party in Connecticut was reluctant to advertise

[48] *Ibid.*, March 15, 1869. The accounts of Uncle Nasby during 1869 and 1870 are both an excellent indication of public opinion and a clever vehicle to mold it.

[49] *Ibid.*, February 25, 1869.

[50] *Ibid.*

[51] *Ibid.*, March 3, 12, 13, 24, 31, April 1, 1869.

[52] *Ibid.*, April 1, 1869.

[53] Norwich *Weekly Courier*, March 4, 1869.

[54] Hartford *Daily Courant*, March 22, 1869.

[55] *Ibid.*, March 30, 1869; Norwich *Weekly Courier*, March 4, 1869.

[56] Hartford *Daily Courant*, March 27, 1869. The number of Negro voters mentioned ran between 1,200 and 1,500. Rarely was the *Courant* so candid as when it boasted that, unlike the view of Fairfield County Democrats of the Fifteenth Amendment being a "death blow to a republican form of government," the Amendment instead was a real "hit from the shoulder right between the eyes of the Democratic party" (March 13, 1869).

the fact during the campaign.[57] Other arguments of political expediency, such as Grant's support of the Amendment and the certainty of ratification, were also suppressed. Republicans, then, made their appeal to principle not to expediency. It was good politics.[58]

The election gave Republicans a victory. Incumbent Democratic Governor James E. English was defeated by Republican Marshall Jewell by a slim majority of 411 votes. Republicans increased their majority in the Senate by two. In the House of Representatives, where Republican control was precarious, they increased their majority by eleven seats.[59] Reaction was swift and sharp on the Republican side. The victory was interpreted as a mandate for ratification of the Fifteenth Amendment,[60] and the *Courant* concluded that the Democratic " salt has lost its savor: their old bugbears frighten no longer." [61] Democrats, who had talked so long and so hard about the Amendment, were silent for the most part.[62] One major Democratic paper, the New Haven *Register*, predicted ratification.[63]

The election returns were somewhat less conclusive than the Republican editorials suggested. Recapturing the governorship and regaining strength in the legislature clearly indicated that the controversial issue of Negro suffrage could not by itself defeat the Republican state ticket. However, Republicans could not claim that their victory constituted a mandate for ratification of the Fifteenth Amendment, because the election was fought on other issues as well, and fewer people voted in 1869 than in 1868.[64] The Republican gubernatorial majority of 411 was the second smallest during Reconstruction,[65] and seemed to indicate that the Amendment might have reduced the Republican turnout. Republican majorities on the county level in 1868 and 1869 were reduced in Hartford, Litchfield, Middlesex, and Fairfield counties.

[57] *Ibid.*, March 25, 1869.

[58] *Ibid.*, March 26, 1869.

[59] *Tribune Almanac for 1870*, p. 50; *Tribune Almanac for 1869*, p. 64.

[60] Bridgeport *Daily Standard*, April 6, 1869.

[61] Hartford *Daily Courant*, April 6, 9, 1869.

[62] Editorial of the Hartford *Times*, quoted in Providence *Morning Herald*, April 8, 1869.

[63] Niven, " Time of Whirlwind," p. 400.

[64] Hartford *Daily Courant*, April 6, 1869.

[65] *Tribune Almanac for 1872*, p. 58. Republicans won the governorship in 1871 by 103 votes.

These, except for Litchfield, were represented by legislators who soon divided closely on the vote to ratify the Amendment. Feeling against it ran so strong in Litchfield that two Republicans bolted from the party and were elected to the legislature on the Democratic ticket on a pledge to oppose ratification. The only significant Democratic loss was in New Haven county. Irish defections may have contributed to the lower turnout there, but the reason was not support of the Amendment. In short, it would appear that Republicans won the state in spite of the Negro suffrage issue.[66]

Prediction of passage was borne out by the action of the General Assembly. The atmosphere in the Senate was brisk. Democratic motions to refer the Amendment to committee, to delay consideration for six days, to forward the Amendment to all town meetings in the state for action, and to postpone consideration indefinitely were all defeated by the Republican majority.[67] On the same day, the Senate then voted along strict party lines to adopt the Amendment. The final vote was thirteen Republicans in favor, six Democrats in opposition.[68] One Democrat and one Republican were absent.

In the House of Representatives, where Republican control was less secure,[69] the fight was more intense and the debate longer. House Republican leaders were as grim in their determination to pass the Amendment as Democrats were stubborn in their hope to block it.[70] Debate consumed three days. Democrat Selah Strong of Milford (New Haven county) said that if more Negroes immigrated to Connecticut, " in close towns they would hold the balance of power and elect your senators and representatives." [71] Democrat Enoch L. Beckwith from Litchfield predicted that the practical effect of the ratification of the Amendment would " place political

[66] *Tribune Almanac for 1869*, p. 64; *Tribune Almanac for 1870*, p. 50. In Litchfield County the Democratic majority increased while in other counties Democratic voting did not.

[67] Connecticut, *Journal of the Senate*, May Sess. (1869), p. 51; Hartford *Daily Courant*, May 8, 1869.

[68] Connecticut, *Journal of the Senate*, May Sess. (1869), p. 51; Hartford *Daily Courant*, May 8, 1869; E. McPherson, p. 488.

[69] *Tribune Alamanac for 1870*, p. 50. In the Senate, Republicans outnumbered the Democrats almost two to one, but in the House, Republicans held 134 seats and Democrats 103.

[70] Connecticut, *Journal of the House of Representatives*, May Sess. (1869), pp. 65–66; Hartford *Daily Courant*, May 12, 1869.

[71] Hartford *Daily Courant*, May 13, 1869.

power in the hands of the Republican opposition." [72] Republicans had little to say about the Amendment. Republican George Pratt rejected the charge that the Amendment was a party measure which would be passed by using party whips and spurs; for since no caucus had been held on it, and " there had been no extraneous effort employed to influence any member beyond his convictions," [73] he concluded that all the Democratic speeches amounted to was " a mere jargon of dead issues." [74] Rejecting Democratic charges that the Republicans were trying to perpetuate themselves in power, Republican William W. Welch contended that Negro suffrage was more important in the South than in the North. He conveniently avoided the question of the need for Republican Negro votes in Connecticut, maintaining that the Amendment was justified because it was right. He further dismissed the forecast that the rule of the ignorant would come; no Republican, he said, objected to the literacy requirement for voting in Connecticut. He concluded that the " negro should have a fair chance; this is all we propose." [75]

On May 13, when the oratory was finished, the Democrats tried at the last minute to postpone consideration, but the Republicans would have no more delays.[76] Democratic opposition had been " thorough and persistent," [77] but it was a lost cause. The House then approved the Amendment by a party division, with a vote of 126 Republicans for the Amendment and 105 Democrats, with one conservative Republican, against.[78] The vote revealed that representatives from western Connecticut, where anti-Negro feeling was strong, Democratic support widespread, and New York and southern influences persistent, were firmly opposed. Those from eastern Connecticut, where men were abolitionist, Republican, and Boston and Providence oriented, supported ratification.

[72] Ibid., May 14, 1869.
[73] Ibid.
[74] Ibid.
[75] Ibid.
[76] Ibid.; Connecticut, Journal of the House of Representatives, May Sess. (1869), pp. 85–86.
[77] Bridgeport Daily Standard, May 8, 1869.
[78] Connecticut, Journal of the House of Representatives, May Sess. (1869), pp. 86–87; Hartford Daily Courant, May 14, 1869; E. McPherson, pp. 488–89. James C. Walkley cast the only vote of a Republican against the Amendment. Walkley, a representative from Haddam in Middlesex county, was elected as an independent or conservative Republican by Democrats on a local railroad issue.

The usual political pattern of each county in state and presidential elections repeated itself in the vote on ratification. Where there was a close county vote for President, there was usually a close county vote on the Amendment. Those counties with a high absolute or large proportionate Negro population strongly opposed the Amendment, while the counties with the least Negroes were overwhelmingly in favor of it.[79] The men who were absent on the vote usually came from closely divided towns and had good reason not to take a stand.

In early 1870 Connecticut Democrats were in serious trouble while Republicans predicted victory. Republican politicians counted on the Negro vote for the election of April, 1870, if the Amendment was ratified by then. They were also aided by a new registration law that probably would disfranchise poor foreigners because it required documents and personal appearance during specified hours of registration. But owing to the stringent registration law, ratification of the Fifteenth Amendment would have to be secured before the middle of March; otherwise Connecticut Negroes could not vote.

Near the end of February, Republican politicians in Connecticut became anxious, for the Amendment had not been proclaimed in force. Former Governor Joseph R. Hawley, who now edited the Hartford *Courant*, wrote a confidential letter to E. Rockwell Hoar, Grant's Attorney General. Hawley supposed that the administration would not proclaim the Amendment in effect until Texas and Georgia were readmitted to Congress and the ratifications by these states became legally admissible. " Now we in Connecticut," he added, " are most anxiously awaiting the event. It will give the Republicans about 1,200 additional votes, perhaps more. But we shall not get a single one this year unless the proclamation shall have been made a few days before March 14th." Hawley asked for Hoar's opinion as to the prospects for official ratification,[80] and in reply Hoar stated that the proclamation would be issued as soon as the administration received official notice of ratification from Texas; he hoped that the proclamation would be made by March 10.[81] Mention of Republican desires was made

[79] Hartford *Daily Courant*, May 14, 1869; *Tribune Almanac for 1870*, p. 50; Bureau of the Census, *Ninth Census*, I, 17.

[80] Hawley to Hoar, February 26, 1870 (enclosure from Hoar to Hamilton Fish, February 28, 1870), Hamilton Fish MSS, Library of Congress.

[81] Hoar to Fish, February 28, 1870, *ibid.*

in the *Courant*.[82] The same day that Hawley wrote to Hoar, Republican Governor Marshall Jewell wrote to President Grant. Grant's personal secretary, Horace Porter, replied, also on February 28, that " every effort will be made " to issue the proclamation in time for Negro registration for the Connecticut election.[83]

As pressure mounted, however, the matter was brought up at a cabinet meeting on March 1. Secretary of State Hamilton Fish wrote in his diary that the " moving cause for an early issue of the proclamation is the approach of elections in Kentucky and Connecticut and the town elections in New York and elsewhere." [84] After some discussion President Grant decided against Hoar's advice and accepted Fish's plan that no proclamation would be issued until the states had been readmitted by Congress.

After they received the news of the decision to postpone the date of the proclamation, panic apparently seized Connecticut Republicans. United States Senator Orris S. Ferry, for one, applied pressure to the administration. He pushed through the Senate a resolution requesting the Secretary of State to inform Congress about the number of states that had ratified the Amendment. Benjamin F. Butler advised Fish to refuse to answer the question for the present and to avoid discussion of the status of Georgia.[85] Butler's position was endorsed by Georgia Governor Rufus B. Bullock,[86] and President Grant concurred.[87] Thus there was a clear conflict of interest between what was best for the administration in making a valid ratification and for Republicans in Georgia, who wanted no debate or further action by Congress on their affairs, and on what was needed desperately by the Connecticut Republican organization.

Because of these developments the Hartford *Courant* became jittery. Still, Negroes were advised to apply to their registrar of voters before March 14.[88] The race with time continued until Benjamin Perley Poore reported that the proclamation of the Fifteenth Amendment would be made too late to benefit Con-

[82] Hartford *Daily Courant*, February 28, 1870.

[83] Porter to Jewell, February 28, 1870, Letterbook, Ulysses S. Grant MSS, Library of Congress.

[84] Diary, I, March 1, 1870, Fish MSS.

[85] Butler to Fish, March 6, 1870, Fish MSS.

[86] Bullock to Butler, March 8, 1870, Benjamin F. Butler MSS, Library of Congress.

[87] Diary, I, March 7, 1870, Fish MSS.

[88] Hartford *Daily Courant*, March 7, 1870.

necticut Republicans.[89] By March 25, 1870, the *Courant* became exasperated. It observed that the Fifteenth Amendment was approved but that the Negro could not vote in Connecticut.[90] Moreover, what infuriated the *Courant* was the Democratic switch on the Amendment. Earlier during the campaign Democrats had said they opposed only the way the Amendment had been ratified and not its objectives. When it was obvious by the end of March that Connecticut Negroes would not be able to vote, however, Democrats reverted to their old tactics of stirring up prejudice and denouncing Negroes.[91] Although the Democratic candidate for governor, James E. English, said that the Amendment was a " settled matter," [92] his party platform considered it anything but settled.

When the official Proclamation of Ratification came on March 30, one hundred guns thundered forth at Hartford. The *Courant* called it a " glorious consummation of Reconstruction," [93] but regretted that the efforts had been too late to admit Negro voters in Connecticut. Just before election day the *Courant* inveighed against the Democrats who had resuscitated the doctrine of white supremacy for one more election: " The Connecticut democracy, more southern than the southerners, more rebellious than the rebels, talk of fighting the fifteenth amendment," [94] while Democrats in Delaware, Maryland, and the South make appeals to get Negro votes. Republican frustration was compounded by the fact that Republicans were caught in a trap of their own making: their stringent registration law, designed to reduce the Irish vote, had prevented the registration of the Negroes.[95]

To complete the comedy of errors, the election was a disaster

---

[89] *Ibid.*, March 18, 1870. Nevertheless, the Democratic New York *World* felt that the proclamation, although late, was intended to get the Negro vote in Connecticut ([New York] *The World*, March 31, 1870).

[90] Hartford *Daily Courant*, March 25, 1870.

[91] *Ibid.*

[92] *Ibid.*, April 2, 1870.

[93] *Ibid.*, March 31, 1870; the New York *Herald*, April 1, 1870. Old abolitionists, like Francis Gillette of Hartford, lauded the Amendment (Hartford *Daily Courant*, April 6, 1870). Gideon Welles, unfriendly to Negro suffrage, growled that the Amendment amounted to " false philanthropy " and " false protection " (" Remarks on the usurpation and bad faith involved in what is called The 15th Amendment," [March, 1870] Gideon Welles MSS, Huntington Library).

[94] Hartford *Daily Courant*, April 4, 1870.

[95] Niven, " Time of Whirlwind," p. 401.

for the Republican party. Incumbent Republican Governor Jewell was defeated by Democrat English; control of the General Assembly was no longer secure; and Republicans were reduced to a majority of one in the Senate and ten in the House of Representatives.

Reaction to the election returns was brisk. The Hartford *Courant* observed tartly that " if the reelection of a few of the Republicans of the [U. S.] Senate had depended upon the result " [96] of the ratification of the Fifteenth Amendment and the readmission of Texas and Georgia, then the whole thing might have been done six weeks before. " The fifteenth amendment would then have been proclaimed in season to give the Republicans a net gain of a thousand or twelve hundred from the colored vote," [97] resulting in a majority for the Republican ticket. The New York *Tribune* agreed; it felt that Republicans of Connecticut had been " ruthlessly slaughtered " by the " procrastinators and flaw-pickers " [98] in the Congress, because victory could have been achieved through the Negro vote in Connecticut if Congress had acted more promptly.

An analysis of the election returns justified Republican charges that the Negro vote could have changed the result and elected a Republican instead of a Democratic governor. The Democratic majority was 843, while a potential Negro vote would have come close to 1,378.[99]

The meaning of the election was less clear. The Democrats asserted that it was a verdict against Negro suffrage.[100] Yet although the loss of the governorship and the Democratic gains in the General Assembly were obviously a Republican defeat, Negro suffrage was not a major issue and the popular vote for governor further declined from that of 1869.[101] Probably, the

[96] Hartford *Daily Courant*, April 5, 1870.
[97] *Ibid.*
[98] New York *Tribune*, April 6, 1870.
[99] Bureau of the Census, *Ninth Census*, I, 17. One-seventh of the total Negro population would be 1,378 eligible voters. This approximation seems reliable, because during the 1871 election the actual Negro vote numbered 1,438. (Niven, " Time of Whirlwind," pp. 404, 413.) The Negro vote in Hartford County would be approximately 250, and the Democratic majority in 1870 was 104.
[100] Niven, " Time of Whirlwind," p. 404.
[101] There was a decline in turnout in the gubernatorial election in 7 out of 8 counties whichever party was in the majority, but no county switched to another party. Republican defections were larger than Democratic losses. Except in Fair-

outcome was due to apathy, not revolt. Republicans could not claim an endorsement of their ratification of the Amendment. Radical prejudice and opposition to Negro suffrage were still very strong. But Democrats could not maintain that the vote represented repudiation of the Amendment, because the Democratic candidate for Governor had scrapped his party platform when he had stated that the Fifteenth Amendment was settled.[102]

Actually, the election proved that the Republicans were lucky. In the short run they could be grateful that the Fifteenth Amendment had been passed in 1869, for their slim majorities in the legislature in 1870 might have prevented ratification. Republicans congratulated Negroes on getting needed Negro votes in the election of 1871, when they at last elected a Republican governor. An editorial praised newly enfranchised Negroes: " this acknowledgment is due to our colored voters: the result would have been different without them! . . . LET THE EAGLE SCREAM! " [103] In the long run, too, Republicans would need and would receive Negro help to keep the Nutmeg State Republican.[104]

The bitterly partisan battle in Connecticut showed that of the New England states only Connecticut would be politically affected by the ratification of the Fifteenth Amendment. Her politics conformed to the middle Atlantic rather than the New England pattern, for they showed that Republicans had a vested interest in Negro voting, and Democrats in maintaining only white voting, but that neither party could afford to ignore the vital interests of the other. An evenly divided electorate, strict party voting, bitter campaigns, evasion of and straddling of the suffrage planks of each party's platform illuminated the critical importance of the Negro vote, which could indeed alter the balance of party power.

---

field county, where the Democratic majority actually increased, nothing changed except the most important total vote. (*Tribune Almanac for 1871*, p. 50; *Tribune Almanac for 1870*, p. 50.)

[102] Hartford *Daily Courant*, April 6, 1870. This position of Governor English's did not prevent him from denouncing the Amendment in his Inaugural Address (Connecticut, *Journal of the Senate*, May Sess., 1870, pp. 24–25).

[103] Hartford *Daily Courant*, April 4, 1871.

[104] Robert A. Warner, *New Haven Negroes* (New Haven, Conn.: Yale University Press, 1940), pp. 177–81, 288–91.

CHAPTER VII

MIDDLE WESTERN CONFLICT

Ratification in the older Middle West constituted the most formidable hurdle for the Amendment. From the beginning it was clear that ratification would prove difficult in Indiana,[1] for Democrats threatened to stall proceedings. John R. Coffroth told fellow representatives that because Indiana Republicans had promised during the campaign of 1868 to let the people of Indiana decide whether the Negro should vote, Democrats should not allow Republicans to force a fraud on the people by ratifying the Fifteenth Amendment.[2] An editorial in a major Democratic newspaper, the Indianapolis *Daily State Sentinel*,[3] was even bolder: " It will be the duty of every Democrat and every member in the present General Assembly opposed to action upon it until it is submitted to the people, to use any and all means at his control—even to bolting or resignation—to defeat it." [4]

On March 5, 1869, the Democratic legislators followed this advice. Thirty-eight Democratic representatives and seventeen Democratic senators resigned from the legislature, leaving three Democrats in the Senate and six in the House of Representatives.[5] The legislature floundered for three more days without a quorum of two-thirds of the total membership. Parliamentary squabbling continued but no legislative business was conducted.[6] The regular

[1] Indiana, *Brevier Legislative Reports: Embracing Shorthand Sketches of the Journals and Debates of the General Assembly*, 46th Sess. (1869), pp. 589–90.

[2] *Ibid.*, pp. 70, 589–90. Both the Republican platform and the governor had so promised. See Emma Lou Thornbrough, *The Negro in Indiana: A Study of a Minority* (Indianapolis: Indiana Historical Bureau, 1957), pp. 242–43.

[3] Quoted in the Evansville *Journal*, March 3, 1869.

[4] *Brevier Reports*, 46th Sess., p. 489.

[5] *Ibid.*, pp. 591, 598; William C. Gerichs, " The Ratification of the Fifteenth Amendment in Indiana," *Indiana Magazine of History*, IX (September, 1913), 139.

[6] *Brevier Reports*, 46th Sess., pp. 594–600.

session adjourned on March 8, but Republican Governor Conrad Baker ordered special elections for March 23 to fill the vacancies of the Democratic members who had resigned, and called a special session of the legislature for April 8.

Republican editorial reaction indicated general disgust with the Democratic bolt, because a general appropriation bill had not passed,[7] and newspapers predicted that the bolt would not alter the balance of power in the legislature even if all the Democrats were re-elected.[8]

But Republicans themselves quarreled over whether the ratification of the Fifteenth Amendment was desirable, or even necessary. The Evansville *Journal*, speaking for Republicans in southern Indiana, considered it "the wrong thing at the wrong time," because it was "keeping up a hubbub about the negro."[9] In an area where southern ways were ingrained and anti-Negro feeling ran high, southern Indiana Republicans recognized that ratification would play into the hands of the Negro-baiting Democrats. It was no coincidence, then, that three of the four Republican senators who were opposed to the Amendment came from sharply competitive counties in southern Indiana.[10] Republicans further contended that the Amendment lacked the support of the people and legislature,[11] and that ratification would constitute repudiation of a party pledge.[12] But party demands were insistent.[13] The Republicans had at stake a potential Negro vote of 6,000 to 8,000 out of a Negro population of 24,560.[14] Indiana Negroes let Republican politicians know that once they were given the ballot, they would become good Republicans. "We would vote the way we

---

[7] The Evansville *Journal*, March 5, 1869; editorial of [Indianapolis] *Journal*, *ibid.*, March 6, 1869; "Address of the Republican Members of the Legislature to the People of the State of Indiana," *ibid.*, March 10, 1869.

[8] Editorial of the Cincinnati *Commercial*, in the Evansville *Journal*, March 9, 1869; "Address of the Republican Members," *ibid.*, March 10, 1869.

[9] *Ibid.*, March 3, 4, 1869.

[10] *Ibid.*, March 9, 1869; *Tribune Almanac for 1869*, p. 70.

[11] The Evansville *Journal*, March 3, 4, 5, 8, 1869. Even Republican legislators acknowledged division in the ranks of the party over ratification ("Address of the Republican Members," *ibid.*, March 10, 1869).

[12] *Ibid.*, March 9, 1869.

[13] *Ibid.*, March 12, 1869.

[14] [Indianapolis] *Journal*, March 23, 1869, cited in Gerichs, *Indiana Magazine*, IX, 148; [Indianapolis] *Journal*, June 25, October 20, 1869; Thornbrough, *Negro in Indiana*, p. 252; Bureau of the Census, *Ninth Census*, I, 26–27.

shot," declared one Negro.[15] Another predicted that Negroes would vote Republican " as naturally as water flows downward." [16] Republican politicians needed these votes.

By 1868 Indiana was a closely divided state. Governor Baker had won the governor's chair in 1868 by a majority of only 961 in a total vote of 342,189.[17] President Grant carried Indiana in the same year by the slim margin of 9,572,[18] and during the campaign politicians had worried about Indiana's thirteen electoral votes. Since Republicans had never won a presidential election by more than 53 per cent of the vote during Reconstruction, and frequently their majority was less,[19] Republican politicians were willing to risk some alienation of southern white Indianans for a solid Negro vote.

To Democrats the prospect of Negro voters was a nightmare. Democratic journalists and politicians therefore defended the bolt of the legislature, proclaiming that duty demanded their resignation.[20] Good Democrats should prevent Republicans from breaking their own campaign pledges by ratifying the Amendment and prevent the inferior Negro from degrading the ballot box. The Republican Cincinnati *Commercial*, for example, commented that " the phantom of the Fifteenth Amendment was sufficient to drive them in terror out of the State House and into retirement," in order to forestall Negro voting,[21] which could threaten a Democratic incumbent in Marion County (Indianapolis) and present obstacles in other counties. But because of its location, the Negro vote constituted a danger not to Democratic legislators but rather to the Democratic state and national tickets.[22] Democrats would have to devise some method to neutralize Negro voting yet retain party strength, and it would be difficult for them to reduce the number of eligible Negro voters by imposing educational and

[15] [Indianapolis] *Journal*, January 2, 1867, quoted in Thornbrough, *Negro in Indiana*, p. 251.
[16] [Indianapolis] *Journal*, June 25, 1869, *ibid.*
[17] *Tribune Almanac for 1869*, p. 70.
[18] *Ibid.*
[19] Burnham, *Presidential Ballots*, pp. 161, 391.
[20] Gerichs, *Indiana Magazine*, IX, 141–44.
[21] Editorial of the Cincinnati *Commercial*, quoted in the Evansville *Journal*, March 9, 1869.
[22] There were 7 counties in Indiana where the Negro population was over 1,000 in 1870. In 5 of these counties Republicans had normal majorities. (Bureau of the Census, *Ninth Census*, I, 26–27; *Tribune Almanac for 1869*, p. 70.)

property qualifications that would not eliminate Democratic supporters as well.[23] Perhaps the solution was Democratic conversion: Democrats would become the Negro's best friend. This maneuver was suggested in the press [24] and even joked about. The fictional character "Petroleum V. Nasby" tested Democratic opinion in Indiana concerning the Fifteenth Amendment by masquerading as a Negro. His reception at the hands of Democratic candidates was privately warm, publicly cool, and occasionally ambiguous. Covering his face with burnt cork, Nasby transformed himself into a Negro minister. Purportedly on a mission to collect church contributions for his Negro parish, he arrived in a closely balanced county where neither party had 50 votes to spare but in which there were 100 Negroes who held the balance of power. Nasby first visited the Democratic candidate for sheriff, reporting: " I WUZ NOT KICKT! On the contrary quite the reverse. The gushin candidate kindly, blandly and winningly begged me to be seated; he askt me, with tears uv interest gushin from his eye, ez to the prospex uv our Zion; ez to how many we numbered, male and female, adult and youthful, and whether or not we coodent indulge a reasonable hope that many more uv our color mightn't be indoost to leave the South and settle in the county." Although this Democratic candidate for sheriff had previously denounced "nigger emigration," Uncle Nasby observed that the man now had changed his tune: " Sed he, ' The admirishen I feel for the Afrikins—the respec I hev for thermany qualities uv head and heart make me say in the language uv the inspired writer, ' The more the merrier.' " The Democrat then handed Nasby some money for the Negro church and said: " ' And next fall, after the Amendment is ratified, and your people git the rites which wuz allus theirn, I trust yoo will remember at the polls them wich hev stood yoor friends, uv whom I am wich.' " Nasby was dumfounded and accosted another Democratic candidate for Treasurer, who took him by the arm and accompanied him on his fund raising campaign. Turning a sharp corner, they came upon some convicts. Nasby described the scene:

The minit his [the Treasurer's] eyes struck em he loosed his holt of me and shot ahead, keepin in advance till he hed turned the next corner.

---

[23] Editorial of the Cincinnati *Commercial*, quoted in the Evansville *Journal*, March 9, 1869.

[24] The Evansville *Journal*, May 20, 21, 1869.

"Why this maneuver?" askt I, thankful that he had even that much uv originel Democratic feelin in him. "Dear sir!" replied he, "Yoo will exuse me, but the fact is, I'm in a prekarious sitooashen. I'm a candidate, its close. Them gentlemen with the ball and chain hev votes, and they hev a most crocil prejoodis agin those uv your color. We must humor their idiosyncrasies, till we kin correct em. The time is comin, and I'm laborin for it nite and day, when it will all be removed. My deer sir, at the polls this fall will yoo and your flock remember the sacrificis I hev made and am makin?"

Nasby was invited to dinner with the Democratic candidate for Treasurer, but forgot he was still disguised as a Negro. When he washed his hands the cork on his skin came off. Seeing that Nasby was a white, the Democrat kicked him out of his house. Nasby concluded his yarn with this moral:

Ez a nigger I wuz welcomed; when it wuz known that I wuz a white man I wuz ignominiously kickt! Is this the beginin uv a new order uv things? Is the niggers to receive all the smiles hereafter uv Dimocrats who want office? I fear me. No sooner is ther a probability uv this race gittin a vote than the Dimocratic leaders, forgottin ther proud Caucashen blood, forgitten the difference in the anatomical structure uv the two races, and forgitten that the minit they give the nigger a vote, their daughters must marry niggers; they forgit all this, and cuddle with 'em the same ez they alluz hev with other inferior classes.[25]

Democrats would have to be as careful in recruiting Negro voters as the Democratic candidates had been in talking to Uncle Nasby. Recruitment of Negroes in private was one thing, but Democrats in public would have to act prudently to suit the tastes of old-fashioned Democratic constituents. The Democrats could never, for example, elect Negroes to hold office. Whatever the solution, Negro suffrage gave Democrats headaches and Republicans laughs.

Stakes, then, were high in the fight over the Amendment. The special election called by the Governor was not, however, a general referendum on Negro suffrage. Instead, the special ballot secured the one-sided re-election of all the resigning Democrats, most of whom came from safe Democratic districts, particularly the southern Indiana stronghold.[26] In many counties and senatorial

[25] *Ibid.*, May 13, 1869.

[26] The bulk of Democratic strength was in southern Indiana. There were 22 Democratic counties south of Indianapolis, but only 12 north of Indianapolis. (*Tribune Almanac for 1869*, p. 70.) Of the Democratic senators who resigned, 6 came from northern Indiana, 11 from downstate (*Brevier Reports*, 46th Sess., p. 591).

districts the Republicans did not offer opposition candidates and the vote was light.

Democrats did not report for duty at the special session until four days after it convened. Apparently they had decided to take their seats in the legislature only after they had reached an understanding with the Republicans to delay consideration of the Amendment until late in the session. Republicans recognized that delay was the best tactic, because the Democrats could block Senate action with their twenty-three out of fifty votes.[27] This awkward situation was duplicated in the House.[28]

But delay was not going to solve the problem, for Democrats planned to repeat their walkout.[29] Senator Thomas Gifford contended that he would " resign at every full change of the moon, if necessary, to defeat this measure." [30] Republican supporters of ratification tried to counter Democratic obstruction and bypass a bolt by calling a joint meeting of both houses of the legislature to act on it,[31] but such tactics failed for want of Republican support.[32]

The parties headed for a showdown as each met in caucus at noon on May 13. Republicans had a formidable reinforcement from Washington. The former Governor and wartime dictator of Indiana, United States Senator Morton, attended the Republican caucus, trying to bolster timid legislators and bring pressure upon Republican opponents. He argued that the Fifteenth Amendment could be ratified without the presence of Democratic legislators because a quorum could be achieved by two-thirds of the legislators present. Members who resigned were no longer members, he claimed, and could not be counted as such. This maneuver had been suggested earlier, but the words and advice of Senator Morton commanded greater assent.[33] Party pressure must have been great,[34] since the caucus decided to ratify the Amendment

[27] *Brevier Reports*, 46th Sess., pp. 42–43.

[28] *Brevier Reports*, Spec. Sess. (1869), p. 40.

[29] The Evansville *Journal*, April 29, 1869.

[30] *Brevier Reports*, Spec. Sess. (1869), p. 43. This position was taken by other Democrats (*Ibid.*, p. 202).

[31] *Ibid.*, pp. 41–43.

[32] *Ibid.*, pp. 42, 44, 222.

[33] William D. Foulke, *Life of Oliver P. Morton Including His Important Speeches* (2 vols.; Indianapolis: The Bowen-Merrill Co., 1899), II, 113.

[34] Indicative of southern Indiana Republican opinion, the Evansville *Journal*, which had energetically fought the Amendment, capitulated in its issue of April

with or without the Democrats. Emboldened Republicans returned to the chambers to do battle with their opponents, who had decided in caucus to resign as a group so that there would be no legislative quorum.

In the Senate the doors were ordered locked and the roll was called.[35] It was learned subsequently that though sixteen Democratic senators had resigned, some remained in the chamber and were counted as present by the Republican presiding officer, who declared a quorum. When Democrats protested this procedure, Republicans pointed out that nothing in writing had been submitted to the presiding officer.[36] The statement was true; written resignations had been submitted only to the Governor. Frustrated Democrats condemned the ruling, but they were shouted down by Republicans.[37] The Fifteenth Amendment was quickly put to a vote and passed, twenty-seven to one. Eleven Senators were declared present but not voting, while eleven were absent.[38] The session was speedily adjourned.

In the House of Representatives, during the same afternoon, the Speaker ruled that business could not be conducted because the withdrawal of the Democrats prevented a quorum.[39] Twenty-four hours later, however, the Speaker was not so sure of his ruling. Despite the fact that twenty-seven Democratic representatives had quit the chamber, leaving eleven fewer than the quorum of two-thirds of the total membership of the chamber required by the Indiana constitution, the Speaker remarked that " on the question of ratifying an amendment to the Constitution of the United States—in absence of any precedent in the legislation, or in the Constitution of our State, in the absence of any law of Congress as to what shall constitute a quorum for the purpose of ratifying a Constitutional Amendment—the question never can be decided and settled unless it is decided in this way." [40] He then ruled that the Amendment could be taken up.

21, 1869, by chiding the Democrats for blocking progress, and implied its endorsement of the Amendment. Republican opposition was dwindling by April.

[35] *Brevier Reports*, Spec. Sess. (1869), p. 222.

[36] *Ibid.*, p. 224.

[37] *Ibid.*, p. 225.

[38] *Ibid.*, p. 224. Republican Senator Thomas C. Jaquess from southern Indiana was the lonely opponent (Indiana, *Journal of the Senate*, Spec. Sess., 1869, pp. 474–76).

[39] *Brevier Reports*, Spec. Sess. (1869), p. 228.

[40] *Ibid.*, p. 239.

Debate was largely confined to parliamentary procedure. After the standard arguments were repeated,[41] the Fifteenth Amendment was passed by fifty-four Republicans who voted "yes"; no one voted "no," but three representatives, including one Republican, were declared present but not voting.[42] In other words, the Amendment was passed by a quorum of fifty-seven members, although Indiana law required, in effect, a quorum of sixty-seven.[43]

The extraordinary tactics that Indiana politicians used in the fight over ratification indicated that the party stakes were high. Humanitarian considerations appeared to have played no decisive role in the outcome: it was the future Negro voter who mattered to most Republican legislators. Professional politicians dominated the stage and party advantage dictated their actions. The customary sectional alignment of northern against downstate Indiana played an important role by dictating tactics and determining tone.[44] But it was significant that when the showdown came, the Republicans from downstate, with two exceptions, voted to ratify the Amendment. Democrats, however, fought a resourceful guerilla battle. Perhaps a majority of Indianans opposed Negro

[41] *Ibid.*, pp. 241, 243.

[42] *Ibid.*, p. 240; Indiana, *Journal of the House of Representatives*, Spec. Sess. (1869), pp. 604–5; E. McPherson, p. 491. The lone Republican was James V. Mithell of Morgan County, which is southwest of Indianapolis. The other two men were the remaining Democrats in the chamber.

[43] Gerichs maintains that ratification by the House was invalid (*Indiana Magazine*, IX, 165–66). This position assumes that Indiana law was in force when the House acted on the Amendment; that the legislative action in each chamber must be judged separately; and that a quorum is an absolute entity determined by the total membership of each chamber, rather than a relative number based on the number of members present. Ample precedent would reject this view (Foulke, *Morton*, II, 113–17; the Evansville *Journal*, May 18, 1869). The ratification was valid, if irregular, because the substance of state authority was expressed and, most important, the ruling of the chair was not overruled. The federal Secretary of State held that the Indiana ratification was binding. The U. S. Supreme Court, moreover, ruled that passage and ratification of the Amendment was valid in *Neal v. Delaware*, 103, U. S., 370 (1880), and further ruled at a later time that quorum can be based on members present. Nevertheless, Indiana ratification did cause concern in Washington and even worried Morton (Diary, November 22, 1869, Fish MSS). Morton wrote Charles Sumner that "the adoption of the Amendment may yet turn on the vote of Indiana" (Morton to Sumner, May 28, 1869, Sumner MSS).

[44] Henry E. Cheaney, "Attitudes of the Indiana Pulpit and Press toward the Negro, 1860–1880." (Ph. D. dissertation, Dept. of History, University of Chicago, 1961), pp. 158–59, 449–50, 453. Only southern Indianan papers refused to accept the Fifteenth Amendment once ratified.

suffrage,[45] but the politicians voted otherwise. Although the burden of racial prejudice was very strong, to party men the necessity of party success proved stronger.

Close elections generated partisan heat and worsened race relations in the short run.[46] Republican enfranchisement of the Negro backfired,[47] and Democrats seized control of the legislature in 1871 for the first time since before the Civil War. In the long run, however, Republican investment in the Negro voter seemed to yield rich dividends. The word " nigger " disappeared from stump speeches, as Hoosiers accepted Negro voters.[48] Negroes remained Republican and their number mounted.[49] Negro voting must have been fairly substantial—substantial enough for Republican Negro politicians to be elected to the General Assembly only eleven years after Negroes had started voting.[50] Although they may have resented their exploitation by the Republicans,[51] they did receive patronage and recognition, while Republican politicians in a politically unsafe state were delighted with the election returns from Negro districts in the 1870's and 1880's.[52]

Ratification in Ohio posed problems and revealed patterns similar to those in Indiana, and their injured tone and hot tempers had more in common with border state than with middle Atlantic Democrats. Southern Ohio remained for the most part strongly southern in outlook, stanchly Democratic in politics, and violently anti-Negro in feeling. Ohioans had rejected Negro suffrage in 1867, and the cause continued unpopular in the state in 1869. A Democratic legislature in April, 1869, rejected ratification [53] along strict party lines. Like Indiana, the potential Negro vote was important in Ohio. Republican state majorities were usually less than 7,000 votes, and an additional 10,600 Negro votes would help.

[45] Thornbrough, *Negro in Indiana*, p. 245.
[46] Cheaney, " Attitudes," pp. 451–53.
[47] Thornbrough, *Negro in Indiana*, p. 249.
[48] Cheaney, " Attitudes," pp. 149–59.
[49] Thornbrough, *Negro in Indiana*, pp. 206–7.
[50] John W. Lyda, *The Negro in the History of Indiana* (Terre Haute, Ind.: privately printed, 1953), p. 90.
[51] Thornbrough, *Negro in Indiana*, p. 315.
[52] *Ibid.*, pp. 288, 291.
[53] On April 1, 1869, the House of Representatives rejected ratification, 47 to 36 (Ohio, *Journal of the House of Representatives*, 58th Gen. Assembly, Adj. Sess., 1868–69, p. 628; Ohio, *Journal of the Senate*, 58th Gen. Assembly, Adj. Sess., 1868–69, p. 671; E. McPherson, pp. 496–97).

There were however significant differences between Indiana and Ohio. Ratification in Ohio was important to more than state politics, for Ohio might decide the fate of the Fifteenth Amendment in the most critical months of the ratification struggle. Moreover, the timing and effect of Ohio ratification were far more crucial than in any other state. Yet the outcome was more precarious in the Ohio legislature of 1870 than in any other state because the balance of power in the legislature was held by the Reform party, a coalition elected from Hamilton county, Cincinnati. Democrats had lost control of the legislature in the 1869 elections, but Republicans did not regain it. In the Senate, Republicans held eighteen seats, Democrats seventeen, and Reformers two. In the House of Representatives, Republicans controlled fifty-three legislators, Democrats forty-nine, and Reformers ten.[54]

The uncertainty of ratification and the critical importance of Ohio's action brought requests for aid. Republican Governor Rutherford B. Hayes had earlier pressed President-elect Grant to endorse ratification in order to ensure its success and to remove some of the pressure on state candidates, like himself, who would run for re-election on a pledge of support for the Amendment.[55] After his re-election Hayes exerted pressure on the Grant administration when he wrote Vice-President Schuyler Colfax of Indiana that Ohio would ratify " *but it is not a certainty. . . .* We *may need help* in Ohio." [56]

Washington, in turn, harassed Columbus. Chief Justice Salmon P. Chase, whose home was in Cincinnati, wrote letters to members of the Reform delegation, sounding them out on ratification. Chase tried hard to get Ohio ratification without publicizing his efforts or expressing firm views on the provisions of the Amendment. This influence upon and friendship among the Cincinnati Reformers proved an important but delicate operation for a Chief Justice. Chase walked a tightrope, first bowing to restrained sympathizers of Negro suffrage on one side, and then nodding furiously to supporters of reconciliation with the South on the other, and all the time virtually double talking on the Amendment's enforcement powers, depending on who was listening.[57]

---

[54] The Cincinnati *Gazette*, October 16, 1869; *Tribune Almanac for 1870*, p. 60.
[55] Rowland E. Trowbridge to Rutherford B. Hayes, February 15, 1869, Rutherford B. Hayes MSS.
[56] Hayes to Schuyler Colfax, October 22, 1869, *ibid.*
[57] Chase to Thomas H. Yeatman, October 19, 1869, Chase MSS, Historical and

United States Senator John Sherman also exhibited interest and exerted influence in securing Ohio's ratification.[58] Senator Morton wrote Hayes that " vast interests depend on the vote of Ohio," [59] whereas another Justice of the United States Supreme Court, Noah H. Swayne, also from Ohio, wrote to Hayes expressing deep interest in ratification.[60] In no other state did so many prominent men actively intervene.[61]

More important than Chase's work in securing ratification was that of Governor Hayes and such Republican politicians as state Senator Benjamin F. Potts [62] and Representative Robert B. Dennis,[63] who kept Republican legislators in line. Hayes wrote one legislator not to resign from the legislature until ratification had been secured.[64] Hayes stayed at his post [65] and apparently made deals to secure it, rewarding loyal supporters by emphatic endorsements for state and federal patronage.[66] He came to regard Ohio ratification as a personal triumph.[67]

Four skirmishes and one major battle were involved in the war over ratification in the legislature. The first skirmish broke out over the organization of the legislature, assignment of committees, and distribution of patronage. The victors were the Reform men and the Democrats, who seized control of both chambers and elected Reform presiding officers. An effort of the Reformers to build up their bargaining position appeared to be the motive behind this maneuver. Probably Democrats were given favorable

Philosophical Society of Ohio; Yeatman to Chase, January 22, 1870, Chase MSS, Historical Society of Pennsylvania; Chase to George H. Hill, January 7, 1870, Letterbook, Chase MSS, Library of Congress.

[58] Potts to Sherman, January 6, 1870, Sherman MSS, Library of Congress.

[59] Oliver P. Morton to Hayes, January 4, 1870, Hayes MSS. Hayes advised Morton, "If you can help us in any way, do not fail to do it." See Hayes to Morton, January 6, 1870, *ibid.*; [Washington] *New Era*, January 13, 1870.

[60] Harry Barnard, *Rutherford B. Hayes and His America* (New York: Bobbs-Merrill, 1954), p. 248.

[61] One Democratic newspaper published a report that the Grant administration offered salary or contracts as bribes for a vote for ratification (the Cincinnati *Daily Enquirer*, January 3, 14, 17, 1870). Republicans denied the charge.

[62] Potts to Sherman, January 12, 1870, Sherman MSS.

[63] Hayes to Columbus Delano, July 8, 1870, Hayes MSS.

[64] Hayes to Potts, December 21, 1869, *ibid.*

[65] Hayes to Birchard, January 14, 1870, *ibid.*; Diary, December 2, 1869, *ibid.*

[66] Hayes to Delano, July 8, 1870, *ibid.*; the Cincinnati *Commercial*, January 22, 1870.

[67] Diary, April 19, 1870, Hayes MSS; Hayes to J. Irving Brooks, March 1, 1870, *ibid.*

assignments by the Reformers in return for some hint by Democrats of support for the Amendment.[68] Some Democrats did favor ratification, but their strength was negligible. When party leaders decided to make opposition a test of party loyalty, Democrats who favored the Amendment or would dodge a vote had no choice but to oppose it or commit political suicide.[69] It would appear, however, that the Democratic decision to oppose was taken earlier in October or November. Ohio opposition was to be in concert with opposition elsewhere.[70]

The second and third skirmishes occurred on the critical battleground of the House of Representatives. Democrats tried to change the rules governing joint resolutions from a simple majority to an absolute majority of all members elected. They also tried unsuccessfully to unseat two Republican members from contested districts. Both maneuvers were regarded as devices to reduce Republican strength in order to defeat ratification.[71] The final skirmish was an attempt by the Democrats to submit the Fifteenth Amendment to the voters or to postpone consideration. All these tactics were defeated by Republicans in a desperate holding action against the assaults of Democrats who were ready to do anything to defeat ratification. Democrats were becoming panicky; they were staking everything on defeat of the Amendment.

During the strategic battle, debate started. Consuming six days,[72] it was uninspired and uninspiring. The main questions were whether the Fifteenth Amendment was an issue in the recent campaign and whether the election returns constituted a mandate

[68] The Cincinnati *Commercial*, January 20, 21, 22, 1870; the Cincinnati *Daily Gazette*, January 3, 4, 1870.

[69] The Cincinnati *Daily Gazette*, January 3, 15, 18, 1870; Hayes to Morton, January 6, 13, 1870, Hayes MSS.

[70] Llewellyn Baber to Andrew Johnson, October 26, 1869, Johnson MSS. Library of Congress; Baber to Johnson, November 10, 1869, *ibid.* Baber, a member of the Democratic State Executive Committee and the man who later publicly accused Chase of intervening in the ratification fight, wrote former President Johnson of Democratic plans to strangle the Fifteenth Amendment by co-operation between the Democratic legislatures of New York, New Jersey, Kentucky, and Tennessee, to defeat the Amendment and stamp out " radicalism." There were vague reports in the press of co-operation among Ohio and New York Democrats to defeat the Amendment.

[71] The Cincinnati *Commercial*, January 14, 15, 20, 1870; Toledo *Daily Blade*, January 14, 15, 1870.

[72] The Cincinnati *Daily Gazette*, January 14, 15, 20, 21, 1870.

for ratification. Politicians drew conclusions according to partisan interest.[73] One perceptive reporter, J. P. Loomis, observed that although some Democrats denounced the qualifications of Negro voters, most did not. Recognizing the future use of the Negro vote, Democrats launched tirades against Congress, predicting despotism, but avoided discussing the qualifications of the Negroes.[74] After an extensive debate, on January 14, 1870, Senators voted to ratify the Fifteenth Amendment by a strict party vote of nineteen to eighteen.[75] Both Reform senators voted for ratification.

The showdown in the House of Representatives was an incredible affair. It was not enough that friends of the Amendment had to wade through the flood of words; they had to conquer a literal flood as well. On their return to Columbus from Cincinnati, several Reform members who favored the Amendment encountered heavy rains that forced them to cross treacherous streams and dragoon a freight train to arrive in Columbus in time for the vote.[76] One legislator was even tricked into returning to Cincinnati, but discovering that he had been deceived by the Democrats, he returned to the state capitol in time to vote.[77]

When every other maneuver and trick had failed, Democrats retorted to a filibuster and threatened to prevent a vote. They were noisy, disorderly, and defiant, and their tactics, temper, and threats enraged the Republicans. The galleries, packed with white and Negro spectators, started shouting, but the Reform Speaker demanded order and ruled that the Amendment must be voted upon.[78] And, as predicted, the Fifteenth Amendment, on January 21, 1870, was ratified by a vote of fifty-seven to fifty-five. All Republicans voted in favor and all Democrats voted against. The Reformers split, four "yes" and six "no." As in the Senate, there were no absences.[79] When the tally was announced there

[73] Newspapers also sided along party lines. The Republican Cincinnati *Daily Gazette* (January 8, 13, 21, 1870), which had opposed the Fifteenth Amendment in 1869, endorsed it in 1870, and regarded the gubernatorial election as a mandate, while the Democratic Cincinnati *Enquirer* which opposed the Amendment, found no mandate for ratification.

[74] The Cincinnati *Commercial*, January 22, 1870.

[75] Ohio, *Journal of the Senate*, 59th Gen. Assembly, 1870 Sess., pp. 43–44.

[76] The Cincinnati *Commercial*, January 19, 1870.

[77] *Ibid.*, January 21, 1870.

[78] *Ibid.*, and January 22, 1870; Cincinnati *Evening Chronicle*, January 21, 1870.

[79] Ohio, *Journal of the House of Representatives*, 59th Gen. Assembly, 1870

were screams of joy and outbursts of applause from the representatives and the crowd in the galleries, followed by hisses and catcalls from the Democrats.[80] The war was over. Patience and persistence had brought victory.

The following day President Grant wrote a friend that with the ratification by Ohio, the future of the Fifteenth Amendment was assured.[81] Members of Congress were so elated that they signed a letter congratulating the Ohio legislature upon its ratification of the " Crowning Measure of reconstruction." [82] There could be little doubt now that the proposed Fifteenth Amendment would shortly be an article in the United States Constitution.

The Proclamation of Ratification of the Amendment by Secretary of State Fish met with an intensely partisan response. Republican newspapers praised the Amendment, but the bitter tone of the Democratic press was striking. The Cleveland *Plain Dealer* considered the Fifteenth Amendment a clear example of " might makes right," [83] because it had been adopted by fraud and intimidation in the South and by political trickery in the North. The Cincinnati *Enquirer* characterized the proclamation of its adoption as an " official lie indorsing a bastard as legitimate," [84] since it had been adopted by force and fraud.

Within a week of the proclamation, Negroes voted in elections in Cincinnati. There was no opposition to them, and they voted almost solidly Republican.[85] Their support was so overwhelming that the German voters became alarmed that Republicans might ignore German interests to curry favor with the Negro vote.[86] In both the short and the long run, Republicans and Negroes benefited from their partnership: Negroes were elected to the

Sess., p. 189; E. McPherson, p. 562. The Reform delegation from Cincinnati was composed of 5 former Republicans and 5 former Democrats. James H. Hambleton, a former Republican, voted with the Democrats to reject the Amendment.

[80] The Cincinnati *Commercial*, January 21, 22, 1870.

[81] James G. Wilson (ed.), *General Grant's Letters to a Friend, 1861–1880* (New York: T. Y. Crowell, 1897), p. 64.

[82] Schuyler Colfax, John Sherman, and other Republican members of Congress to Hayes, January 21, 1870, Hayes MSS.

[83] The Cleveland *Daily Plain Dealer*, March 31, 1870.

[84] The Cincinnati *Daily Enquirer*, April 1, 1870.

[85] Diary, April 4, 19, 1870, Hayes MSS; Hayes to Charles Nordhoff, April 5, 1870, *ibid.*; Hayes to William K. Rogers, April 6, 1870, *ibid.*; the Cincinnati *Daily Gazette*, March 31, 1870.

[86] Cincinnati *Volksblatt*, quoted in Mobile *Daily Register*, April 29, 1870.

legislature and Republican politicians got much-needed Negro votes.

The violent tone and reckless tactics of Ohio and Indiana Democrats contrasted sharply with the more moderate style of the middle Atlantic Democrats. On the other hand, the middle western states were similar but not identical in their partisan responses to ratification. In Illinois, for example, although the Negro suffrage issue divided the state along traditional north-versus-south lines, and caused dissension within Republican ranks as well, the Fifteenth Amendment did not provoke a legislative brawl, as it did in Indiana and Ohio. With overwhelming strength in the state legislature, adroit Republican leaders handled ratification expertly. First, surprise and speed shocked Democratic legislators and restricted debate; then firm parliamentary control demoralized opposition. The endorsement of ratification by President Grant and approaching adjournment paved the way for ratification. Despite downstate grumbling, Republican legislators supported it, with only one deserter.[87]

Different again was the reaction in Wisconsin, Minnesota, Iowa, Nebraska, Michigan, and Kansas, where the Fifteenth Amendment did not create much of a storm. The first four states already allowed the few Negroes living in their states to vote. Although radical Republicans in Wisconsin were restive over what they termed a half-way Amendment, and Democrats were in an obstructive mood, the ratification resolution was pushed through the Wisconsin legislature with telegraphic speed during early March, 1869.[88] In Minnesota ratification was an anticlimax, since Minnesotans had voted three times on Negro suffrage and only in the last election did it win. Republican support of the Fifteenth Amendment in January, 1870, made Minnesota Negroes loyal to the Republican party, which in turn rewarded its new supporters.[89] In Iowa ratification was a Republican formality during January, 1870.[90]

[87] Illinois, *Journal of the House of Representatives*, II, 741–42; E. McPherson, p. 490; Illinois, *Journal of the Senate*, 26th Sess. (1869), II, 262.

[88] Wisconsin, *Journal of the Assembly*, 21st Sess. (1869), pp. 689, 708–9; *Journal of the Senate*, 21st Sess. (1869), pp. 601–2.

[89] Minnesota, *Journal of the Senate*, 12th Sess. (1870), p. 9; *Journal of the House of Representatives*, 12th Sess. (1870), p. 27.

[90] Iowa, *Journal of the Senate*, 13th Sess. (1870), p. 45; *Journal of the House of Representatives*, 13th Sess. (1870), p. 128.

The problem with Nebraska was not whether she would ratify but when. The Nebraska legislature was scheduled to convene in January, 1871, yet by the fall of 1869 the chances of ratification by twenty-eight states seemed poor. Republican Governor David Butler was reluctant to call a special session and presidential pressure was required. On November 23, 1869, President Grant firmly suggested that Butler " consider the propriety of convening the legislature in extra session for this purpose, and if the proposition should meet with your views, I request that a proclamation be issued to that effect at as early a period as you may deem expedient." [91] Governor Butler followed orders from the General and a special session met on February 17, 1870. Within fifteen minutes ratification was secured.[92]

Both in Michigan and in Kansas, as elsewhere in the country, prejudice against Negroes remained strong. In Michigan, Negro suffrage had been postponed indefinitely or defeated repeatedly by conservative Republicans and Democrats. But the party call had been sounded, and Republican legislators fell into line, ratifying the Amendment in March, 1869.[93] Kansans also were unfriendly to Negroes, but on the question of ratification, party came first.[94] This avowal of party loyalty came at a high price for some Republicans whose political future in a state with a high proportion of Negroes was adversely affected. As in other states motivation appeared to be largely political, not humanitarian, in origin. Ratification was not popular but it was a party measure; its adoption was interpreted as a party victory.

In any event, the Middle West approved the Fifteenth Amendment. The Republican strongholds were stanch for ratification. New England had made her mark in the Western Reserve in Ohio, in northern Indiana, Illinois, and Michigan, and in Minnesota and Iowa. Adroit parliamentary and political maneuvers,

[91] Grant to Butler, November 23, 1869, Letterbook, Grant MSS, Library of Congress; John M. Mayer to Charles Sumner, October 13, 1869, Sumner MSS; David Butler to Sumner, October 30, 1869, *ibid.*
[92] Nebraska, *Journal of the House of Representatives*, Spec. Sess. (1870), p. 19; *Journal of the Senate*, Spec. Sess. (1870), p. 18.
[93] Michigan, *Journal of the Senate*, 1869 Sess., p. 739; *Journal of the House of Representatives*, 1869 Sess., pp. 1103–4.
[94] Kansas, *Journal of the House of Representatives*, 10th Sess., (1870), pp. 55–56; *Journal of the Senate*, 10th Sess. (1870), p. 95. Kansas had previously ratified the wrong version of the Amendment. See Kansas, *Journal of the House of Representatives*, 9th Sess. (1869), p. 914; *Journal of the Senate*, 9th Sess. (1869), p. 587.

particularly in Illinois and Wisconsin, yielded rich dividends. Generally, the states with the smallest number of Negroes were those most disposed to be broad in sympathy and liberal in outlook.

To sum up, where the Democrats were strong and where their kin were Southern, ratification temporarily hung fire. In close states where the Negro vote mattered, the fight was sustained and vicious. But it was a lost cause for caste was crumbling.

CHAPTER VIII

NEW ENGLAND ACCEPTANCE AND FAR WESTERN REJECTION

The pattern of ratification in New England, where there were few Negro inhabitants, posed different problems than in the middle Atlantic and older middle western states. Although every New England legislature approved the Amendment, the kind of support and opposition varied, depending on the relative strength and cohesion of each political party. In the one-party states of Maine and Vermont ratification was easy, but in the more competitive states of New Hampshire and Massachusetts, Democratic opposition was sharp. Ethnic cleavage deflected the course of ratification in heavily Republican Rhode Island. Yet ratification did not affect any of these states since all allowed the Negro to vote. State power thus determined Democratic loyalty, while fear paralyzed Republican action for a time in Rhode Island.

In Maine and Vermont ratification presented no difficulty. Completely dominated by Republicans, both states ratified without a fight. Generally, Democrats either supported ratification or were conspicuously absent. In the Maine House of Representatives, for example, Representative William Dickey, "the venerable Democratic warhorse,"[1] led his fellow Democrats to join the Republicans to make ratification unanimous in that chamber. In Vermont three Democrats joined Republicans to approve the Amendment, while half the Democratic Representatives were absent, and these defectors and dodgers were taken to task for their apostasy.[2] Party leadership then opposed the Amendment,

---

[1] Bangor *Daily Whig and Courier*, March 11, 1869; Maine, *Journal of the Senate*, 48th Sess. (1869), pp. 293, 324; *Journal of the House of Representatives*, 48th Sess. (1869), pp. 309, 326, 339; E. McPherson, p. 492.

[2] St. Johnsbury *Caledonian*, October 29, 1869; Vermont, *Journal of the House of Representatives*, Ann. Sess. (1869), pp. 48–49; *Journal of the Senate*, Ann. Sess. (1869), pp. 41–42; E. McPherson, pp. 560–61.

but fear of individual defeat in the next election was a more pressing consideration for Democrats in a Republican and abolitionist constituency. Vermont Democrats sacrificed national party for state party interests, thereby illustrating their political isolation. In both states there was little fuss over the Amendment, and its ratification provoked little comment in the press.

Unlike Maine and Vermont Republicans, those in Massachusetts and New Hampshire had to contend with fractious Democrats. Consideration of the Fifteenth Amendment generated partisan voting and sparked controversy. Long-winded speechmaking and hot partisan tempers erupted in New Hampshire. Some Democrats, sensing public opinion, advocated a referendum. Others preached prejudice and advocated postponement of ratification or outright rejection. Republicans joined battle.

Each party proved its discipline by strict party votes. Observing this partisan flavor, one New Hampshire newspaper characterized the vote on ratification as the only party vote of the session.[3] Democratic politicians apparently used the Fifteenth Amendment to gain publicity in a potentially competitive state. Whatever the motive, New Hampshire had the lowest percentage of affirmative votes for the Amendment in northern New England.

Though adoption was certain in Massachusetts, prejudice was still strong enough for Republicans there to dodge the Negro suffrage issue in 1868. They retained solid control of the General Court, and that fact decided ratification. Debate was brief, consideration swift, and voting followed strict party lines.[4] Massachusetts Democrats did not share the broader sympathies of the Maine Democracy, probably because they reflected strong anti-Negro feeling in their Boston Irish constituencies and retained some loyalty to national Democratic policy.

Public opinion concerning the Fifteenth Amendment naturally varied according to political persuasion and antislavery background, but in general, Massachusetts citizens seemed more preoccupied with liquor laws and railroad subsidies. Also, the Amend-

[3] *The Portsmouth Journal of Literature and Politics*, July 17, 1869; New Hampshire, *Journal of the House of Representatives*, June Sess. (1869), pp. 177–79; *Journal of the Senate*, June Sess. (1869), pp. 102–3; E. McPherson, pp. 494–95, 559.

[4] Massachusetts, *Journal of the Senate*, 1869 Sess., pp. 171–72; *Tribune Almanac for 1869*, p. 63; Massachusetts, *Journal of the House of Representatives*, 1869 Sess., pp. 224–27; E. McPherson, pp. 492–93.

ment was something of an anticlimax, for Massachusetts men had debated and settled Negro suffrage long before. Yet there were many editorials and much news about it. Of course general acceptance of the Amendment was not to be mistaken for enthusiasm about its limitations. One leading Republican journal measured the Fifteenth Amendment by the yardstick of the possible and by the intent of the framers: " It has been shorn of everything foreign to its original purpose, and will go before the state legislatures purely on the merits of Impartial Suffrage, and with the least possible risk of defeat." [5] Nevertheless, all the important Massachusetts reformers, including William Lloyd Garrison and Wendell Phillips, endorsed the Amendment and worked for its adoption.[6]

Stiffest opposition came from Democrats. Protest was emphatic and penetrating. The Boston *Morning Journal* observed significantly that the " rebel organs themselves do not object to this recommendation of the President's so much as some of our Northern Democratic sheets." [7] The Boston *Post* commented that from the beginning of congressional consideration, " it has been perfectly clear that this is a party measure, driven through Congress on the ruffianly plea of ' now or never,' and to be forced through the requisite numbers of legislatures with the whip and spur of party command." [8]

In fact, the Amendment changed nothing in Massachusetts, and ratification brought no trouble for Republican politicians. Despite some grumblings from more radical Republicans, the Republican legislators did their duty, and there was enough opposition from the Democrats to cause a strict party division.

Rhode Island agonizingly delayed ratification until 1870, because

[5] Boston *Daily Advertiser*, March 1, 1869.

[6] *Ibid.*; Garrison to John Oliver, April 18, 1870, copy, Carter G. Woodson Collection of Negro Papers, Library of Congress. Garrison regarded the Amendment as the " keystone of the arch of emancipation." The major abolitionist organizations, such as the New England Anti-Slavery Convention, the American Anti-Slavery Society, and the Pennsylvania Anti-Slavery Society, supported ratification and adopted Phillips' reasoning ([New York] *National Anti-Slavery Standard*, May 15, June 5, November 27, September 25, December 18, 1869). Phillips and veteran abolitionists clearly recognized that the northern Negro vote would prove highly beneficial to the Republican balance of power in the North (*Ibid.*, March 6, April 3, June 26, July 24, 1869).

[7] Boston *Morning Journal*, March 9, 1869.

[8] Boston *Post*, March 2, 1869.

Republicans were paralyzed by the Amendment. The brawl seems curious at first glance, because Negroes had been voting in Rhode Island since 1842, when they were rewarded for opposing the Dorr Rebellion. The controversy instead centered on Irish, not Negro, voters. Some Republicans were tricked into thinking that the word " race " in the Fifteenth Amendment could mean nativity and would invalidate state suffrage restrictions, which required naturalized citizens to own $134 worth of real estate. The practical effect of this qualification was to bar most naturalized citizens from suffrage who could not afford and, as aliens until 1868, were not allowed to buy property.[9] The Irish and other foreign-born residents who were pro-Democratic were successfully kept from influencing, or perhaps deciding, elections.[10] A desire to keep Rhode Island Republican was reinforced by the frantic need of old Yankee Protestants to keep " foreigners " in their place.

Though social tensions were high, all Republicans were not united about keeping the ethnic groups out of the State House and denying them influence within the Republican party. Apparently Governor Seth Padelford [11] and Congressman Thomas A. Jenckes [12] led one Republican faction favoring extension of the suffrage and endorsing ratification. United States senators Henry B. Anthony [13] and William Sprague,[14] along with Congressman Nathan F. Dixon,[15] wanted no liberalization of the suffrage and opposed ratification. Perhaps the personality clashes and power rivalries between these two factions cut more deeply than did ethnic jealousy.

The effort to achieve ratification was especially frustrating because no one seemed to know exactly what effect the Amendment would have on ethnic suffrage. Wendell Phillips spoke to Rhode

[9] *Woonsocket Patriot and Rhode Island State Register*, January 14, 1870.

[10] The Irish numbered 31,534 in a total foreign-born population of 55,396 in Rhode Island in 1870. The native population was 161,957, while the normal Republican majority was about 11,000. (Bureau of the Census, *Ninth Census*, I, 320, 336–42, 370.)

[11] Providence *Morning Herald*, May 28, 1869.

[12] J. R. Kimball to Thomas A. Jenckes, January 18, 1870, Thomas A. Jenckes MSS, Library of Congress.

[13] Providence *Morning Herald*, March 2, 1869; Providence *Evening Press*, January 18, 19, 1870.

[14] Providence *Daily Journal*, January 19, 1870. In the showdown of 1870 Sprague did not oppose the Amendment.

[15] Providence *Evening Press*, January 19, 1870.

Island legislators and unwisely asked them to act against their own interest. If by ratifying the Amendment the Irish could vote, Phillips said, so be it, but in the same breath he denied that the Amendment would invalidate state suffrage regulations, commenting that " Rhode Island hesitates to ratify on account of these four letters; r—a—c—e. She is being frightened with a shadow." [16] The Democrats shared Phillips' confusion, not being able to make up their minds whether to vote against the Amendment because it guaranteed Negro suffrage or to vote for it because it might give the Irish the vote.[17]

The upshot of this confusion was a stalemate. The Senate postponed consideration of the Amendment from the January session to the session of May 23, 1869,[18] during which the Senate ratified it by a party vote.[19] But the House of Representatives postponed consideration until 1870.[20] One reporter wrote that many Republicans were afraid of the Amendment, not because they liked the Negroes less, but because they feared the Irish more.[21] On the vote in the House of Representatives enough Republicans joined Democrats to defeat ratification. Republicans and Democrats voted on exactly opposite grounds: [22] Republicans voted against the Amendment because it would, Democrats because it would not, give the Irish the vote.

By January, 1870, the situation became critical. Failure of Rhode Island to ratify might jeopardize success. In a strong editorial the Providence *Evening Press* denounced the timid delay of ratification, which it termed stumbling over a shadow. Inaction had " contributed to the doubt and uncertainty hanging over the measure . . . the friends of the Amendment were discouraged and

[16] Providence *Morning Herald*, May 28, 1869.

[17] Providence *Evening Press*, January 18, 1870.

[18] Rhode Island, MS Journal of the Senate, 1868–71, XXVI, March 24, 1869, Rhode Island State Archives.

[19] *Ibid.*, May 27, 1869; E. McPherson, p. 497. The final vote was 23 ayes and 12 nays.

[20] Rhode Island, MS Journal of the House of Representatives, 1869–71, XIII (May Sess., 1869), 159–60, Rhode Island State Archives. The vote was 35 to 20. Of the 35 votes for postponement, 23 were cast by Republicans and the rest by Democrats. Only Republicans voted against postponement. (E. McPherson, p. 497.)

[21] Providence *Morning Herald*, May 28, 1869; *Harper's Weekly*, XIII (June 26, 1869), 403.

[22] Providence *Evening Press*, January 18, 1870.

its enemies elated." [23] The *Woonsocket Patriot* felt ultimate rejection of the Amendment would disgrace the good name of Rhode Island.[24] Governor Padelford, in his message to the legislature in 1870, gently but firmly exerted pressure:

A difference of opinion prevails, whether this Amendment may not materially affect certain rights in our own State Constitution. As the general government is embarrassed by the present situation of the question, and as the adoption of the article by the constitutional majority of the States will tend to be restoration of the Union of the States lately engaged in rebellion, I would earnestly recommend the early action of the General Assembly on this important question.[25]

The battle was not yet over, but last minute attempts to submit the Amendment to the voters of the state failed. Representative Lucius C. Ashley, leader of the ratification forces, answered objections that the Amendment would not allow naturalized citizens to vote by saying that if it did, then a literacy test would be imposed to keep ethnic groups from voting.[26] On January 18, 1870, the vote was taken and the Amendment approved, though four Republicans bolted the party to vote against it.[27] The crowd in the lobby stamped their feet furiously to hail what was interpreted as a personal victory for Thomas A. Jenckes.[28] The fight was furious, the outcome until the last minute, doubtful; but Rhode Island ratificationists triumphed in spite of partisan feuding, factional quarreling, constitutional confusion, and ethnic tensions. The New England pattern was ratification and Rhode Island followed it, for Republicanism was too strong and antislavery sentiment too entrenched.

On the Pacific coast the Chinese question dominated politics, and the Democrats linked the issue to the question of the rati-

[23] *Ibid.*, January 15, 1870.

[24] *Woonsocket Patriot and Rhode Island State Register*, January 14, 1870.

[25] Rhode Island, *Message of Seth Padelford, Governor of Rhode Island to the General Assembly its January Session, 1870* (Providence, R.I.: Providence Press Co., 1870), p. 15.

[26] Providence *Daily Journal*, January 19, 1870.

[27] Rhode Island, MS Journal of the House of Representatives (January Sess., 1870), p. 187; E. McPherson, p. 560. The final official vote was 57 to 9, but McPherson records the vote as 59 to 10. According to E. McPherson, 4 Democrats voted in favor of the Amendment, and this fact is omitted from the tally in Republican Congressional Committee, *Suffrage*, p. 3.

[28] Providence *Evening Press*, January 18, 1870; Kimball to Jenckes, January 18, 1870, Jenckes MSS.

fication of the Fifteenth Amendment. With other far western Democrats, Governor Henry Haight of California developed a bizarre theory that the federal Constitution did not really provide for its own amendment. For their part, Republicans in California, Oregon, and Nevada tried hard to dissociate the Chinese question from the Fifteenth Amendment. They opposed Chinese suffrage and citizenship, avoided the issue of Negro suffrage, and offered only grudging support of ratification. Underlying the debate on constitutional powers and the separationist strategy was an almost hysterical fear of the Chinese, a fear deftly manipulated by Democratic politicians.

These forces and their interplay found classic formulation during the 1869 campaign in California, where the Chinese question tyrannized over state politics for forty years after 1867. Population figures tell part of the tale: in the California of 1870 there were almost half a million whites and 49,310 Chinese, but only 4,272 Negroes.[29] For Democrats the Chinese issue was fertile campaign material, because Republicans had signed the Burlingame Treaty, which provided that Chinese could become legal residents of the United States. In addition, as the issues of the Civil War became increasingly irrelevant to far-off Californians, who were preoccupied with local questions even in presidential elections, the Democrats stood to gain further party advantages.

The campaign started at the Democratic state convention in June, 1869. Democrats asserted that the Fifteenth Amendment would enfranchise the Chinese, create a Chinese voting bloc controlled by the railroads, and eventually encourage greater Chinese immigration, which in turn would increase competition between whites and Chinese both on the job and at the polls. In short, they argued, a Negro-Chinese voting combination would degrade public life. Predictably, the Democratic platform appealed strongly to race prejudice.[30]

At their state convention Republicans tried as nearly as possible to downgrade the Negro issue and substitute instead Grant, Union, and Peace. In their platform they attempted to separate the Chinese question from the Fifteenth Amendment; to do otherwise would have been political suicide. Thus the convention strongly opposed

[29] Bureau of the Census, *Ninth Census*, I, 15.
[30] Winifield J. Davis, *History of Political Conventions in California, 1849–1892* (Sacramento, Cal.: California State Library, 1893), pp. 290–91.

Chinese suffrage and Chinese citizenship at the same time that it avoided taking a strong stand on Negro suffrage by denying the existence of any Negro issue: " the negro question has ceased to be an element in American politics," [31] Republicans declared with a mixture of sharp tactics and sincere wishful thinking. The platform then proceeded to urge ratification of the Fifteenth Amendment, quickly adding that all southerners should be pardoned and allowed to vote. Republicans found balancing state needs and national demands a tricky business.[32]

The campaign was wild. Democratic shouts of " nigger " vote and " pagan " hordes turned into a roar of bigotry. Democrats termed the Amendment the monster to be quelled lest the Chinese take over. General W. T. Wallace devoted half of one speech to the Amendment, accusing Republicans of deceit: " The State [Republican] Convention, though in favor of the Fifteenth Amendment, say they are opposed to Chinese suffrage; yet it is one and the same thing." [33] General Wallace also met head on the Republican argument that it did not matter how California voted on ratification since the Amendment would be ratified without California: " Believe it not; it is a snare. But if California and Oregon vote against it, they cannot count enough states to ratify it." [34] In general, Democrats hammered away at the theme that a vote for Republicans was a vote for ratification and Chinese suffrage.[35]

Republicans were not slow to attack Democratic tactics. The *Union* declared that it was now a contest between Republican principles and Democratic prejudices.[36] The *Mercury* condemned the Democrats: " The truth is all the talk about the fearful results of the adoption of the Fifteenth Amendment is a bugaboo to frighten ignorant voters into the Democratic ranks." [37] The Negro paper, *The Elevator*, charged that California Democrats had made " opposition to the Fifteenth Amendment the principal plank in its platform, or declaration of principles." [38] Democrats, declared

[31] *Ibid.*, pp. 293–94.
[32] Sacramento *Daily Union*, August 30, 1869.
[33] [San Francisco] *Daily Alta California*, August 31, 1869.
[34] *Ibid.*
[35] The San Francisco *Daily Herald*, August 30, September 1, 1869.
[36] Sacramento *Daily Union*, August 31, 1869.
[37] San Jose *Weekly Mercury*, August 12, 1869.
[38] [San Francisco] *The Elevator*, August 20, 1869.

The Elevator, were using the question of Chinese suffrage to defeat ratification of the Amendment and keep Democratic control of the legislature.

Meanwhile, most Republican papers tried to play down the Amendment as an issue. In San Francisco, where one-third of the Negro population was concentrated and where potential Negro voters could be important,[39] one paper stressed such local issues as city corruption, and others followed suit.[40] Republicans everywhere repeated that the Chinese question had nothing to do with ratification,[41] because the Chinese could not become citizens. There was also a definite effort to minimize the powers of the Amendment and to champion an education test.[42] These efforts became more frantic as election day approached, because some Republicans were frightened and others intimidated. But there were refreshing exceptions, such as the Vallejo *Advertiser*, which endorsed the Fifteenth Amendment because it recognized the mind, not the skin, of a man.[43]

After the feverish election campaign, which probably generated more violent anti-Negro rhetoric than anywhere else in the country, the Democrats captured control of the legislature with a landslide victory. The new legislature rejected the Fifteenth Amendment in January, 1870.[44]

Oregon was the only state in the Union not to take action on the Amendment before it was proclaimed in effect. Republicans in Oregon were conservative and did not campaign for it. Democrats, who were opposed to the Amendment, won control of the

[39] Bureau of the Census, *Ninth Census*, I, 15; Burnham, *Presidential Ballots*, p. 301. There were 1,330 Negroes in San Francisco county. In the 1868 Presidential election the Democratic ticket carried the county by 1,399 votes. But in 1872 the Republican ticket carried the county by a slim 714 votes. Assuming that one-seventh of the Negroes were eligible and voted Republican, a Negro vote of 200 would probably make an important contribution to the result.

[40] [San Francisco] *Daily Alta California*, September 1, 1869; Sacramento *Daily Union*, September 3, 1869.

[41] Sacramento *Daily Union*, August 31, 1869; San Jose *Weekly Mercury*, August 12, 1869.

[42] San Jose *Weekly Mercury*, August 12; Sacramento *Daily Union*, August 30, 31, 1869.

[43] Vallejo *Advertiser*, August 7, 1869, quoted in [San Francisco] *The Elevator*, August 13, 1869.

[44] California, *Journal of the Senate*, 18th Sess. (1869–70), p. 245; *Journal of the House of Assembly*, 18th Sess. (1869–70), pp. 295–96.

state and in a perverse gesture rejected it in October, 1870, six months after it had become part of the Constitution.[45]

Nevada was the only far western state to approve the Fifteenth Amendment. Ratification in March, 1869, was secured [46] shortly after a telegraphic dispatch notified the legislature of its passage; the speed and the advice to ratify quickly reflected pressure from Washington, particularly from Senator Stewart, who had composed and sent the telegram and made sure that the telegraph office in Carson City would stay open all night to receive and acknowledge it.[47] Senator Stewart sent another telegram informing the legislators that Grant was in earnest about securing ratification.[48] He also telegraphed Federal Judge A. W. Baldwin that the " word ' nativity ' was stricken from the original draft of the Constitutional Amendment so as to allow the exclusion of Chinese from its benefits." [49] Party pressure was applied in the legislature as well. One Republican assemblyman, Curt Hillyer, declared that " any Republican member that voted against it, should be put within the pale of the party." [50] He warned that the national Republican organization would forsake Nevada Republicans with a possible loss of federal patronage unless Republicans ratified the Fifteenth Amendment.[51]

Counterpressure from constitutents was tremendous, since anti-Chinese feeling,[52] Democratic strength, and reaction to party pressure were gaining momentum. One Republican assemblyman, for example, protested that Congress had no right to " boss Nevada around." [53] Another irate Republican legislator vowed that even if he was thrown out of the Republican party he would still vote against ratification.[54] Though it was widely predicted that Nevada

---

[45] Oregon, *Journal of the Senate*, 6th Sess. (1870), p. 655; *Journal of the House of Representatives*, 6th Sess. (1870), p. 512.

[46] Nevada, *Journal of the Senate*, 4th Sess. (1869), p. 251; *Journal of the Assembly*, 4th Sess. (1869), pp. 243–44.

[47] Brown, *Reminiscences*, pp. 237–38.

[48] [San Francisco] *Daily Alta California*, March 2, 1869.

[49] The Chico *Courant*, March 19, 1869; Carson City *Daily Appeal*, March 3, 1869. The telegram was sent on March 1, 1869, and was published in the Virginia City *Enterprise*, date unknown.

[50] Carson City *Daily Appeal*, February 28, 1869.

[51] [San Francisco] *Daily Alta California*, March 2, 1869.

[52] *Ibid.*, February 28, March 2, 1869; the San Francisco *Daily Herald*, February 27, 1869; Sacramento *Daily Union*, March 2, 1869.

[53] Carson City *Daily Appeal*, March 3, 1869.

[54] *Ibid.*

would not ratify,[55] she paid in full her debt to the Republican party for securing her statehood.[56] Since, like most states of the Union, Nevada was pro-Republican but not pro-Negro,[57] her ratification combined good luck, excellent timing, and shrewd politics.

Except for Nevada, the far western states resembled the border state pattern of rejection in both strategy and tone, but with a distinctive Chinese flavor. Violence and the exploitation of the Negro and ratification issues to win votes was characteristic in the operations of both sections, and in both, Republicans were clearly intimidated and on the defensive.

New England acceptance and Pacific coast rejection represent the extreme positions in the northern fight for ratification.

---

[55] The San Francisco *Daily Herald*, February 27, 1869. Newspapers throughout the nation predicted rejection.

[56] William Hanchett, "Yankee Law and the Negro in Nevada, 1861–1869," *Western Humanities Review*, X (Summer, 1956), 241–49.

[57] *Ibid.*

CHAPTER IX

WHIRLWIND OF CAUTION

Though the ratification fight consumed only thirteen months, it was hard and the outcome uncertain. Ratification was easy in safe Republican territory (the South, New England, and in most of the Middle West), but the fight was tougher in the middle Atlantic states and in Indiana and Ohio. In Democratic border states and on the Pacific coast, Republicans were paralyzed and did not work hard for ratification.

In clearcut conflicts of interest between state and national Republican party organizations, the national party was everywhere victorious despite the political risks. Mutinies in Rhode Island and Georgia were suppressed. Republicans were in power in Washington and had rich patronage to offer. The national administration, led by President Grant, could and did exert influence. But Republican politicians who held—or who aspired to hold—national office really spurred the ratification drive. The persistence and resourcefulness of Senator Oliver P. Morton, who influenced Indiana ratification and helped secure it for Texas, Mississippi, Virginia, and Georgia, proved as indispensable as Grant's inaugural endorsement. Grant himself maneuvered to win Nebraska to the cause; Senator Stewart fought with characteristic single-mindedness in Nevada, as did Governor Rutherford B. Hayes and Chief Justice Salmon P. Chase in Ohio, and Congressman Thomas A. Jenckes in Rhode Island. To these and other Republicans the future benefits of the northern Negro vote were worth fighting for, despite widespread opposition among Republicans in the North and white Americans generally. The Amendment received substantial support from veteran abolitionists like Wendell Phillips, old antislavery men like Salmon P. Chase, and Negro reformers like Frederick Douglass. Support was strongest from traditional antislavery strongholds, such as northeastern Connecti-

159

cut and the Western Reserve of Ohio, where Negroes formed only a small percentage of the population. Though moral and emotional forces were important in these regions, by themselves the antislavery sections could not have secured ratification. The Fifteenth Amendment was ratified because in such closely divided states as Connecticut, Indiana, Ohio, and Pennsylvania it made political sense to shrewd politicians who would benefit from the Negro vote.

If the Fifteenth Amendment divided Republicans during the fight for passage in Congress and then united them during the ratification fight, the opposite pattern plagued Democrats. Tension between the northern and southern wings of the Democratic party was evident when Indiana Democrats bolted the legislature to prevent ratification, while southern Democrats wooed Negro voters. Since only on the Pacific coast and in the border states did Democrats substantially benefit from disfranchising or denouncing the Negro, they opposed ratification. Elsewhere, and particularly in the middle Atlantic states, they were torn between traditional policies and inevitable realities. If it was risky to accept the Amendment and bid openly for Negro votes, it was too dangerous to yell "nigger" and alienate Negroes forever. Where their party could make a respectable stand, Democrats fought; otherwise they capitulated, as in Virginia and Vermont, Mississippi and Maine. Significantly, Democratic temper and tone varied from a shriek in California and Kentucky, through shrill tones and rash tactics in Ohio and Indiana, to moderate talk and flexible consideration in New Jersey and New York. The Chinese scare and white supremacy accounted for the mood in the Pacific and border states, while southern ethnic influences determined temper along the Ohio River. The compromising position in the middle Atlantic states indicated a willingness and ability to undertake a new departure to recruit Negro voters once they started voting.

The alternate bullying and wooing of the Negro voter by Democrats suggested both shrewd maneuvering and acute schizophrenia. The need for power was strong, but so too was the compulsion of prejudice. Doubtless many Democrats were sincere; state rights did matter to them. But they lacked the needed wit and will to play the difficult role of a responsible and responsive party of the opposition. Democrats had been so long out of power that they seemed to cultivate political bankruptcy. Their conduct of the presidential campaign of 1868 was duplicated in the ratification fight of 1869: they fled to a past of sterile slogans, inert ideas, and constitutional ghosts. In effect, Democrats repudiated Negro suffrage, the fundamental condition of Reconstruction. They became rigid, inflexible, and politically inept—incapable of moving out of their traditional ruts. The Democracy never fashioned a suitable alternative to the Fifteenth Amendment, such as support for qualified Negro suffrage by state action alone; instead, Democrats lost their heads. Their record on the Fifteenth Amendment and their platform of 1868 together brought the war issues to the surface and generated a solid Republican and stanchly Unionist response. Retention of the strong cohesive power of a Reconstruction issue was just what Republicans needed. The Democrats provided Republicans with suitable occasion to unfurl the bloody shirt and helped to relegate the potentially powerful party of 1868 to a demoralized and divided minority in 1872.

If Democrats expressed unfounded fears, other Americans entertained false hopes when the Fifteenth Amendment was adopted. President Grant, for one, told Congress upon proclamation of ratification that the Amendment " completes the greatest civil change and constitutes the most important event that has occurred since the nation came into life." [1] Such a sweeping statement was echoed by a New York *Times* editor, who wrote that " the final crowning of the edifice of American republicanism " [2] was at hand because the Amendment " italicizes every word of the Declaration of Independence, and harmonizes our Constitution with the highest civilization to which we may aspire." [3] Abolition-

[1] Richardson, *A Compilation of the Messages and Papers of the Presidents*, VII, 55–56. Secretary of State Hamilton Fish, who was away from Washington, was told by telegram to cut short his absence and return immediately to the capital on March 29 to prepare an official proclamation of ratification (J. C. B. Davis to Fish, March 28, 29, 1870, Fish MSS). On March 30 Fish was notified to issue the proclamation, because the bill for the admission of Texas as a state had been received and signed by President Grant (O. E. Babcock to Fish, March 30, 1870, *ibid.*). Apparently Republican Congressman George F. Hoar of Massachusetts persuaded the President to prepare a special message to impress upon the country the " grandeur of the great victory " (*The New York Freeman*, August 29, 1885). President Grant wrote the original lead-pencil draft, which included mention of Negro officeholding—" having the right to vote and be voted "—but this was later deleted. Secretary of the Navy George M. Robeson and Attorney General E. Rockwood Hoar made some changes in the message, and then it was copied. (Fish Diary, entries for February 4, March 1, 7, 15, 30, 1870, Fish MSS.)
[2] The New York *Times*, March 31, 1870.
[3] *Ibid.*

ist rhetoric duplicated these starry-eyed and sentimental pronounce-
ments. And great celebrations matched strong words when one
hundred guns fired their salute in Washington, while ten thousand
Negroes, representing regiments, drum corps, fraternal clubs,
secret lodges, and trade unions, marched through the streets of
Baltimore. Flags and bunting were displayed in Philadelphia,
where Negro women wore shawls of red, white, and blue. Monster
rallies were held, fireworks were ignited, and spread-eagle speeches
poured forth.[4] Victory prevailed.

The war for Negro rights appeared to be won by placing the
keystone of Reconstruction—the Fifteenth Amendment—into position. With the job apparently done, demobilization of the troops
proceeded efficiently, as antislavery societies disbanded and their
newspapers either ceased publication or dropped the words " anti-
slavery " from their mastheads. The war appeared over; the
crusade was finished. Effort thus slackened and interest began
to fade. Regarding the ballot as a panacea, whites could in good
conscience leave Negroes alone now, because Negroes could
protect themselves with the ballot and without the help of government. In short, the celebration of the adoption of the Amendment
underscored the option of whites to be indifferent rather than
to help Negroes to help themselves or to lobby for a civil rights
commissioner to undertake needed responsibilities, create new
agencies, and fashion bold programs. In other words, instead of
thinking about what was needed in the future, there was self-
congratulation about the past. What was indeed a modest beginning struck most Americans as a spectacular ending. The
widespread assumption that the Amendment was self-executing
and thus bound to succeed paved the way for nullification or at
least apathy. The ballot was but a tool; upon its use would depend
its real value. Federal enforcement could make or break the tool;
individual handling and electoral competition would determine
its use.

Soon the unreasonable hopes were dashed by the bleak realities,
but the response was as negative as the political reaction. Whites
seemed no longer to care and now turned their backs on the Fifteenth Amendment as well as on the Negro. Hamilton Fish wrote
in his diary in 1877 that Grant " says he is opposed to the XV
amendment and thinks it was a mistake; that it had done the

[4] [Washington, D. C.] New Era, April 7, 28, 1870.

negro no good, and had been a hindrance to the South, and by no means a political advantage to the North." [5] There were others who echoed such sentiments, which only seemed to prove that the earlier celebration of ratification was as unwarranted as the subsequent denigration of the Amendment. Illusion had soured to disenchantment.

Shrewd Republican politicians, however, entertained no illusions about the Fifteenth Amendment. After all, it was their pessimism about the reliability of the Negro vote in the South and their doubt about the viability of Reconstruction there that had motivated in part the adoption of the Amendment. During the ratification fight William E. Chandler trenchantly observed, " We are bound to be overwhelmed by the new rebel combinations in every southern state. With the New York *Tribune* championing Universal Amnesty and all the Chase men and disaffected soreheaded Republicans reechoing the cry, the negroes deceived, coaxed or bullied and the rebels a solid phalanx in the combination there can be but one result." [6] His prediction proved correct. Overwhelming opposition to Negro suffrage resulted in nullification of the Fifteenth Amendment in the southern and border states. The Amendment became a dead letter everywhere that fraud, bribery, violence, intimidation, difficult registration, literacy tests, read-and-understand tests, poll taxes, grandfather clauses, and white primaries were condoned by public opinion. But if Negro suffrage, the fundamental condition of Reconstruction, was short-lived in the South, it became permanent in the North.

Most constitutional historians have argued that the Fifteenth Amendment failed. It did not guarantee southern Negro voting and, in the former Confederate states, became ineffectual through successful evasion. But it is not altogether fair to condemn the Amendment because of the weakness with which it was enforced. If Presidents, in effect, ignored or repudiated the Amendment after 1874, if Congress failed to provide enough troops, marshals, and money to enforce it,[7] if the Republican party, upon which

[5] Diary, January 17, 1877, Fish MSS. See two brilliantly suggestive essays by C. Vann Woodward, in *The Burden of Southern History* (New York: Vintage Books, 1961), pp. 69–107.

[6] Chandler to Benjamin F. Butler, August 10, 1869, Butler MSS.

[7] See the excellent article by Everette Swinney, " Enforcing the Fifteenth Amendment, 1870–1877," *Journal of Southern History*, XXVIII (May, 1962), 202–18. Swinney has challenged the traditional view that the Enforcement acts were unsound,

the success of enforcement rested, did not retain control of both houses of Congress and the Presidency from 1875 to 1889, if the courts declared unconstitutional provisions of the Enforcement Act of May 31, 1870, and if the people lost interest in free and fair voting, then it was no wonder that the Amendment failed to safeguard Negro voting in the South. The Amendment became what Americans by their habits, values, and practices wanted it to be. However, it did succeed in its primary objective: to enfranchise the northern Negro. "The effect of the amendment," wrote its father, William Stewart, "has been what I supposed it would be, to secure for the negro in the Northern States his right to vote without interruption."[8]

But Senator Stewart did not live to see how northern Negro voters would exert their power in national politics, and how they and others would intensify pressures on Presidents, congressmen, and judges to induce white southerners to allow Negro southerners to vote. When survival of southern politicians came to depend on the good will of Negro voters, then the days of racist appeal were numbered. Implicit, then, in the Fifteenth Amendment is both the source and the vision of political equality—deduced by generally twentieth-century justices in their decisions and expressed by Negro Americans casting their ballots at the polls. The source and the vision were to outlive evasion and to triumph in both constitutional theory and election-day practice. Thus the Fifteenth Amendment was to prove in its own way both bold and prudent: bold in enfranchising Negroes despite opposition and in ordering change by establishing constitutional guide-lines; prudent, as well, in adapting ethics to circumstances so that the Amendment would not only pass Congress and be ratified by the states but would also be enforced and interpreted by men judging the times on their own terms. In other words, the Fifteenth Amendment was to be as capable of growth as the capacity of Americans to mature.

During the nineteenth century the practical effect of the Amend-

---

inefficient, unconstitutional, and iniquitous. He marshals evidence to show that, although initially successful, the Enforcement acts failed after 1874 because the Grant administration lacked political power, adequate authority, and popular support. The Enforcement acts, moreover, were not enforced because of the difficulty of obtaining evidence and securing juries, the lack of co-operation of state and local officials, the shortages of troops, money, and officials, and adverse court decisions.

[8] Brown, *Reminiscences*, p. 236.

ment was to bring the ballot to the Northern Negro and power to the Republicans. The Negro was started along the road to first-class citizenship. He could vote in the North, and the Republicans benefited from a solid Negro vote in the close elections of the 1870's and 1880's. The significance of the Amendment was roughly distilled by the Negro preacher from Pittsburgh, Reverend Peck, who observed that " the Republican Party had done the Negro good but they were doing themselves good at the same time." [9] Partisan but enlightened self-interest was the motive of most Republican politicians, and mutual interest was to develop as a result. The Fifteenth Amendment was thus a shot-gun marriage of practical idealism to political realism.

In short, the politics of the Fifteenth Amendment represented the needs of the Republican party. The primary object of the Amendment was to get the Negro vote in the North, not, as other writers have insisted, to keep Negro suffrage in the South, which was a secondary objective. The Amendment was not radical in design, intent, or result. Instead, it was a moderate, modest, and statesmanlike measure, framed, championed, and secured by generally Republican moderates. The designs of both white supremicists and professional reformers were rejected by men who instinctively knew that fundamental reform was too important to be left to the hallowed bias of the reactionaries and the noble sentiments of the reformers. The extremism of those who wanted to do nothing and the radicalism of those who wanted to do everything were rejected. A pragmatic and *ad hoc* spirit dominated the framing and passage, and the irresistible pressure of political, organizational needs, rather than the remnant of the organized abolitionist movement, secured difficult ratification. Conceived in realism, born in compromise, and raised by partisanship, the Fifteenth Amendment represented a fusion of power and justice.

[9] See Chap. VI, n. 33.

BIBLIOGRAPHY

The largest and most valuable source I tapped was 172 newspapers from 36 states. No other source conveyed the importance and the tone of the issues growing out of the Fifteenth Amendment. In particular, the editorials of the New York *Times*, which reflected the moderate Republican position, were invaluable, as were those of the New York *World*, which vigorously expressed the peculiar opposition of the Democrats. The most persistent fighter, with many of the most radical editorials, was the veteran reformist *Anti-Slavery Standard*, also of New York. In many respects the most interesting confrontation between the moderate and more radical Republican press occurred in California. Newspapers, however, were not only important for opinion but indispensable for news. The major newspaper collection I used was at the Library of Congress. My experience convinces me that libraries everywhere should take greater care of their priceless newspaper collections.

My greatest disappointment was the relative lack of important material to be gleaned from manuscripts, especially concerning passage of the Fifteenth Amendment. Research in manuscripts was undertaken in Massachusetts, Connecticut, New York, New Jersey, Pennsylvania, Ohio, Wisconsin, Oregon, California, Louisiana, Tennessee, and the District of Columbia at 26 libraries. I consulted fruitlessly 165 collections, took notes from an additional 87. I received photo and hand-copied material from other libraries, and received reports from archivists, librarians, and historians in 40 states. The papers of Senator William M. Stewart of Nevada, before 1875 for example, went up in flames in the Virginia City fire of 1875. The papers of critically important members of Congress, such as George S. Boutwell, John A. Bingham, James C. Blaine, Roscoe Conkling, John A. Logan, Oliver P. Morton, Samuel J. Randall, and Henry Wilson, are infinitesimal in size for the period of the passage and ratification of the Fifteenth Amendment. The large manuscript collection of Benjamin F. Butler proved by examination to be as unrewarding as were the voluminous letters of Charles Sumner. The letters of Presidents Johnson and Grant also proved of little value. Access to the papers of William D. Kelley was not granted. In general, letters did not refer to the framing of the Amendment because congressmen had been preoccupied with the new Grant administration which was shortly to take

166

office, and the related matters of appointments, programs, and congressional organization.

The most significant collections I examined were the letters of Chief Justice Salmon P. Chase of Ohio (Library of Congress and the Historical Society of Pennsylvania), the manuscripts of Governor Rutherford B. Hayes of Ohio (Hayes Library, Fremont, Ohio), the Hamilton Fish manuscripts (Library of Congress), the papers of Senator Waitman T. Willey of West Virginia (West Virginia University Library), those of Representative Thomas A. Jenckes of Rhode Island (Library of Congress), the correspondence in the William E. Chandler collection (Library of Congress), and minutes of the Executive Board of the Pennsylvania State Equal Rights League (part of the Leon Gardiner Collection on Negro History at the Historical Society of Pennsylvania).

Federal and state documents were indispensable; generally, copies existed at the Library of Congress. On the whole, archival materials were disappointing. Indispensable aids to research on voting were the almanacs and federal documents, especially the published census reports. Except for the voluminous *Congressional Globe*, a scanty record of debate in the Louisiana House of Representatives, the excellent and extensive Pennsylvania *Legislative Record*, and the Indiana *Brevier Legislative Reports*, there were no official state records of legislative debate, though the various official journals give meager voting records. However, various newspapers in the state capitals were extremely helpful in recording or summarizing debate of individual legislators.

There are few references to the Fifteenth Amendment in published recollections, and fewer that are valuable. The retrospective remarks by James G. Blaine of Maine, George S. Boutwell of Massachusetts, and William M. Stewart of Nevada are useful.

The secondary sources were rather uneven for my purpose. I did not find the general histories of Rhodes and Oberholtzer very rewarding. There are the interesting but extremely brief accounts of the passage of the Amendment by John M. Mathews and by A. C. Braxton. There were more helpful accounts in the story of state ratification: an interesting, almost contemporaneous, but brief account on Georgia by I. W. Avery; more recent but uneven dissertations by John W. Huston on Pennsylvania, and by Sylvia Cohn on New York and Ohio, and an older legalistic but interesting article on Indiana by William C. Gerichs. James McPherson and Everette Swinney have expertly told the stories of abolitionist advocacy during the 1860's and enforcement efforts during the 1870's. Leslie H. Fishel has studied northern Negroes and politics between 1865 and 1900 in his Harvard dissertation and in two articles. Also valuable were William Hanchett's perceptive short article on Nevada Negroes, John A. Munroe's fine but brief account of Delaware Negroes, and a thorough history on Indiana Negroes by Emma L. Thornbrough. A general monograph, which sheds some light on the importance of the northern Negro vote, is an older Princeton politics dissertation by Robert A. Horn. Political monographs and articles on states outside the South during the period of Reconstruction generally were sparse, but one outstanding exception was a Columbia dissertation on Connecticut politics by William J. Niven, Jr. An excellent general bibliography concerning Reconstruction America can be found in J. G. Randall and David Donald, *The Civil War and Reconstruction* (2nd ed.). Finally, I have been influenced by the re-thinking on Reconstruction by such scholars as David Donald, C. Vann Woodward, and Eric McKitrick.

COLLECTIONS OF LETTERS AND MANUSCRIPTS

Samuel J. Bayard MSS, Princeton University Library.
Benjamin F. Butler MSS, Library of Congress.
William E. Chandler MSS, Library of Congress.
Salmon P. Chase MSS, Historical and Philosophical Society of Ohio, Historical Society of Pennsylvania, and Library of Congress.
William P. Fessenden MSS, Library of Congress.
Hamilton Fish MSS, Library of Congress.
Leon Gardiner Collection of Negro History, Historical Society of Pennsylvania.
James A. Garfield MSS, Library of Congress.
Jesod R. Grant MSS, New York Historical Society.
Ulysses S. Grant MSS, Library of Congress.
Rutherford B. Hayes MSS, The Rutherford B. Hayes Library, Fremont, Ohio.
Robert G. Ingersoll MSS, Library of Congress.
Thomas A. Jenckes MSS, Library of Congress.
Andrew Johnson MSS, Library of Congress.
George W. Julian MSS, Library of Congress.
John Sherman MSS, Library of Congress.
Thaddeus Stevens MSS, Library of Congress.
Charles Sumner MSS, Houghton Library, Harvard College.
Samuel J. Tilden MSS, New York Public Library, Main Branch.
Benjamin F. Wade MSS, Library of Congress.
Gideon Welles MSS, Henry E. Huntington Library, San Marino, California.
Waitman T. Willey MSS, West Virginia University Library.
Carter G. Woodson Collection of Negro Papers, Library of Congress.

PRINTED SOURCE COLLECTIONS, OFFICIAL DOCUMENTS, AND MISCELLANEOUS

American Annual Cyclopaedia and Register of Important Events of the Year 1864, and succeeding volumes from 1865 to 1872. New York: D. Appleton and Co., 1865–73.
BURNHAM, W. DEAN. *Presidential Ballots, 1836–1892.* Baltimore: The Johns Hopkins Press, 1955.
Commonwealth of Kentucky. *Journal of the House of Representatives,* Adj. Sess. Frankfort, Ky., 1869.
———. *Journal of the Senate,* Adj. Sess., 1869. Frankfort, Ky., 1869.

Commonwealth of Massachusetts. *Journal of the House of Representatives*, 1869 Sess. Boston, 1869.

———. *Journal of the Senate*, 1869 Sess. Boston, 1869.

Commonwealth of Pennsylvania. *Journal of the House of Representatives*, 93rd Sess., 1869. Harrisburg, Pa., 1869.

———. *Journal of the Senate*, 93rd Sess., 1869. Harrisburg, Pa., 1869.

———. *The Legislative Record*, 93rd Sess., 1869. Harrisburg, Pa., 1869.

Commonwealth of Virginia. *Journal of the House of Delegates*, Reg. Sess., 1869. Richmond, Va., 1869.

———. *Journal of the Senate of Virginia*, Reg. Sess., 1869. Richmond, Va., 1869.

Democratic Party National Convention. *Official Proceedings of the National Democratic Convention, Held at New York, July 4–9, 1868* (reported by George Wakeman, Official Reporter of the Convention). Boston, 1868.

HEWES, FLETCHER W. *Citizen's Atlas of American Politics, 1789–1888, a Series of Colored Maps and Charts*. New York: Charles Scribner's Sons, 1888.

LORD, CLIFFORD L., and ELIZABETH H. LORD. *Historical Atlas of the United States*. New York: H. Holt, 1944.

MCPHERSON, EDWARD. *The Political History of the United States of America during the Period of Reconstruction*. Washington: Philp & Solomons, 1871.

Republican Congressional Committee. *Suffrage and Civil Rights—The Record of the Democracy on the Fifteenth Amendment*. Washington, D. C., 1872.

Republican Party National Convention. *Proceedings of the National Union Republican Convention, 1868* (reported by Ely, Burnham, and Bartlett). Chicago, Ill., 1868.

RICHARDSON, JAMES D. (ed.). *A Compilation of the Messages and Papers of the Presidents, 1789–1897*. 10 vols. Washington: Bureau of National Literature and Art, 1896–99.

State of Alabama. *Journal of the House of Representatives*, 1869–70 Sess. Montgomery, Ala., 1870.

———. *Journal of the Senate*, 1869–70 Sess. Montgomery, Ala., 1870.

State of Arkansas. *Journal of the House of Representatives*, 17th Sess. Little Rock, Ark., 1870.

———. *Journal of the Senate*, 17th Sess. Little Rock, Ark., 1869.

State of California. *Journal of the House of Assembly*, 18th Sess., 1869–70. Sacramento, Cal., 1870.

———. *Journal of the Senate*, 18th Sess., 1869–70. Sacramento, Cal., 1870.

State of Connecticut. *Journal of the House of Representatives*, May Sess., 1869. Hartford, Conn., 1869.

———. *Journal of the Senate*, May Sess., 1869. Hartford, Conn., 1869.

———. *Journal of the Senate*, May Sess., 1870. New Haven, Conn., 1870.

State of Delaware. *Journal of the House of Representatives*, 1869 Sess. Dover, Del., 1869.

———. *Journal of the Senate*, 1869 Sess. Dover, Del., 1869.

State of Florida. *Journal of the Assembly*, Ext. Sess., June, 1869. Tallahassee, Fla., 1869.

———. *Journal of the Senate*, Ext. Sess., June, 1869. Tallahassee, Fla., 1869.

State of Georgia. *Journal of the House of Representatives*, Ann. Sess., 1869. Atlanta, Ga., 1869.

———. *Journal of the House of Representatives*, Ann. Sess., January, 1870. Atlanta, Ga., 1870.

———. *Journal of the Senate*, Ann. Sess., 1869. Atlanta, Ga., 1869.

———. *Journal of the Senate*, Ann. Sess., Jan., 1870. 3 vols. Atlanta, Ga., 1870.

State of Illinois. *Journal of the House of Representatives*, 26th Sess., 1869. 2 vols. Springfield, Ill., 1869.

————. *Journal of the Senate*, 26th Sess., 1869, 2 vols. Springfield, Ill., 1869.

State of Indiana. *Brevier Legislative Reports: Embracing Short-Hand Sketches of the Journals and Debates of the General Assembly*, 46th Sess., 1869. Indianapolis, Ind., 1869.

————. *Brevier Legislative Reports: Embracing Short Hand Sketches of the Journals and Debates of the General Assembly*, Spec. Sess., 1869. Indianapolis, Ind., 1869.

————. *Journal of the House of Representatives*, 46th Sess., 1869. Indianapolis, Ind., 1869.

————. *Journal of the House of Representatives*, Spec. Sess., 1869. Indianapolis, Ind., 1869.

————. *Journal of the Senate*, 46th Sess., 1869. Indianapolis, Ind., 1869.

————. *Journal of the Senate*, Spec. Sess., 1869. Indianapolis, Ind., 1869.

State of Iowa. *Journal of the House of Representatives*, 13th Sess., 1870. Des Moines, Iowa, 1870.

————. *Journal of the Senate*, 13th Sess., 1870. Des Moines, Iowa, 1870.

State of Kansas. *Journal of the House of Representatives*, 9th Sess., 1869. Topeka, Kan., 1870.

————. *Journal of the House of Representatives*, 10th Sess., 1870. Topeka, Kan., 1870.

————. *Journal of the Senate*, 9th Sess., 1869. Topeka, Kan., 1870.

————. *Journal of the Senate*, 10th Sess., 1870. Topeka, Kan., 1870.

State of Louisiana. *Debates of the House of Representatives*, 1869 Sess. New Orleans, La., 1869.

————. *Journal of the House of Representatives*, 1869 Sess. New Orleans, La., 1869.

————. *Journal of the Senate*, 1869 Sess. New Orleans, La., 1869.

State of Maine. *Journal of the House of Representatives*, 48th Sess., 1869. Augusta, Me., 1869.

————. *Journal of the Senate*, 48th Sess., 1869. Augusta, Me., 1869.

State of Maryland. *Journal of the House of Delegates*, 1870 Sess. Annapolis, Md., 1870.

————. *Journal of the Senate*, 1870 Sess. Annapolis, Md., 1870.

State of Michigan. *Journal of the House of Representatives*, 1869 Sess., 3 vols. Lansing, Mich., 1869.

————. *Journal of the Senate*, 1869 Sess., 2 vols. Lansing, Mich., 1869.

State of Minnesota. *Journal of the House of Representatives*, 12th Sess., 1870. St. Paul, Minn., 1870.

————. *Journal of the Senate*, 12th Sess., 1870. St. Paul, Minn., 1870.

State of Mississippi. *Journal of the House of Representatives*, Reg Sess., 1870. Jackson, Miss., 1870.

————. *Journal of the Senate*, Reg. Sess., 1870. Jackson, Miss., 1870.

State of Missouri. *Journal of the House of Representatives*, 25th Sess., 1869. Jefferson City, Mo., 1869.

————. *Journal of the Senate*, 25th Sess., 1869. Jefferson City, Mo., 1869.

————. *Journal of the Senate*, 25th Adj. Sess., 1870. Jefferson City, Mo., 1870.

State of Nebraska. *Journal of the House of Representatives*, Spec. Sess., 1870. Omaha, Nebr., 1870.

————. *Journal of the Senate*, Spec. Sess., 1870. Omaha, Nebr., 1870.

State of Nevada. *Journal of the Assembly*, 4th Sess., 1869. Carson City, Nev., 1869.

————. *Journal of the Senate*, 4th Sess., 1869. Carson City, Nev., 1869.

State of New Hampshire. *Journal of the House of Representatives*, June Sess., 1869. Manchester, N. H., 1869.

————. *Journal of the Senate*, June Sess., 1869. Manchester, N. H., 1869.

State of New Jersey. *Documents*, 93rd Sess., 1869. Hudson City, N. J., 1869.

————. *Documents*, 94th Sess., 1870. Hoboken, N. J., 1870.

————. *Documents*, 95th Sess., 1871. Jersey City, N. J., 1871.

————. *Minutes of the General Assembly*, 94th Sess., 1870. Freehold, N. J., 1870.

————. *Journal of the Senate*, 94th Sess., 1870. Newton, N. J., 1870.

State of New York. *Journal of the Assembly*, 92nd Sess., 1869. Albany, N. Y., 1869.

————. *Journal of the Assembly*, 93rd Sess., 1870. Albany, N. Y., 1870.

————. *Journal of the Senate*, 92nd Sess., 1869. Albany, N. Y., 1869.

————. *Journal of the Senate*, 93rd Sess., 1870. Albany, N. Y., 1870.

State of North Carolina. *Journal of the House of Representatives,* 1868–69 Sess. Raleigh, N. C., 1869.

————. *Journal of the Senate*, 1868–69 Sess. Raleigh, N. C., 1869.

State of Ohio. *Journal of the Senate*, 58th General Assembly, Adj. Sess., 1868–69. Columbus, Ohio, 1869.

————. *Journal of the Senate*, 59th General Assembly, 1870 Sess. Columbus, Ohio, 1870.

————. *Journal of the House of Representatives*, 58th General Assembly, Adj. Sess., 1868–69. Columbus, Ohio, 1869.

————. *Journal of the House of Representatives*, 59th General Assembly, 1870 Sess. Columbus, Ohio, 1870.

State of Oregon. *Journal of the House of Representatives*, 6th Sess., 1870. Salem, Ore., 1870.

————. *Journal of the Senate*, 6th Sess., 1870. Salem, Ore., 1870.

State of Rhode Island and Providence Plantations. MS Journal of the House of Representatives, 1869–71, XXII. Rhode Island State Archives.

————. MS Journal of the Senate, 1868–71, XXVI. Rhode Island State Archives.

————. *Message of Seth Padelford, Governor of Rhode Island to the General Assembly at its January Session, 1870.* Providence, R. I., 1870.

State of South Carolina. *Journal of the House of Representatives*, 1868 Sess. Columbia, S. C., 1868.

————. *Journal of the Senate*, 1868 Sess. Columbia, S. C., 1868.

State of Tennessee. *Journal of the House of Representatives*. 2 vols. 36th General Assembly, 1st Sess., 1869–70. Nashville, Tenn., 1869.

————. *Journal of the Senate*. 2 vols. 36th General Assembly, 1st Sess., 1869–70. Nashville, Tenn., 1869.

State of Texas. *Journal of the House of Representatives,* Prov. Sess., 1870. Austin, Texas, 1870.

————. *Journal of the Senate*, Prov. Sess., 1870. Austin, Texas, 1870.

State of Vermont. *Journal of the House of Representatives*, Ann. Sess., 1869. Montpelier, Vt., 1870.

————. *Journal of the Senate*, Ann. Sess., 1869. Montpelier, Vt., 1870.

State of West Virginia. *Journal of the House of Delegates*, 7th Sess., 1869. Wheeling, W. Va., 1869.

————. *Journal of the Senate*, 7th Sess., 1869. Wheeling, W. Va., 1869.

State of Wisconsin. *Journal of the Assembly*, 21st Sess., 1869. Madison, Wis., 1869.

————. *Journal of the Senate*, 21st Sess., 1869. Madison, Wis., 1869.

STORY, JOSEPH. *Commentaries on the Constitution of the United States: With a*

Preliminary Review of the Constitutional History of the Colonies and States Before the Adoption of the Constitution. 2 vols., 4th ed., with notes and additions by Thomas M. Cooley. Boston: Little, Brown, 1873.

THORPE, FRANCIS N. *The Federal and State Constitutions.* Washington, D. C., 1909.

Tribune Almanac for the Year 1865, and succeeding volumes from 1866 to 1876. New York, 1865–77.

U. S. Bureau of the Census. *Negro Population, 1790–1915.* Washington, D. C., 1918.

――――. *Ninth Census of the United States: 1870.* 3 vols. Washington, D. C., 1872.

U. S. *Congressional Globe.* 39th–41st Cong., 1865–72.

U. S. House of Representatives. *Biographical Directory of the American Congress, 1774–1949.* 81st Cong., 2nd Sess., 1950, House Doc. 607.

U. S. Senate. *The Constitution of the United States of America,* 82nd Cong., 2nd Sess., 1953.

――――. *The Constitution of the United States of America,* 87th Cong., 1st Sess., 1961, Sen. Doc. 49.

――――. *Memorial of a Committee of the Union League Club of the City of New York . . . ,* 40th Cong., 3rd Sess., 1868, Sen. Mis. Doc. 4.

――――. *Ratification of the Constitution and Amendments by the States,* 71st Cong., 3rd Sess., 1931, Sen. Doc. 240.

NEWSPAPERS AND PERIODICALS CITED

Alabama:

> Mobile *Daily Register,* 1869–70
> [Montgomery] *Alabama State Journal,* 1869

Arkansas:

> *Daily Arkansas Gazette,* 1869
> [Little Rock] *Morning Republican,* 1869

California:

> The Chico *Courant,* 1869
> Sacramento *Daily Union,* 1869–70
> [San Francisco] *Daily Alta California,* 1869
> The San Francisco *Daily Herald,* 1869
> [San Francisco] *The Elevator,* 1869
> San José *Weekly Mercury,* 1869

Connecticut:

> Bridgeport *Daily Standard,* 1869
> Hartford *Daily Courant,* 1869–71
> New Haven *Register,* 1869
> Norwich *Weekly Courier,* 1869

Delaware:

> Wilmington *Daily Commercial,* 1869–70

District of Columbia:

> [Washington] *Daily Morning Chronicle,* 1868–69
> [Washington] *Daily National Intelligencer,* 1868–69
> [Washington] *The National Republican,* 1868–69
> [Washington] *New Era,* 1870

Georgia:

    [Atlanta] *The Daily New Era*, 1869
    [Augusta] *Daily Press*, 1869
    [Milledgeville] *Federal Union*, 1869–70
    The Savannah *Daily Republican*, 1869
    Savannah *Morning News*, 1870

Illinois:

    The Chicago *Republican*, 1868
    The Chicago *Tribune*, 1869
    [Springfield] Illinois *Daily State Journal*, 1869

Indiana:

    The Evansville *Journal*, 1869

Kentucky:

    The Louisville *Courier-Journal*, 1869

Louisiana:

    New Orleans *Commercial Bulletin*, 1869

Maine:

    Bangor *Daily Whig and Courier*, 1869

Maryland:

    [Baltimore] *American and Commercial Advertiser*, 1870
    The Baltimore *Gazette*, 1870
    [Baltimore] *The Sun*, 1870
    [Cumberland] *Civilian and Telegraph*, 1870

Massachusetts:

    Boston *Daily Advertiser*, 1869
    Boston *Daily Journal*, 1869
    Boston *Morning Journal*, 1868, 1869
    Boston *Post*, 1869
    The Springfield *Daily Republican*, 1869

Michigan:

    The Detroit *Free Press*, 1869

Missouri:

    [St. Louis] The Missouri *Democrat*, 1870

Nevada:

    Carson City *Daily Appeal*, 1869

New Hampshire:

    The Portsmouth Journal of Literature and Politics, 1869

New Jersey:

    The Paterson *Daily Press*, 1869–70
    [Trenton] *Daily State Gazette*, 1869–70

New York:

    Harper's Weekly, 1869
    The Independent, 1867–68

The Nation, 1866–70
[New York] *National Anti-Slavery Standard*, 1867–70
New York Freeman, 1885
The New York Herald, 1868–69
[New York] *The Evening Post*, 1868–69
The New York *Times*, 1867–70
New York *Tribune*, 1868–69
[New York] *Weekly Journal of Commerce*, 1869
[New York] *The World*, 1868–70
North American Review, 1868–69
Rochester *Daily Union and Advertiser*, 1869–70

Ohio:

The Cincinnati *Commercial*, 1867–70
The Cincinnati *Daily Enquirer*, 1870
The Cincinnati *Daily Gazette*, 1869–70
Cincinnati *Evening Chronicle*, 1870
The Cleveland *Daily Plain Dealer*, 1870
Toledo *Daily Blade*, 1870

Pennsylvania:

The Miner's Journal and Pottsville General Advertiser, 1869
[Philadelphia] *The Age*, 1868–69
[Philadelphia] *The Press*, 1868–69

Rhode Island:

Providence *Daily Journal*, 1870
Providence *Evening Press*, 1870
Providence *Morning Herald*, 1869
Woonsocket Patriot and Rhode Island State Register, 1870

South Carolina:

The Charleston *Daily Courier*, 1869, 1870
The Charleston *Daily News*, 1869
[Charleston] *The Daily Republican*, 1870

Texas:

[Galveston] *Flake's Bulletin*, 1869–70
Galveston *News*, 1870
San Antonio *Express*, 1869

Vermont:

St. Johnsbury *Caledonian*, 1869

Virginia:

Daily Richmond Whig, 1869
[Salem] *Roanoke Times*, 1869

West Virginia:

[Kingwood] *Preston County Journal*, 1870
The Wheeling *Daily Intelligencer*, 1869

PUBLISHED REMINISCENCES, LETTERS, AND OTHER SOURCES

ADAMS, HENRY B. "The Session," *North American Review*, VIII (April, 1869), 610–40.

AVERY, I. W. *The History of Georgia from 1850 to 1881.* . . . New York: Brown & Derby, 1881.

BLAINE, JAMES G. *Twenty Years of Congress: From Lincoln to Garfield.* 2 vols. Norwich, Conn.: Henry Bill, 1884–86.

BOUTWELL, GEORGE S. *Reminiscences of Sixty Years in Public Affairs.* 2 vols. New York: McClure, Phillips, 1902.

BROWN, GEORGE R. (ed.). *Reminiscences of Senator William M. Stewart of Nevada.* New York: Neale Publishing Co., 1908.

CLEMENCEAU, GEORGES. *American Reconstruction, 1865–1870, and the Impeachment of President Johnson.* Ed. Fernand Baldensperger, trans. Margaret MacVeagh. New York: Dial Press, 1928.

HILL, ADAMS S. "The Chicago Convention," *North American Review*, VII (July, 1868), 167–86.

HINSDALE, MARY L. (ed.). *Garfield-Hinsdale Letters, Correspondence between James Abram Garfield and Burke Aaron Hinsdale.* Ann Arbor, Mich.: University of Michigan, 1949.

McCLURE, ALEXANDER K. *Old Time Notes of Pennsylvania.* 2 vols. Philadelphia, Pa.: John C. Winston, 1905.

NORTON, SARAH, and M. A. DE WOLFE (eds.). *Letters of Charles Eliot Norton with Biographical Comment.* 2 vols. Boston, Mass.: Houghton Mifflin, 1913.

PALMER, JOHN M. *Personal Recollections of John M. Palmer: The Story of an Earnest Life.* Cincinnati, Ohio: Robert Clarke, 1901.

WILSON, JAMES O. (ed.). *General Grant's Letters to a Friend, 1861–1880.* New York: T. Y. Crowell, 1897.

MONOGRAPHS

AMBLER, CHARLES H. "Disfranchisement in West Virginia," *Yale Review*, XIV (May and August, 1905), 38–59, 155–80.

———. *A History of West Virginia.* New York: Prentice-Hall, 1933.

BARNARD, HARRY. *Rutherford B. Hayes and His America.* New York: Bobbs-Merrill, 1954.

BRAXTON, ALLEN C. *The Fifteenth Amendment—an Account of Its Enactment Read by A. Caperton Braxton at the Fifteenth Annual Meeting Held at Hot Springs of Virginia, August 21, 22, and 24, 1903.* Richmond, Va.: E. Waddey, 1903.

CHEANEY, HENRY. "Attitudes of the Indiana Pulpit and Press toward the Negro, 1860–1880." Unpublished Ph. D. dissertation, Dept. of History, University of Chicago, 1961.

COHN, SYLVIA. "The Reaction of New York and Ohio to the Ratification of the Fifteenth Amendment." Unpublished M. A. dissertation, Dept. of History, University of Chicago, 1944.

COLEMAN, CHARLES H. *The Election of 1868: The Democratic Effort to Regain Control.* New York: Columbia University Press, 1933.

CURRENT, RICHARD N. *Old Thad Stevens: A Story of Ambition.* Madison, Wis.: The University of Wisconsin Press, 1942.

DAVIS, WINIFIELD J. *History of Political Conventions in California, 1849–1892.* Sacramento, Cal.: California State Library, 1893.

DuBois, W. E. Burghardt. *The Philadelphia Negro: A Social Study.* Publications of the University of Pennsylvania: Series in Political Economy and Public Law, No. 14. Philadelphia, Pa.: Ginn, 1899.

Fishel, Leslie H., Jr. "The North and the Negro, 1865–1900: A Study in Race Discrimination." Unpublished Ph. D. dissertation, 2 vols., Dept. of History, Harvard University, 1953.

———. "Northern Prejudice and Negro Suffrage, 1865–1870," *Journal of Negro History,* XXXIX (January, 1954), 8–26.

Foulke, William D. Life of Oliver P. Morton, 2 vols. Indianapolis, Ind.: Bowen-Merrill, 1899.

Gerichs, William C. "The Ratification of the Fifteenth Amendment in Indiana," *Indiana Magazine of History,* IX (September, 1913), 131–66.

Hanchett, William. "Yankee Law and the Negro in Nevada, 1861–1869," *Western Humanities Review,* X (Summer, 1956), 241–49.

Henry, Selden. "Radical Republican Policy toward the Negro during Reconstruction (1862–1872)." Unpublished Ph. D. dissertation, Dept. of History, Yale University, 1963.

Horn, Robert A. "National Control of Congressional Elections." Unpublished Ph. D. dissertation, Dept. of Politics, Princeton University, 1942.

Huston, John W. "The Ratification of the 13th, 14th, and 15th Amendments to the United States Constitution by the State of Pennsylvania." Unpublished M. A. dissertation, Dept. of History, University of Pittsburgh, 1950.

James, Joseph B. *The Framing of the Fourteenth Amendment.* Illinois Studies in the Social Sciences, XXXVII, No. 37. Urbana, Ill.: The University of Illinois Press, 1956.

Lyda, John W. *The Negro in the History of Indiana.* Terre Haute, Ind.: privately printed, 1953.

McKitrick, Eric L. *Andrew Johnson and Reconstruction.* Chicago: The University of Chicago Press, 1960.

McPherson, James M. *The Struggle for Equality: Abolitionists and the Negro in the Civil War and Reconstruction.* Princeton, N. J.: Princeton University Press, 1964.

Mathews, John Mabry. *Legislative and Judicial History of the Fifteenth Amendment.* Johns Hopkins University Studies in Historical and Political Science, Series XXVII, Nos. 6–7. Baltimore, Md.: The Johns Hopkins Press, 1909.

Munroe, John A. "The Negro in Delaware," *The South Atlantic Quarterly,* LVI (Autumn, 1957), 428–44.

Niven, William J., Jr. "The Time of the Whirlwind: A Study in the Political, Social and Economic History of Connecticut from 1861 to 1875." Unpublished Ph. D. dissertation, Dept. of History, Columbia University, 1954.

Riegel, Robert E. "The Split in the Feminist Movement in 1869," *Mississippi Valley Historical Review,* XLIX (December, 1962), 485–96.

Swinney, Everette. "Enforcing the Fifteenth Amendment, 1870–1877," *Journal of Southern History,* XXVIII (May, 1962), 202–18.

Thornbrough, Emma L. *The Negro in Indiana: A Study of a Minority.* Indianapolis, Ind.: Indiana Historical Bureau, 1957.

Warner, Robert A. *New Haven Negroes: A Social History.* New Haven: Yale University Press, 1940.

Woodward, C. Vann. *The Burden of Southern History.* New York: Vintage Books, 1961.

INDEX

THE JOHNS HOPKINS UNIVERSITY
STUDIES IN
HISTORICAL AND POLITICAL SCIENCE

, , .

, . .

THE JOHNS HOPKINS PRESS
BALTIMORE

THE JOHNS HOPKINS UNIVERSITY STUDIES IN HISTORICAL AND POLITICAL SCIENCE

A subscription for the regular annual series is $8.00. Single numbers may be purchased at special prices. A complete list of the series follows. All paperbound unless otherwise indicated.

viii

3. Slave States in the Presidential Election of 1860. By Ollinger Crenshaw O. P.
Paper 4.00; Cloth O. P.

SIXTY-FOURTH SERIES (1946)

1. Great National Project: A History of the Chesapeake and Ohio Canal. By W. S. Sanderlin.................. O. P.
2. Richard Hildreth. By Donald E. Emerson 3.50
3. William Rufus Day: Supreme Court Justice from Ohio. By Joseph E. McLean 3.00

SIXTY-FIFTH SERIES (1947)

1. British Block Grants and Central-Local Finance. By Reynold E. Carlson.... 4.50
2. Landowners and Agriculture in Austria, 1815-1848. By Jerome Blum........ 5.00

SIXTY-SIXTH SERIES (1948)

1. French Freemasonry Under the Third Republic. By Mildred J. Headings.. 5.00
2. Science and Rationalism in the Government of Louis XIV, 1661-1683. By James E. King.................... O. P.

SIXTY-SEVENTH SERIES (1949)

1. Capitalism in Amsterdam in the 17th Century. By Violet Barbour....... O. P.
2. The Patent Grant. By Burke Inlow.. O. P.
3. Saint Mary Magdalene in Mediaeval Literature. By Helen Garth......... 3.00

SIXTY-EIGHTH SERIES (1950)

1. The Organization of State Administration in Delaware. By Paul Dolan... 3.50
2. The Theory of Inter-Sectoral Money Flows and Income Formation. By John Chipman 3.00
3. Congressional Differences over Foreign Affairs, 1921-41. By George Grassmuck .... O. P.

Bound Volumes Discontinued Beginning with the Sixty-Ninth Series.

SIXTY-NINTH SERIES (1951)

1. Party and Constituency: Pressures on Congress. By Julius Turner........ O. P.
2. The Legates of Galatia From Augustus to Diocletian. By Robert K. Sherk.. 2.50

SEVENTIETH SERIES (1952)

1. Federal Examiners and the Conflict of Law and Administration. By Lloyd D. Musolf 4.00
2. The Growth of Major Steel Companies, 1900-1950. By Gertrude G. Schroeder .... O. P.

SEVENTY-FIRST SERIES (1953)

1. The Revolt of 1916 in Russian Central Asia. By Edward D. Sokol......... 4.00
2. Four Studies in French Romantic Historical Writing. By Friedrich Engel-Janosi .... O. P.

SEVENTY-SECOND SERIES (1954)

1. Price Discrimination in Selling Gas and Electricity. By Ralph Kirby Davidson .... O. P.
2. The Savings Bank of Baltimore, 1816-1866. By Peter L. Payne and Lance E. Davis 3.50

SEVENTY-THIRD SERIES (1955)

The Paris Commune in French Politics, 1871-1880. By Jean T. Joughin. . . .
Two vols. .... O. P.
1. Volume I: The Partial Amnesty
2. Volume II: The Final Amnesty

SEVENTY-FOURTH SERIES (1956)

1. Robert Oliver, Merchant of Baltimore, 1783-1819. By Stuart Weems Bruchey 6.00
2. Political Theory and Institutions of the Khawārij. By Elie Adib Salem....... 3.00

SEVENTY-FIFTH SERIES (1957)

1. Britons in American Labor: A History of the Influence of the United Kingdom Immigrants on American Labor, 1820-1914. By Clifton K. Yearley, Jr. 5.00
2. The Location of Yamatai: A Case Study in Japanese Historiography. By John Young .... O. P.

SEVENTY-SIXTH SERIES (1958)

1. Trends in Birth Rates in the United States since 1870. By Bernard Okun. O. P.
2. The Dynamics of Supply: Estimation of Farmers' Response to Price. By Marc Nerlove ....Cloth 5.00

SEVENTY-SEVENTH SERIES (1959)

1. Republicans Face the Southern Question—The New Departure Years 1877-1897. By Vincent P. De Santis.
Paper 4.00; Cloth 6.00
2. Money, Class, and Party: An Economic Study of Civil War and Reconstruction. By Robert P. Sharkey..Cloth 5.50

SEVENTY-EIGHTH SERIES (1960)

1. The Nobility of Toulouse—An Economic Study of Aristocracy in the Eighteenth Century. By Robert Forster.
Cloth 5.00

2. The Union Pacific Railroad—A Case in Premature Enterprise. By Robert William Fogel. . . . . Paper 3.00; Cloth 3.50

SEVENTY-NINTH SERIES (1961)

1. Enterprise and Anthracite: Economics and Democracy in Schuylkill County, 1820-1875. By Clifton K. Yearley, Jr.
Cloth 5.00

2. Birth Rates of the White Population in the United States, 1800-1860: An Economic Study. By Yasukichi Yasuba.
Paper 5.00

EIGHTIETH SERIES (1962)

1. The Road to Normalcy: The Presidential Campaign and Election of 1920. By Wesley M. Bagby
Paper 4.00; Cloth 4.50

2. The Decline of Venetian Nobility as a Ruling Class. By James C. Davis.
Paper 3.50; Cloth 4.00

EIGHTY-FIRST SERIES (1963)

1. The First Ottoman Constitutional Period: A Study of the Midhat Constitution and Parliament. By Robert Devereux. . . . . Cloth 6.00

2. Elbeuf During the Revolutionary Period: History and Social Structure. By Jeffry Kaplow. . . . . Cloth 6.50

EIGHTY-SECOND SERIES (1964)

1. A Rural Society in Medieval France: The Gâtine of Poitou in the Eleventh and Twelfth Centuries. By George T. Beech . . . . Cloth 5.00

2. United States Policy and the Partition of Turkey, 1914-1924. By Laurence Evans . . . . Cloth 7.95

EIGHTY-THIRD SERIES (1965)

1. The Right to Vote: Politics and the Passage of the Fifteenth Amendment. By William Gillette . . . . Cloth 4.50